Understanding the New Testament and the End Times

Second Edition

Understanding the
New Testament
and the End Times

Second Edition

Rob Dalrymple

WIPF & STOCK · Eugene, Oregon

UNDERSTANDING THE NEW TESTAMENT AND THE END TIMES,
Second Edition

Copyright © 2018 Rob Dalrymple. All rights reserved. Except for brief quotations in critical publications or reviews, no part of this book may be reproduced in any manner without prior written permission from the publisher. Write: Permissions, Wipf and Stock Publishers, 199 W. 8th Ave., Suite 3, Eugene, OR 97401.

Wipf & Stock
An Imprint of Wipf and Stock Publishers
199 W. 8th Ave., Suite 3
Eugene, OR 97401

www.wipfandstock.com

PAPERBACK ISBN: 978-1-5326-4947-9
HARDCOVER ISBN: 978-1-5326-4948-6
EBOOK ISBN: 978-1-5326-4949-3

Manufactured in the U.S.A.   04/05/18

All Scripture quotations, unless otherwise noted, are take from the New American Standard Bible ®, copyright © 1960, 1962, 1963, 1968, 1971, 1972, 1973, 1975, 1977, 1995 by The Lockman Foundation. Used by permission.

To the loving memory of my mom
You are my hero

Contents

Acknowledgments / ix
Preface / xi
Preface to the Second Edition / xiii

1. My Story / 1
2. Introduction to Understanding The New Testament and the End Times / 8
3. Jesus: Reading the Bible Christologically / 17
4. Jesus, the End Times, and the Arrival of the Kingdom / 28
5. Understanding Prophecy and the End Times / 43
6. The End Times and the Temple / 57
7. The End Times, the Temple, and the New Testament / 79
8. The Tribulation and the People of God / 100
9. Understanding the Second Coming of Christ / 119
10. Understanding the "Signs of the Times" / 136
11. The War of Armageddon / 155
12. Understanding The New Testament and the End Times: Why It Matters! / 166

Bibliography / 181

Acknowledgments

THERE HAVE BEEN MANY people who have helped in the writing of this book. Without their tireless efforts I am not sure this project would ever have been completed. I would like to thank Josh Jonas, Clint Rutledge, Vinnie Angelo, Jim Sawyer, Paul Hinsberg, and Fr. Leo Arrowsmith for their help with the early drafts of this book. Most notably, I wish to thank my brother Bill, who has always been a great encouragement, and for the great input with regard to most of the manuscript. I am quite indebted to the detailed assistance of Ian Spencer who offered tremendous aid in the final draft of this book. Tom Biesiada was also of great help. Tom read most of the manuscript and graciously provided invaluable insights. This work would not have been completed with any degree of quality without their efforts.

Much thanks must go to my wife Toni, who has always supported me and my research. She has sacrificed greatly to allow me to devote the time necessary to do the writing and research that made this project happen. I am glad that the Lord has blessed me with such a wonderful spouse.

Finally, thanks to my students who have allowed me to process this material on them!

Preface

SOMETIMES A BOOK JUST needs to go to print. Even before perfection arrives. I hope that you, the reader, will give me grace. For this book has indeed gone to print before perfection arrived. I know that I have omitted much. I know, also, that I have not been flawless in my communication of all that I am trying to convey. And for that I apologize.

I have at times engaged with some of the popular eschatological positions. I know for some of you that these viewpoints are held onto in earnest. I understand, for I too once held such views. I hope that I have adequately represented the popularist viewpoint. I have represented it as I have known it. I realize that this may not completely represent it as you have known it.

Please read with the grace that characterizes the body of Christ. I have done my best to write with such grace.

My primary interest is not to present a critique of the popular eschatology. Instead, I have aimed at providing a positive framework for understanding Scripture eschatologically. I believe that the Gospel of Christ is simply so much richer and more comprehensive than many have ever imagined. And it is the greatness of the biblical story that I hope you see as you read.

Rob Dalrymple
February 2013

Preface to the Second Edition

We chose to produce a second edition for one simple reason. I believe even more deeply now than I did five years ago when I published the first edition of this book (under the title *Understanding Eschatology: Why it Matters*) that the perspective presented in this book is critical for Christians—both in terms of our understanding of the Bible and for the discernment of our call as Christians to take the gospel to the nations. This was and remains the central purpose of this book.

I also wrote this book to provide an understanding of the New Testament and the end times that will help counter some of the popular misconceptions. It is my conviction that such misconceptions have had at least two significant effects: First, the popular conception that the end times are something wholly future and, for those who espouse a pre-tribulation rapture theology, something that Christians are somehow exempt from enduring has contributed to a widespread complacency among many Christians. Why bother really living as Christ has called us when, even if the tribulation were to come tomorrow, we will be taken out of the way? Secondly, the failure to understand the church's mission in terms of carrying forward the kingdom of God, as inaugurated by Christ, has contributed to a failure on the part of the Church to remain focused on our mission.

These two motivations for writing this book remain. In fact, I believe even more deeply than before that the material in this book is vital for the Church today. There was, however, one consistent bit of negative feedback on the first edition: because many did not know what "eschatology" (the study of the end times) meant, the title turned them off from the book.

So Wipf and Stock and I decided to publish a second edition under a new title (*Understanding the New Testament and the End Times: Why it Matters*) that is more understandable and yet perhaps more accurately captures the essence of the book, which is to help readers understand the New Testament and the end times so that they might recognize the significance of the New Testament's message for their lives.

Preface to the Second Edition

The text of the original edition is largely unchanged. The most consistent alteration has been to exchange "eschatology" in most of its occurrences for "end times." Note that this is not always possible. There are some instances in which the word "eschatology" is just necessary. The reader, however, will find that in those few instances the meaning of "eschatology" (the study of the end times) should be fairly apparent.

In Christ
Rob Dalrymple
Mar 2018

1

My Story

Introduction

IN 1989, I HAD come to conclude that the end times and the book of Revelation were a mystery that would only be solved when everything was over. If anyone proposed that they knew what it meant, they were not to be trusted, for no one knows what it means. Now, you must understand that prior to this time I had been fascinated with the end times and all of the hype that went along with it.

After all, I was born in 666—honestly: June 1966. After coming to faith in Christ at a young age, I grew up in an evangelical, fundamentalist Christian tradition. I strived to live as a faithful Christian and, by God's grace, my faith remained strong. Throughout my youth I read dozens of books on the end times and earnestly strove to determine the meaning of the book of Revelation and the end times according to the New Testament (NT). I even spent hours in the local library one day to determine the number of earthquakes and other such "signs" that had occurred in the last generation, with the conviction that this data would confirm that the return of Christ was indeed near.

As a product of a well-intentioned, evangelical, fundamentalist upbringing, I was taught that the Bible was to be interpreted in a particular manner—with a wooden literalism—and in accord with a well-delineated evangelical worldview. I was convinced that this was the only true way to interpret the Bible. In fact, I was confident that Jesus, Paul, and for that matter Moses, David, and the rest, must also have thought and reasoned like me. Furthermore, I was also convinced that all other interpretations were the result of liberal assertions, which were intended to undermine the truth of God, Christ, the Bible, and ultimately Christianity itself.

Now, in all of this I was very well intentioned. I was a sincere and genuine follower of Christ. I read the Bible as a moral guidebook. It told me what was right and what was wrong. It told me that if I believed in Jesus then I should do what was right. The Bible was merely a handbook of dos and don'ts, which I was attempting to follow. I worked hard at being a good Christian.

When it came to the study of the end times, I was taught that things were fairly well spelled out. We were to look for certain events that were precursors to the return of Jesus, including the rebuilding of the temple in Jerusalem and the rise of an anti-Christ, who will rise to power in a restored Roman Empire and will impose a one-world, end-times government.

Problems began to surface for me along two lines. First, I began to realize that there were tremendous disagreements in the popular literature over the meaning of Revelation and the end times. I became increasingly uneasy in my heart as I grappled with these things, not knowing whom to believe. Secondly, by the middle of the 1980s, I began to realize that many of the prophecies, which I had been told we were seeing fulfilled in our generation, never seemed to come to fruition. I had read many books that assured me that Jesus would return by the mid 1980s.[1] By 1989, and the fall of the iron curtain, I was totally disillusioned. I had begun to realize that not only were the events not being fulfilled as these popular writers had assured me, but the things that I was told were "signs" of the imminent fulfillment were all moving in the opposite direction. The Russians were certainly not about to invade Israel; they seemed more concerned with how they might feed their own soldiers.

Now, the Lord has a way of being quite humorous. For, by the early 1990s, in the midst of my disillusionment with the book of Revelation and the study of the end times, I was blessed with the opportunity to teach New Testament studies at a Christian college. Immediately I was confronted with a problem. How could one teach an "Introduction to the New Testament" course and omit the book of Revelation? For I truly wanted to omit it. After all, I certainly did not know what it meant.

I decided to prepare by consulting some commentaries on the book of Revelation. Now, in my studies of the New Testament I had gained much insight from several series of standard evangelical commentaries. As I read through these standard, scholarly, evangelical commentaries on

---

1. Among them were Swihart, *Armageddon 198?*; and Lindsey, *The 1980's*.

My Story

the book of Revelation, I began to realize several things. First, there was a significant amount of agreement among scholars as to what the book of Revelation was saying. Secondly, the book of Revelation made great sense when approached carefully through the lens of the Old Testament (OT) and Jesus' fulfillment of it. Thirdly, the message of the book is incredible! As a result, I began to fall in love again with the book of Revelation and the study of the end times!

Over the next few years I immersed myself in the study of the end times and apocalyptic literature. I soon discovered that the message of the NT must be understood from within an eschatological ("end times") context; and that God's eschatological plan was not only fulfilled in Christ, but was continuing to unfold through his people, and that all of this climaxes in the New Jerusalem.

As I continued to examine the Scriptures I became aware that the message of the NT is that God has called us—his people—to participate now in the building of his kingdom! The kingdom that Jesus began is the same kingdom that God has prepared for us to build. Eschatology is missional! That is, understanding the end times, and that they have begun in Christ, provides us with the framework for understanding the work of God in the present: namely, his bringing about the New Creation!

This all came to a climax for me during the years of my graduate and doctoral work. For, it was then that I came to fully grasp that the manner of interpretation of the Scriptures that I had followed, and its accompanying worldview, was not the approach/worldview of Jesus, Paul, Moses, David, or anyone in the biblical world. When I initially came to an awareness of this fact, I was somewhat okay with it. For how and why should I suppose that anyone in the ancient world thought like me (even though I had been raised to think that they did!)? But, I was also uncertain how to proceed—for I knew that I could not go back. What I was learning was true. For Paul thought like a first-century Jew, Luke was well at home in the Roman world, and Moses' writings make perfect sense when read from within an Ancient Near Eastern (ANE) perspective.

At the same time, I found myself in awe of the beauty and depth of the Scriptures as I was now beginning to see them. They were not merely a simplistic manual on right and wrong and how to be a good Christian until I go to heaven. The Scriptures were far grander, much richer, and more magnificent than I had ever thought! They exhibited a depth and beauty beyond anything I had ever imagined. I was beginning to see that God and his plan were far more majestic than I could possibly conceive!

Understanding the New Testament and the End Times

Throughout this time I was continuously stimulated by the new found riches revealed in Scripture.

But I was also fearful. On the one hand, I was beginning to see that Scripture contained so much more for me to discover. It was as though I had stumbled into Narnia and there before me was a whole new world to explore beyond the wardrobe! But, on the other hand, I was nervous. My prior convictions had been the bedrock of my faith. If this bedrock was nothing more than sand, then upon what would I now stand? If my preconceptions in all these areas were unfounded, then might my whole faith implode? For months, and even years, as I continued to grapple with this newfound understanding of God and Scripture, I struggled with these constantly mixed emotions: excitement over newly discovered riches, and concern over a quickly eroding foundation. For, if this foundation were removed, then with what would it be replaced? How was I now to read the Bible?

Then I found Jesus. Not in a personal sense—I already knew him in that regard. I mean that I found that Jesus was the answer! Jesus became my new foundation for understanding the Bible. That is, the Bible is about Jesus—the Jesus who transcends all comprehension: the God whose thoughts are not my thoughts and whose ways are not my ways.[2] Jesus is the key to a proper understanding of the Bible. Christ himself became my new bedrock for interpreting the Scriptures. And I found that the centrality of Christ was a more sure foundation than any method of interpretation that I had previously employed. I discovered that if we come to fully understand the significance of the person and work of Jesus, that is, truly understand it without limitations, then the Scriptures and the mission of God all begin to fall into place.

This new perspective (new for me of course, but one that I soon found out was commonplace among most scholars today and the church historically) radically influenced my understanding of the overall nature and purpose of Scripture. Suddenly, the overall story of the Bible—the person, nature, and mission of God; the person of Christ and his fulfillment of God's mission; and the calling of God on people to be the means by which he continues to build his kingdom—have all come into a much sharper focus. Now I see that Scripture relays for us a dynamic story in which God has guided and moved history in a tremendously fascinating and complex manner: the grand plan of God's cosmic design unfolds throughout the narrative of Genesis to Revelation. God's sovereign plan,

---

2. Isa 55:8.

My Story

in which he wills to dwell among his people, is disclosed through the pages of Scripture. That plan is about Jesus.

What I hope to share in the pages of this book are the implications of all this for understanding the end times, the mission of God's people, and why it matters. Why is this important? After all, there is so much speculation about the end times, and much of it has proven to be false over the years, that one may well wonder if it even matters—let alone if anyone could possibly know what the end times hold. Well, it matters alright! It matters greatly. It matters because this plan is one in which God has called us to participate!

Reading This Book

As for the general presentation of this book: I am confident that, for the most part, much of the basic argumentation within each chapter, though perhaps new to many, will appear reasonable and stimulating. Most readers who have not ventured too far into this field of study will agree with the overall conclusions and find them exciting. At times, however, I will take some of these conclusions and draw inferences from them that, though widely acknowledged among the scholarly community, and well within the historical understanding of the church, will prove to be a challenge for many readers.

One of the reasons for this challenge is that much of contemporary Christianity has unknowingly been influenced by Western rationalism and modernism. This influence of Enlightenment and post-Enlightenment thinking is so deeply engrained in our psyche that many of us are unprepared and, perhaps, even unwilling to think differently. I know, for I too thought this way.

Unfortunately, the theological perspectives of twentieth-century popular Christianity have become such dogma that many find it impossible to think any other way. All other boxes are deemed a concession to liberalism, scientism, humanism, and many other -isms. The thought that Jesus, Paul, Moses, et al. did not think within the context of a modernistic worldview is unconscionable. Indeed, I am speaking from my own experience here. I remember distinctly thinking that Jesus must have thought like me because we, in the post-Enlightenment West, have learned how to think and to know in all fields with absolutes. Since this manner of thinking is deemed "correct" in an absolute sense, and since Jesus must have thought "correctly," then he too must have thought like me. My worldview, in fact, was built on the edifice that this was the proper and only way to think and reason.[3]

I assure you that the conclusions presented in this work will serve to confirm the core of Christian theology. The primacy of Christ is a conviction that all Christians share. This book will not only affirm the primacy of Christ, but demonstrate that much of Christian theology has not emphasized enough the centrality of Christ's person and work, especially when it comes to interpreting the Bible. At this point, most readers will not only find themselves in hearty agreement, but will sense a level of enthusiasm as the Scriptures come alive with far more force than previously imagined. The problems for some will arise when I extend these conclusions and the accompanying implications to their natural conclusions. For, the ramifications of a proper christological perspective in Scripture are grand—and at times convicting.

Another reason why some may struggle with the framework presented here is that a number of the conclusions derived at in this book will demand a new way of thinking as we approach the Scriptures. New always presents challenges for us. For, we do not know what to do with new. We are comfortable with the old. Consequently, the easiest thing to do is to reject the new and remain comfortable. Of course, we should immediately remind ourselves that Jesus brought the new wine![4]

Thus, many readers may well be challenged in regards to some fundamental conceptions of Jesus, Scripture, the end times, and the mission of the church. Indeed, some of my conclusions may well shake the foundations of things that you have always considered as true. For others, this journey will be as exciting as it was and continues to be for me. For those who are uncertain what to think, I only ask that you join me with an open mind and heart in this endeavor to find truth. For, it is only as we honestly approach the Scriptures, fully willing to allow our conceptions to become subject to him who made all things, that we can even begin to discern truth.

Finally, and equally important, if in the end we disagree on some matters, may we never allow our differences to divide us as brothers and

---

3. Now, in saying this I am not suggesting that we abandon modernism and jump on the bandwagon of the latest and greatest new thing: postmodernism. In fact, neither modernism nor postmodernism are Christian worldviews. Since this is not a textbook on Christian worldviews I cannot proceed much further here. I simply want readers to be assured that I am advocating neither a wholesale abandoning of modernism nor an embrace of a postmodern worldview.

4. Cf. Matt 9:17; Mark 2:22; Luke 5:37–39.

sisters in Christ! We have a gospel to proclaim and lights that must shine. Lord, help us if we ever begin by snuffing out each other's lamps!

2

Introduction to Understanding The New Testament and the End Times

From first to last, and not merely in the epilogue, Christianity is eschatology, is hope, forward looking and forward moving, and therefore also revolutionizing and transforming the present. The eschatological is not one element of Christianity, but it is the medium of Christian faith as such, the key in which everything in it is set, the glow that suffuses everything here in the dawn of an expected new day.[1]

Introduction

MANY CHRISTIANS SURRENDER EVEN an attempt to wade through the muck and mire of the seemingly endless array of speculative materials regarding the alleged "signs" of the imminent fulfillment of biblical prophecy, including the presence of the "anti-Christ," the rebuilding of the Jewish temple, the nearness of the rapture, and the time of Jesus' return. Unfortunately, the church has never ceased to have self-professed prophetic experts who, according to their own insights, have calculated the precise times of these events. Others have more cautiously offered us only a general roadmap of events that would inevitably, according to their insights, end with the return of Christ and the destruction of the planet within a matter of years.

A study of church history reveals that such interpretations of contemporary events and how they have been "foretold" in the Bible runs through the centuries.[2] Our generation has likewise had no shortage of

---

1. Jürgen Moltmann, *Theology of Hope*, 16.
2. See Kyle, *Last Days are Here Again*. Kyle chronicles many of the instances

prophetic voices warning us of the impending doom. This has tragically caused great apathy among many regarding biblical eschatology, and especially the younger generation of Christians within our churches. Many of them have no interest in regard to matters that "no one can know."

But eschatology (the study of the end times) matters. It matters because one cannot understand Scripture apart from eschatology. Eschatology does not merely address the things to come. Instead, it is foundational to the message of the New Testament. Furthermore, a proper grasp of eschatology is vital to our understanding of the call and the mission of the church today. That is, a proper eschatological framework provides a correct understanding of God's purpose in creation, his call upon Abraham and Israel, the work of Christ, the sending of the Spirit, the continued mission of the church, and ultimately the consummation! Thus, eschatology is not merely about the future. It is inherently historical and missional.

The Bible as Story

The Bible is an incredible and fascinating book. It is far from being merely a list of moral guidelines, or an instruction manual on "How to Get to Heaven in Ten Easy Steps." Instead, when read in terms of the overall story of God's work within creation, it reveals a depth and beauty that transcends comprehension. Unfortunately, for many Christians, the notion of reading and teaching Scripture in terms of the overarching story of the Bible has been vacant. Instead of understanding the grand narrative and its majestic portrait of God and his redemptive activity, the Bible has unfortunately become the repository of rules and regulations. This is not to say that the Bible does not have such an ethical code, but only that in failing to see God's mission within creation as unveiled in the biblical narrative, we have neglected the vital storyline that runs from Genesis to Revelation (from garden to garden!).[3]

It is this story that I want to explore in more depth. For, it is my contention that a proper understanding of eschatology begins with a complete grasp of the entire story of the Old and New Testaments. For, when we place the life and ministry of Jesus into the overarching story of God's mission,

---

throughout history in which men have attempted to predict the time of Jesus' return.

3. Some good works that provide an understanding of the biblical story in terms of the overall narrative of the Bible include: Wright, *Mission of God*; and Roberts, *God's Big Picture*.

then we may begin to discern the eschatological significance of Christ's life, death, and resurrection, and the coming of the Spirit at Pentecost.[4]

And it is here that eschatology becomes relevant for the church today! Our mission as followers of Christ is to carry forward the mission begun by Christ, which itself was an inauguration of the eschaton (the "end"). You see, eschatology is not simply a bunch of ramblings about the future and what will happen, but it is intimately tied to the life of the church today. That is, understanding Jesus, both his person and his work, in the context of the biblical story and through the lens of eschatology, correlates directly to a proper understanding of the mission of God's people today.

The Need for a High Christology

Perhaps the primary presupposition presented throughout this book is that a proper understanding of biblical eschatology begins and ends with a very high Christology.[5] The basis for this exceedingly high view of Jesus is found in Paul's affirmation, "For as many are the promises of God, in him they are yes" (2 Cor 1:20). It is this high view of Jesus, though relevant in many ways beyond what we can possibly engage here, that will enhance our understanding of the Bible in general and the issues pertaining to the end times in particular. It is, in fact, my contention that many evangelical Christians have failed to grasp the significance of the first coming of Christ (his life, death, and resurrection, as well as the coming of the Spirit) in terms of the end times. The result is that many have also failed to adequately understand both the mission of the people of God in the present, as well as the unfolding of end times events (e.g., temple, tribulation, second coming, Armageddon) throughout the NT.

---

4. What I am saying here, as I intend to clarify throughout this work, is that the life, death, and resurrection of Jesus has significant implications for a proper understanding of eschatology.

5. Christology is simply the study of Christ. By a "high Christology" I mean that we must understand the person and work of Christ as central to everything in Scripture. That is, Jesus fulfilled the entirety of the Scriptures and has inaugurated the eschaton ("end times," also known as "the age to come"; see ch. 8). At his return he will consummate all things. This is counter to the all too common understanding that in his first coming Jesus only fulfilled various isolated prophecies, mostly relating to his role as the Suffering Servant, or his atoning death, and that in his return Jesus will fulfill the remaining prophecies related to his role as the King (this is proposed by Swihart, *Armageddon 198?*, 264). The latter view, I will contend, has a poor conception of the person and work of Christ.

Introduction to Understanding The New Testament and the End Times

The tragedy, then, that many Christians have become apathetic towards eschatology resides in the fact that the mission of the people of God in the present is an eschatological mission. Discerning this is central not only for our understanding of Scripture, as well as the person and work of Christ, but also for our awareness of what it means to be a disciple of Jesus today. Thus, a proper understanding of Scripture is at stake. But, also at stake is a proper understanding of the mission of God's people and, as we shall see, the ethical manner in which we are to carry out that mission. Understanding the end times indeed matters!

The Hermeneutical Problem

It is important also to understand that the debate over which perspective of the end times is most warranted is not simply a matter of differing interpretations of isolated passages. Instead, the debate begins and ends with a proper hermeneutical perspective.[6]

Hermeneutics seeks to answer the questions of how a given passage, as well as the Bible as a whole, is to be understood. Unfortunately, many Christians have come to accept a basic set of assumptions with regard to how the Bible is to be interpreted that is highly suspect. This questionable set of assumptions has been manifested most significantly in the area of the end times. Two of the key elements of popular evangelical hermeneutics for our purposes are that the Bible must be interpreted literally as much as possible and that the end times relate primarily, if not strictly, to the future.

What I intend to suggest is that those who place so much emphasis on the future aspect of the end times and the need for a "literal" fulfillment have not only failed to properly understand the person and work of Christ in his first coming, as well as the implications of this for the fulfillment of Scripture, but they have failed to maintain a consistent hermeneutical approach.

Now, since this work is not intended to be an introduction on how to interpret the Bible, we are going to approach this issue from a different angle. What I aim to show is that a proper understanding of the person and work of Christ and a consistent approach to biblical interpretation results in an understanding of the end times that runs counter to many of the popular conceptions within evangelical Christianity—even though it

---

6. Hermeneutics is the "science of interpretation."

accords with both the majority opinions of the scholarly community today as well as the general historical understanding of the church.

What Do You Mean By "Eschatology"?

Part of the difficulty with regard to the debate over eschatology relates to the meaning of the terms employed. The view held throughout this book is that eschatology, or the "end times," has a past, a present, and a future fulfillment. That is, I will contend that the end times/eschaton/last days are defined in Scripture as the period of time in history that was inaugurated by the life, death, and resurrection of Jesus and the coming of the Holy Spirit, and climaxes at the return of Christ. This does not in any way deny that there is a future to eschatology. We do indeed anticipate a future coming of Christ in glory. And we join the heavenly chorus in affirming, "Amen, come Lord Jesus" (Rev 22:20). We long for the time when the New Jerusalem comes "down out of heaven" to the earth (Rev 21:10).

The point is that the "last days" in Scripture refers to events that are characteristic of the past, the present, and the future. This is what scholars have termed the "already/not yet." That is, the end times have "already" come and they have "not yet" been fully consummated. For example, we see that in 1 Corinthians Paul affirms (referring to the present reign of Christ) that "He must reign until he has put all his enemies under his feet" (1 Cor 15:25).[7] Thus, Jesus presently reigns! His kingdom has "already" come. At the same time, however, Paul may also proclaim, "Come O Lord" (1 Cor 16:22). In another instance, Paul acknowledges that Jesus has risen and begun the eschaton,[8] while at the same time he notes that we have not yet been raised.[9] Likewise, Paul asserts that sin and death have already been defeated,[10] and yet sin and death remain.[11] In all of these examples, the former elements are the present characteristics of the eschaton/last days/end times, while the latter features confirm that the consummation of the kingdom has not yet occurred. Therefore, we may conclude that the "last days" are "already" here[12] and that the return of Christ and the final consummation are "not yet."

7. See 1 Cor 15:20–28.
8. Cf. 1 Cor 15:20.
9. Cf. 1 Cor 15:22.
10. Cf. 1 Cor 15:54–55.
11. Cf. 1 Cor 15:26.
12. Cf. Acts 2:17; 2 Tim 3:1.

Introduction to Understanding The New Testament and the End Times

Understanding the End Times and Why It Matters

This book endeavors to lay a foundation for understanding Scripture in general and biblical eschatology in particular. I will attempt to move beyond the impasse and the confusion that often convolutes the issues. The goal is not just to provide a framework for understanding the end times, but always to ask the question, "Why does this matter?" In the end, I will contend that a proper understanding of the end times is more than just helpful; it is in fact essential for the life of God's people today.

Underscoring each of the central chapters of this book (chs. 6–11) will be the importance of understanding the significance of these issues as it relates to the present life of the people of God. That is, much of the popular ideas on the end times, with its fascination with contemporary world events and how such may fulfill prophecy, is the assumption that the end times are primarily about the future. This future focus can be potentially dangerous for the life of the Christian. For it can lead to apathy. This, as I see it, is a significant problem for many in the church today—especially among the younger generation. For many of them, end times speculations are not worth the time and energy. And I understand why they might say this.

But if, as I will argue, there is a present importance to the temple, the tribulation, and Armageddon, then we may need to heed the biblical exhortations related to each theme as it relates to us. That is, if we are the temple of God, then should we not strive for holiness now? And, if the notion of tribulation refers to some extent to the life of the follower of Christ now, then should we not be prepared to overcome? And if the notion of Armageddon refers to the present lives of the people of God throughout history, then should we not prepare to endure and to provide for our brothers and sisters in Christ who are enduring such today?

Furthermore, understanding the end times matters because the very nature of Scripture is such that the eschatological promises of the OT have been inaugurated in Christ. Understanding the end times, then, is vital. For to understand the end times is to understand the biblical story that the kingdom has begun. More than that, if we, the people of God, are missionally called to carry forth this kingdom, then understanding the end times is central for the very mission of God's people.

Understanding the New Testament and the End Times

Overview of This Book and Its Conclusions

I will begin in chapters three and four by examining the hermeneutical issues that are the primary source of the many differences among evangelicals. I will contend that a proper method of biblical interpretation has Jesus at the center. In chapter 3, I contend that the NT writers understood the entirety of the OT story as applying to Jesus. That is, he is the fulfillment of the story of Israel and the OT, and not merely certain isolated verses.[13] In chapter 4, I will further suggest that we must also understand the life, death, and resurrection of Jesus, the coming of the Spirit, and the mission of the NT people of God from the perspective of the end times. Thus, the New Creation has come in Christ, continues in the life of God's people, and looks forward to the consummation.

Chapter 5 will then include a look at the nature of biblical prophecy. I will note that the prophets were very concerned with the people of their day and their obedience, or the lack thereof, to the covenant. Thus, I will contend that the prophets must be understood in light of the historical era in which they prophesied. Our study of the prophets will include a look into their use of apocalyptic language.

After these opening chapters, I will turn our focus to four issues that are commonly misunderstood in regards to the end times. First, in chapters 6 and 7 we will explore the theme of the temple throughout Scripture in order to determine the nature and purpose of the temple and how this relates to the end times. I will begin by contending that one of the goals of creation is for God to dwell among his people. In light of this, I will show that Eden is understood in Scripture in terms of a temple, with Adam as a priest in the garden-temple. Moreover, I will contend that after the expulsion of humankind from Eden, God permitted temporary structures to serve as the place of his dwelling among his people. These included the tabernacle of Moses and the temple of Solomon. After the destruction of Solomon's temple, the prophets looked forward to a restoration of the presence of God among his people—that is, a future temple—in terms more fitting of Eden than of a physical building in Jerusalem. We will see that, contrary to some of the popular suggestions that a future temple will be rebuilt in Jerusalem prior to the return of Christ, all of these OT promises find their fulfillment in Jesus. I will also note that the theme of the temple in Scripture does not end with Christ and his resurrection. For,

13. Note: This chapter is the most complex chapter of the book. The argument of chapter 3 is helpful for understanding the rest of the book, but not necessary. If the reader has too much difficulty, feel free to move on to chapter 4.

Introduction to Understanding The New Testament and the End Times

Paul refers to the people of God as the temple in the exact same manner as Christ. Furthermore, the Scriptures look forward to the New Jerusalem as the consummation of God's promises regarding the temple. That is, the New Jerusalem is itself a temple, a restored Eden, and the climax of the dwelling of God among his people.

Chapter 8 will then examine the notion of "tribulation" in Scripture. The popular conception of the tribulation is that it represents a seven-year, or three-and-a-half-year, period of time immediately prior to the return of Jesus. As such, the tribulation is often viewed as exclusively in the future. We will observe, however, that the NT's focus on "tribulation" and "affliction" relates consistently to the current plight of the people of God. That is, the people of God are to be fulfilling the mission of God in building his kingdom, but to do so we must endure tribulation.

Chapters 9 and 10 will then examine what the Bible says about the second coming of Jesus. I will contend that the NT affirms three "signs" related to the time of Jesus' return, and that these signs relate to the present conduct of the people of God. First, the nations will be converted before Christ returns. Secondly, the holiness of the people of God will hasten the day of Christ. Finally, the suffering of God's people will ultimately cause him to delay no longer. I will note that each of these three elements have tremendous implications for Christian living. For, instead of passively watching for the alleged signs of Jesus' imminent return in the newspaper, the people of God are to be busy studying Scripture, applying it to our lives and our witness, and preparing to suffer for the sake of the kingdom!

In chapter 10, I will conduct a brief excursus and examine Jesus' end-times sermon (Matt 24–25; Mark 13; Luke 17, 21). This sermon is often understood as Jesus' message that delineates the events that will occur prior to his return. Instead, I will contend that, in light of the fact that Jesus does not know the hour of his return, the focus of this message is not on the signs that will occur immediately prior to his coming, but on the readiness of the people of God. That is, Jesus was not giving us details of what will transpire before his return so that we will know when his coming is near. Instead, Jesus was primarily concerned with what we are doing until he returns! Thus, again, the end times are missional and ethical!

In chapter 11, I will look at the use of "Armageddon" and "war" in the book of Revelation. I will contend that Revelation depicts a battle waged between Satan and God. Satan empowers the kings of the earth to do his bidding. But, instead of waging a pointless war against God himself, Satan employs the kings of the earth to attack the people of God.

Understanding the New Testament and the End Times

In chapter 12, I will endeavor to take all that we have learned and ask what all this might mean for the people of God today. I will affirm that a proper understanding of the end times is essential for the life of the people of God in the present and for how we are to understand the Scriptures. I will conclude that, in light of the whole of the biblical story, the New Creation has already begun in Christ, continues by means of the Spirit in the life of church, and that we look forward to its consummation in the New Jerusalem. This New Creation is a restoration and glorification of God's creation in Eden. And, this restoration is one in which God's people are called to participate. Our participation in God's work of restoration entails tribulation and suffering now! But, it ultimately results in our resurrection, when there will be no more suffering, pain, or death!

3

Jesus: Reading the Bible Christologically

Peter's depth of insight and the dexterity of his memory in Acts 2 reveal what might be the single most significant theological shift among the apostles: Jesus' resurrection and the profound experience with the Holy Spirit at Pentecost led the apostles into a "hermeneutical revolution." They suddenly had new eyes to reread and reinterpret the Old Testament from the perspective of the Story of Jesus.[1]

For as many as may be the promises of God, in Him they are yes. (2 Cor 1:20)

Introduction

THE FABRIC UPON WHICH the Bible was penned must be viewed as one garment. In the book of Revelation we see Genesis fulfilled. The whole Bible coheres and centers around the fact of God's redemption and restoration of both humankind and the whole of creation.[2] The entire Bible weaves a beautiful story of God's work in creation and, because of the fall, his subsequent effort to restore his creation. That is, its primary subject matter is God's redemption of his people and creation. Moreover, the central character in the biblical story is Jesus. Jesus is the means by which God is redeeming and restoring humankind and the creation. It is my contention that to properly interpret Scripture we must have Jesus as the center of our hermeneutic.[3] That is, the Scriptures are about Jesus!

1. McKnight, *King Jesus Gospel*, 117.
2. Cf. Rom 8:18–25.
3. Hermeneutics is the science of interpretation. The use of "hermeneutic" here is in the context of a set of assumptions that influence how one interprets the Bible. Thus, I am saying that to properly interpret the Scriptures we must understand that the central aspect of the biblical story is that it is about Jesus. When we understand that

The claim that a proper biblical hermeneutic centers on Jesus does not intend to suggest that he is simply the central character of the Bible—as though he were the primary character among many characters and subplots. Instead, I am suggesting that Jesus is the story! Everything is about Jesus! Indeed, there are the stories of Abraham, Moses, and David. But underlying the entire story of Scripture is the fulfillment of God's plan of redemption, which God has provided in Jesus. That is, even the stories of Abraham, Moses, and David point us to the ultimate fulfillment in Jesus.

In Jesus we have two central features of the biblical story coming to a climax. First, the Scriptures primarily relate to us God's desire to be made known and to be worshipped within his creation.[4] Secondly, and closely related, God is vitally concerned with the redemption of both humankind and of creation. What these two central features of the biblical story point to is the fact that Jesus is both God made known[5] and he is the means of redemption.[6]

In light of this we can say that the Bible is Christocentric (Christ centered) and, therefore, a proper hermeneutical starting point for all biblical interpretation is Christ. Jesus is our central hermeneutic. That is, the Bible must be understood in light of Jesus. As Paul asserts, "For as many as may be the promises of God, in Him they are yes" (2 Cor 1:20).[7]

Understanding the Entirety of the Bible in Light of Jesus

In suggesting that the entire story is about Jesus, I am not saying that Jesus merely fulfilled some isolated verses that prophesied his life, death, and resurrection (e.g., Isa 7:14; Isa 53; Micah 5:2). Instead, I am suggesting that we should understand that the whole story points to Jesus. That is, the entire story, and not merely certain isolated references, is fulfilled by Jesus.

Now I am not suggesting that the OT is merely allegorical and has no reference to real events. For example, the story of Joseph is a true historical account of a man named Joseph who became a significant ruler

---

the Bible is about Jesus we can then begin to explore the importance of this in regards to others matters, including eschatology.

4. See Wright, *Mission of God*.

5. Cf. John 1:18: Jesus is the "One and only" who "makes Him [the Father] known"

6. Cf. Eph 1:7: 'In Him we have redemption."

7. Richard Hays refers to the apostles' shift in understanding the entire story of the OT as fulfilled in Jesus as the "conversion of their imagination" (*Conversion of the Imagination*).

in Egypt. But it also looks forward to Christ, who similarly was betrayed by "those who were his own" (John 1:11)! The story of Joshua leading the Israelites into the promised land is a true historical account. Yet, it also looks forward to Jesus who leads his people into the ultimate promised land. Neither am I suggesting that we read every verse and find some application or fulfillment in the life of Jesus. But, instead, the story as a whole is to be read in light of Jesus.

It is only when the entirety of the Bible is read in light of Jesus that we can truly comprehend the grand narrative of the Bible and both the mission of Jesus and the mission of the people of God today. It is here that the end times and a proper understanding of the Bible become paramount. For if we fail to understand the mission of Jesus in light of the entirety of the biblical story, then we will likely fail to grasp the nature and significance of our mission.

This is the key. For many, a common perception of the Bible is that it contains stories and principles by which the Christian life is to be lived. Amidst the stories are predictions (prophecies if you will) that point to God's work in Jesus. Jesus' work, however, is often perceived of only in terms of his atoning for our sins and his leading us to heaven. This overly simplistic understanding of Scripture is problematic on a number of fronts. Primarily, in failing to view the entire story in light of God's plan for redeeming the entire creation, and Jesus' fulfillment of that plan, and the role of the people of God in carrying out that fulfillment, we fail to understand the nature and purpose of the people of God and our mission. Instead, the Bible becomes a moral handbook telling us what we should do—honor your father and mother—and not do—do not murder, steal, lie, commit adultery, and covet.

It is in understanding the Bible in terms of God's grand narrative and Jesus as the fulfillment of that narrative that the Bible comes to life. The story is exciting. It is also empowering, as we begin to realize that the work of building God's kingdom continues in the life of the NT people of God. All of this will climax in the coming of the New Jerusalem.

Though I think most readers are ready to move forward and see what this all means for us, it is perhaps worthwhile to provide some justification for my thesis that Jesus is the focus of the biblical story.

Understanding the New Testament and the End Times

Luke 24 and Jesus as the Fulfillment of All the Scriptures

That Jesus is the key to understanding the entirety of the Bible is evident from the accounts of the resurrected Jesus in Luke 24:13–35. Here Luke records two events that occurred on the day of the resurrection. First, we see the resurrected Jesus coming alongside two disciples of Jesus walking from Jerusalem to the village of Emmaus. They were followers of Jesus who were apparently bewildered by the events of the last several days. Jesus, whom they had hoped would restore God's kingdom to Israel, had been crucified by the Romans.[8] Earlier that same day, however, some of the women who had followed Jesus, as well as some of Jesus' disciples upon visiting his tomb, found it empty.[9] The two recounted all these events to Jesus—whom they were unable to recognize.[10] Suddenly, Jesus interjects, in what may be taken as an admonishment: "'O foolish men and slow of heart to believe in all that the prophets have spoken! Was it not necessary for the Christ to suffer these things and to enter into His glory?' And beginning with Moses and with all the prophets, He explained to them the things concerning Himself in *all the Scriptures*" (Luke 24:25–27).[11]

A second appearance of Jesus occurred later that evening in Jerusalem. The two men with whom Jesus spoke on the road returned to the rest of the disciples in Jerusalem. While these two were recounting the events and their meeting with Jesus, he suddenly appeared in the room. Jesus, then explained to them all, "'These are My words which I spoke to you while I was still with you, that *all things* which are written about Me in the Law of Moses and the Prophets and the Psalms must be fulfilled.' Then He opened their minds to understand the Scriptures, and He said to them, 'Thus it is written, that the Christ should suffer and rise again from the dead the third day'" (Luke 24:44–46).[12] Consequently, on both occasions Jesus appears to assert that the entire OT is fulfilled in himself.[13]

---

8. Cf. Luke 24:19–21.
9. Cf. Luke 24:22–23.
10. Cf. Luke 24:16.
11. Note: "Moses and all the prophets" (Luke 24:27) is a common first-century Jewish manner of referencing the entirety of the OT.
12. Note the threefold designation for the entirety of the OT: "Law of Moses, Prophets, and the Psalms" (Luke 24:45). This is merely another common designation for referencing the entire OT.
13. In both instances Jesus has the entire OT in view: First, He utilized the twofold designation of "Moses and the Prophets" (Luke 24:27); then he refers to it according to the threefold designation of "Law, Prophets, and the Psalms" (Luke 24:44). Both, however, customarily refer to the entirety of the OT from Genesis through Malachi

Jesus: Reading the Bible Christologically

Now, at this juncture some may suggest that Jesus was merely identifying isolated prophesies that he had fulfilled. However, in Luke 24:25 Jesus states directly, "O foolish men and slow of heart to believe in *all* that the prophets have spoken." Jesus' words strongly suggest that he was referencing "all" the Scriptures and not merely "all that refer to me." The best reading of this text is that Jesus viewed the entirety of the OT witness as fulfilled in himself.

General Statements That Show That Jesus Is the Fulfillment of All the Scriptures

Secondly, that the NT views Jesus as the fulfillment of the entirety of the OT story is seen in that the person and work of Jesus is presented in terms of the overall story of the Bible and not just in light of the fulfillment of isolated verses. This concept is a bit more difficult to grasp. But, the fact is that there are instances in the NT in which Jesus claims to be fulfilling the Scriptures and yet we have no corresponding prophecy in the OT. That is, we cannot find any passage in the OT that corresponds to Jesus' claim.

For example, Luke records:

> And He took the twelve aside and said to them, "Behold, we are going up to Jerusalem, and all things which are written through the prophets about the Son of Man will be accomplished. For He will be delivered to the Gentiles, and will be mocked and mistreated and spit upon, and after they have scourged Him, they will kill Him; and the third day He will rise again. Thus *it is written*, that the Christ would suffer and rise again from the dead the third day." (Luke 18:31–33)[14]

The difficulty here is that we do not know of any verse that "prophesies" that the Christ (Hebrew: "Messiah") would rise again on the third day.

That Jesus, in Luke 18, is not referencing a particular prophecy is evident first from the fact that he references "the prophets." That is, Jesus refers to the prophets in general, which may well be understood to refer more generically to the Scriptures, and not to a particular prophet or any particular saying of the prophets.[15]

---

as we know it.

14. Cf. Mark 9:12; Luke 24:46.

15. "The prophets" can be a general reference to Scripture, which was commonly referred to as "the Law and the Prophets" (Matt 7:12; 11:13; 22:40; Luke 16:16; 24:44; John 1:45; Acts 13:15; 24:14; 28:23; Rom 3:21) or "the Law, the Psalms, and the

Understanding the New Testament and the End Times

Secondly, though specific passages can be found in the OT that suggest that the people of God will suffer,[16] there are no corresponding references that indicate in the least that the Christ would rise on the third day.[17] That is, there are no verses in the OT to which we can turn to and say, "Jesus was referring to this passage." The best we can come up with is the reference in Hosea 6:2: "He will revive us after two days; He will raise us up on the third day that we may live before Him." This passage, however, contains no direct messianic overtones, but instead references the promised restoration of Israel (note "us").

If, however, we are to understand that the overarching narrative theme of the Bible is God's redemptive and restorative work, and that this work reaches its fulfillment in Jesus, then the promise of the restoration of God's people, announced in Hosea 6:2, indeed finds its fulfillment in Jesus. That is, if we understand that Jesus is the fulfillment of the entirety of the OT, then we have no real difficulty with Jesus saying that the Christ must "rise again from the dead the third day" (Luke 18:31–33).

Jesus' claim in Luke 18:31–33 is problematic, however, if we assume that Jesus fulfills only isolated verses. For there are no verses in the OT that could be cited as referencing the Christ dying and rising again on the third day. There is no problem, however, if we assume that Jesus has in view the entirety of the story of the OT. One could simply reference Hosea 6:2 and see Jesus as the embodiment of the people of God and, thus, the fulfillment of this passage.

Jesus' claim that he will rise on the third day may also be understood in light of the story of Jonah. This finds support in that Luke has already associated Jesus' death and resurrection with account of Jonah: "For just as Jonah became a sign to the Ninevites, so shall the Son of Man be to this generation" (Luke 11:30). A direct link between Jesus' death and resurrection and the account of Jonah is also supported by the parallel in Matthew:

Prophets" (Luke 24:44).

16. For example, Isaiah 52:13—53:12. This passage, which is widely recognized by Christians to refer to the Messiah, is perhaps in its original context of Isaiah about the people of Israel (cf. Isa 44:1, where the servant is explicitly called Israel and Jacob). There is no doubt that the NT understands it as fulfilled in Jesus! The point is that Jesus is fulfilling a prophecy that relates to the suffering of the people. That is, Jesus is the people of God and the fulfillment of the seed of Abraham (Gal 3:16).

17. Joel Green acknowledges, "One would be hard-pressed to locate specific texts that make these prognostications explicit. Even to attempt to do so would be wrongheaded, however. The point of Jesus' words is not that such-and-such a verse has now come true, but that the truth to which all of the Scriptures point has now been realized!" (Green, *Luke*, 857).

"for just as Jonah was three days and three nights in the belly of the sea monster, so shall the Son of Man be three days and three nights in the heart of the earth" (12:40).

But again it must be noted that there are no explicit prophesies in Jonah regarding the Messiah rising on the third day. There is no problem, however, if we view Jesus as the fulfillment of the story of Jonah. This is how Matthew can draw the parallel between Jonah's being three days and nights in the belly of the fish and Jesus' death and resurrection.

Therefore, when the NT refers to Jesus as the fulfillment of the OT, it is not merely referring to him as the fulfillment of specific OT passages, but to the overall story of Scripture. Jesus is the hermeneutical key to understanding the Bible. The entire narrative of the Bible is about Jesus!

The Gospel of John and Jesus as the Fulfillment of All the Scriptures

Another example that all of the Scriptures are about Jesus, and not just certain isolated prophecies, is evident from even a cursory look at the Gospel of John. For example, in John 5:39, 45–47 Jesus asserts, "You search the Scriptures, because you think that in them you have eternal life; and it is these that bear witness of Me. . . . The one who accuses you is Moses, in whom you have set your hope. For if you believed Moses, you would believe Me; for he wrote of Me. But if you do not believe his writings, how will you believe My words?" When these verses are read in light of the whole of the Gospel of John it becomes clear that Jesus is not simply referring to isolated prophecies within the Torah/Pentateuch,[18] but to the entirety of it.

First, that Jesus was referring to the whole of the Torah/Pentateuch and not just select messianic verses, it is important to note that Jesus claims that they do not believe "My words" (John 5:47). That is, it is the teachings of Jesus that the Jewish leaders at the time missed. They failed to see that what Jesus was saying was fully in accord with the words of Moses. But, that Jesus was referring to the whole tenor of the Torah of Moses, and not to any particular teaching, is evident in that Jesus does not appeal to a

---

18. "Torah" generally refers to the first five books of the OT, which are traditionally attributed to Moses. In these instances it is equivalent to the Christian designation the "Pentateuch" (five rolls or books). "Torah" may also have a broader meaning that includes the entirety of the OT, and occasionally it can include the entirety of Jewish teaching and practices.

particular chapter and verse to support his argument. That is, if Jesus had in mind a particular verse, or set of verses, in the writings of Moses that he was fulfilling, then why did he not reference them? It would certainly have been compelling for Jesus to point out a specific reference in the writing of Moses and show them that he was indeed fulfilling it. We can imagine that John's readers would certainly like to have known to which verses Jesus might have been referring. That Jesus does not appeal to any passage suggests that it is the whole of his teachings that fulfills the whole of the Torah.

Secondly, one of the major thrusts of John's portrait of Jesus is in regards to Jesus as the fulfillment of the OT—not just as the Messiah but also in terms of the institutions, symbols, and festivals of Judaism.[19] Jesus in the Gospel of John conforms to Paul's affirmation that "the old has gone, the new has come" (2 Cor 5:17). Thus, in the Gospel of John, the waters of purification are fulfilled with the new wine,[20] the temple finds its fulfillment in Jesus,[21] the old birth looks to the new birth of the Spirit,[22] the water from Jacob's well looks forward to the Spirit who is the living water,[23] and worship in Jerusalem and Gerizim looks forward to the true worship, which is "in spirit and truth."[24]

Also, in John 5–10, the events of Jesus' ministry are consistently dated in relation to a feast. John then uses both the narratives of the events related to the feast and the speeches of Jesus associated with these feasts to demonstrate that the feasts of Israel find their fulfillment in Jesus. In doing so, John affirms that Jesus has fulfilled the Jewish festivals. For example, in chapter 5, the true meaning of Sabbath and work points to Christ.[25]

Furthermore, in chapter 6, Jesus is the true "bread of God" that "comes down out of heaven" (6:33) in fulfillment of the Feast of Passover.[26] Jesus' declarations that he is the "light of the world" (8:12; 9:5) and the source of "living water" (7:39) take place during the Feast of Tabernacles.[27] The significance of these proclamations is that during the seven (or eight?)

---

19. The following relies heavily on my entry on "John" in Longman, *Baker Illustrated Bible Dictionary*.
20. John 2:1–11.
21. John 2:12–25.
22. John 3:1–21.
23. John 4:7–15; 7:37–39.
24. John 4:20–24.
25. John 5:1–47.
26. John 6:1–71.
27. John 7:1—9:41.

days of the Feast of Tabernacles elaborate water ceremonies and the lighting of four huge lamps in the temple's Court of Women took place.[28] Jesus' declaration of himself as the source of "living water" and as the "light of the world" during this feast strongly suggests that he was declaring himself to be the fulfillment of light and water for which this feast looked towards. This is all the more likely in light of the fact that John consistently portrays Jesus as performing acts and making speeches that link Jesus with the fulfillment of the feast.

Finally, Jesus declares himself to be the "good shepherd" (John 10:11, 14) during the Feast of Dedication.[29] The significance of this is that Jesus was alluding to Ezekiel 34, which affirms that the leaders of Israel were called to shepherd the people of God. The failure of the leadership at the time of Ezekiel led to his rebuke and the declaration that God himself will

> search for My sheep and seek them out. . . . I will seek the lost, bring back the scattered, bind up the broken, and strengthen the sick. . . . I will deliver My flock. . . . Then I will set over them one shepherd, My servant David, and he will feed them; he will feed them himself and be their shepherd. (Ezek 34:11, 16, 22, 23)

It is evident that John understands Jesus' declaration to be the "good shepherd" in light of Ezekiel 34. Jesus is the shepherd of Israel and the fulfillment of God's promise that he himself will be the shepherd of Israel. That Jesus makes this declaration during the Feast of Dedication is highlighted by the fact that Ezekiel 34 formed part of the liturgy for the Feast of Dedication![30] Thus, Jesus is again declaring that he is the fulfillment of all that this feast points towards and not simply isolated verses within the texts.

Conclusion: What Does It Mean to Say That the OT Finds Its Fulfillment in Jesus?

It is reasonably clear then, even from this fairly quick glance into the NT, that "as many as may be the promises of God, in Him they are yes" (2 Cor 1:20). That the promises of the OT find their fulfillment in Jesus is one of the most significant factors to understanding the end times in the NT. Scot

---

28. The Mishnah states, "He who has not seen the joy of the place of water-drawing has never in his life seen joy" (Mishnah *Sukkah* 5:1–4).
29. See John 10:1–39.
30. Burge, *John*, 288.

McKnight concludes, "Each of the four witnesses [Matthew–John] tells us the same thing about the gospel. It is the Story of Israel that comes to completion in the saving Story of Jesus, who is the Messiah of Israel, Lord over all, and the Davidic Savior. There is one and only one gospel, and it was preached by Jesus, by Paul, and by Peter. To gospel is to tell that story about Jesus."[31]

Now it is important to understand that this does not mean that everything in the OT has already reached its consummation. For, we see that the kingdom of God has come in Christ in fulfillment of the OT promises, and yet the kingdom of this world remains.[32] The point is that when one is looking at the issues related to the end times and pondering the prophesies of the last days, one must first ask, "How, and in what manner, might the fulfillment of these prophesies have been inaugurated by Christ?"

At this point I am fully aware that some readers may still find it difficult to accept that all of the Scriptures are about Jesus. This may stem from an understanding of Scripture that asserts that a given verse must be interpreted in light of its immediate context. This understanding is of course quite true. Yet, here it seems that I am arguing that Jesus took a passage out of its immediate context and applied it to himself. This creates a crisis of belief. Either we suggest that Jesus was wrong in doing so, which very few of us would concede, or we must consider the possibility that our assertion is incomplete.

Ultimately, I am suggesting that there is nothing wrong here. Our high view of Scripture can still be maintained, though we are in need of a slight addition to our paradigm. If we conclude, as I am suggesting, that the entirety of the Scriptures—that is, the overarching narrative of God's plan to make himself known and to redeem and restore his creation—is about Jesus, then we may also conclude that Jesus is certainly correct to claim that a passage, which on the surface appears to be about the restoration of Israel, is about him. That is, the restoration of Israel finds its fulfillment in Jesus. Consequently, we must both determine the meaning of a passage in light of its original context and determine how this points us to Jesus!

Thus, the entirety of the story is about Jesus. This is what Jesus was telling the two on the road to Emmaus and the disciples later that same evening! "It was about me! The whole story was leading to me!" Jesus, then, does not simply affirm that he came to fulfill parts of the Law and the

---

31. McKnight, *King Jesus Gospel*, 131.
32. This thought will be developed more fully in ch. 8.

Prophets, namely, those parts that applied to him. Instead, the entirety of the Law and the Prophets is fulfilled in Jesus.

4

Jesus, the End Times, and the Arrival of the Kingdom

And after John had been taken into custody, Jesus came into Galilee, preaching the gospel of God, and saying, "The time is fulfilled, and the kingdom of God is at hand; repent and believe in the gospel" (Mark 1:14–15)

The end times are a present reality since the first coming of Jesus. This is the conviction of Peter, Paul, John, Jude, and the author of the epistle to the Hebrews. The conviction that the present time is the "end time" derives from the belief of the apostles that Jesus is Israel's promised Messiah in whose person, ministry, death, and resurrection God has fulfilled his promises of salvation.[1]

Introduction

IN THE PREVIOUS CHAPTER it was argued that the Bible must be read in light of Jesus. He is the fulfillment of the entirety of the narrative of God's work of redemption and restoration. Now I wish to venture further and suggest that the coming of Christ must not only be understood in terms of the fulfillment of the OT story, but also in terms of the inauguration of the kingdom of God, which itself is the beginning of the eschaton (i.e., end times, last days, etc.). Thus, in contrast to many of the popular conceptions that suggest that the end times are future, it is my contention, which is widely acknowledged among the scholarly world, that they began with the coming of Christ, continue in the present through the work of the Spirit, and await the consummation at his return.[2]

---

1. Schnabel, *40 Questions*, 25.
2. I am not making any claims as to the nature and timing of the millennium.

Jesus, the End Times, and the Arrival of the Kingdom

The importance of understanding that the kingdom of God has come in and through Christ cannot be overstated. For the central thesis in this book is that eschatology matters. It matters because we are living in the eschaton. We are not waiting for it to come. We are not called to scour the newspapers and Internet to discern if the "signs of the times" are being fulfilled in our generation. Instead, we are to be busy living in the kingdom as agents of the kingdom! Thus, understanding the NT from the perspective that in Jesus the eschaton has arrived not only provides a needed clarity to the message of the NT, but it also more clearly delineates the nature and mission of God's people. To say that Christ came the first time to be our Savior and to die for our sins and that he will return to become the king not only overly simplifies things, but also fails to understand the mission of Jesus and the nature of the kingdom of God.

The question I wish to investigate, then, throughout this chapter is: Does viewing the NT and the life of Jesus from an eschatological perspective provide the best foundation for understanding the NT? G. K. Beale, in fact, suggests, "Just as when you put on green sunglasses, everything you see is green, so Christ through the Spirit had placed eschatological sunglasses on his disciples so that everything they looked at in the Christian faith had an end-time tint."[3]

Understanding the NT in Light of the End Times

I often ask my seminary students several questions that appear on the surface to be simple Bible trivia. The answers, however, are not straightforward. In fact, I would suggest that these conundrums are only solvable when one reads the NT from the perspective that Jesus was ushering in, and did usher in, the eschaton!

First, I will ask, "Why was Jesus baptized?" It is interesting to watch graduate students wrestle with what on the surface appears to be a very simple question—after all, the event must have been important since it is

---

For the reader who is aware of such theology, I will only say that whether the millennium is present or future is secondary at this time. I am fully aware of the theological intricacies of premillennialism, postmillennialism, and amillennialism. However, I do believe that proponents of each of the views should be able to affirm the main thrust of this chapter and this book as a whole.

3. Beale, *New Testament Biblical Theology*, 18. On the same page Beale adds, "This means that the doctrine of eschatology in NT theology textbooks should not merely be one among many doctrines that are addressed but should be the lens through which all the doctrines are best understood."

either described or referenced in each of the four Gospels.[4] It doesn't take long for the students to begin speculating: "He did so in order to be an example to us." This is the most common assertion.

The problem is that the NT never says that Jesus was baptized as an example for us. If this were the reason, then one might expect Paul to reference the baptism of Jesus as a model for Christian baptism. But he does not. I would go so far, in fact, as to say that none of Jesus' disciples would have even thought that he was baptized merely as an example for them. Furthermore, if Jesus' baptism primarily served as an example for us, then we might suggest that the Gospel writers would have preferred to omit this event. For, the writers of the NT could well have challenged the first Christians to be baptized in light of the fact that they themselves were baptized, or they could have appealed to the fact that Jesus commanded them to be baptized (Matt 28:18–20). There was no real need to affirm that Jesus was baptized. After all, the baptizing of Jesus with a "baptism of repentance" only raises questions. Why was Jesus baptized with a baptism of repentance when he was without sin? It may well have been easier to simply omit references to Jesus' baptism. Yet, all four Gospels mention John the Baptist, and the Synoptics[5] all have Jesus being baptized by him.

Another conundrum in the NT is: Why does Matthew's Gospel note that the angel tells Joseph to name the child Immanuel (Matt 1:23), yet two verses later they name him Jesus? And, in fact, Jesus is never called Immanuel in the NT! Even more problematic is the fact that Matthew cites Isaiah 7:14 and claims this as the first of his five famed "fulfillment passages."[6] Yet, if Jesus is never named Immanuel then does this really constitute a fulfillment?

Thirdly, why are the first words in the Gospel of John, "In the beginning" (John 1:1)? This is a clear allusion to Genesis 1. But why does John cite Genesis 1 when there appears to be no overt reference to the creation account in the Fourth Gospel?

Finally, why does Matthew begin his Gospel with a genealogy? For most of us genealogies are something found in the OT. Why, then, does the NT begin with one? Many have suggested that Matthew draws

---

4. Cf. Matt 3:13–17; Mark 1:9–11; Luke 3:21–22; John 1:29–34.

5. The word "Synoptics" means "seeing together" and refers to Matthew, Mark, and Luke. The term comes from the fact that these three Gospels are very similar in their overall content.

6. The five "fulfillment passages" in Matt 1–2 are: 1:18–25; 2:1–12; 2:13–15; 2:16–18; 2:19–23. In each account Matthew narrates an event in Jesus' birth and childhood in accord with the OT in order to demonstrate that Jesus fulfilled the Scripture.

a connection to David in his lineage thereby demonstrating that Jesus is qualified to be the king. Such is indeed true. But a closer look at Matthew 1:1–17 confirms that Matthew explicitly draws up his genealogy into three distinct sections, each comprising fourteen generations: "Therefore all the generations from Abraham to David are fourteen generations; and from David to the deportation to Babylon fourteen generations; and from the deportation to Babylon to the time of Christ fourteen generations" (1:17). Yet, a problem arises when one compares the genealogy of Matthew with the corresponding genealogies in the OT[7]; for Matthew, in order to have fourteen generations in each segment, has had to omit names.[8] Why did Matthew do this? Why was it important that he classified Jesus' ancestry into three groups? And why was it important that they be delineated into groups of fourteen generations?

Only after we have sufficiently understood Jesus as the end times prophet[9] who was announcing in his presence and his ministry the fulfillment of all of God's covenant promises, can we begin to fully appreciate these and many other aspects of the life of Jesus. Furthermore, with a focus on Jesus as the end times prophet, not only do many aspects of the Gospel come to life, but only then can we begin to look at our mission as the people of God in an end times context.

The Story Is About Jesus and the Inauguration of the Eschaton

That the coming of Christ in the opening of each of the Gospels is closely viewed in connection with the OT is beyond dispute. Matthew's Gospel commences with a genealogy that clearly serves to identify Jesus with the story of the OT.[10] The Gospel of Mark opens with a composite citation

7. Cf. 1 Chr 2:1–15; 3:10–24.

8. One need only realize that the third section of Matthew's genealogy spans five hundred years and has only fourteen generations to see that names have been omitted. See Leon Morris, *Gospel according to Matthew*, 22.

9. That is, the prophet that ushers in the end times. Now, I fully understand that Jesus was much more than the eschatological prophet. The focus here is merely on this aspect of Jesus' identity and ministry.

10. That Matthew's genealogy serves to identify Jesus with the story of the OT and not merely the lineage of Abraham and David is evident in the intended structure of the genealogy. Matthew notes in 1:17 that there were fourteen generations in all from Abraham to David, and from David to the exile, and from the exile to Jesus. This arrangement of the genealogy suggests that the story of Israel, which moves from Abraham to David, from David to the exile, and the exile to Jesus, finds its consummation

of Isaiah 40:3; Exodus 23:20; and Malachi 3:1 that serves to identify the coming of John the Baptist as the herald of the promise coming of Christ.[11] Luke's opening two chapters contain a plethora of OT citations and allusions.[12] And the Gospel of John begins by quoting Genesis: "In the beginning" (1:1). In each instance, the Gospels are connecting the narrative of Jesus with the OT story.

Upon closer examination, we note that the Gospel writers intended us to see the coming of Christ both as the fulfillment of the entirety of the OT story and as the inauguration of the end times.[13] It is too simple, then, to merely state that John 1:1 alludes to the creation narrative in Genesis. Instead, John wants us to not only see Jesus in light of the creation narrative of Genesis, but also in terms of a new creation. That is, "In the beginning" not only serves to connect the story of Jesus with Genesis and the OT, but also in an eschatological—forward-looking—sense. Thus, with the coming of Jesus we have "in the beginning" a reference to the New Creation.

One may also read the Gospel of Mark in such a light as well. In his opening citation he references Isaiah 40:3; Exodus 23:20; and Malachi 3:1. Each of these verses employs the term "road/way" (Greek: *hodos*). This term occurs in Exodus 23:20 in connection with the exodus of Israel out of Egypt. Isaiah then picks up the term and applies it in the context of the end times return of God and his people in terms of a new exodus.[14] The use of *hodos* in Malachi 3:1 then extends the end times dimension of the restoration of God's people by associating it with the return of God himself to his temple.[15] In citing these verses in the opening of his Gospel, Mark, then, is

---

in Jesus. (Note: The exile refers to the sending out as captives of the people of Israel at the hands of foreign nations. The northern kingdom of Israel was sent out by the Assyrians in 721 BC and the southern kingdom of Judah was sent out in 605 BC.)

11. Cf. Mark 1:2–3.

12. Luke's use of the OT is significant despite the fact that he does not extensively cite the OT. Pao and Schnabel note, "Luke's use of the OT Scripture underlies his conviction that the OT prophetically announced Jesus' life and ministry" ("Luke," in Beale and Carson, *Commentary on the NT Use of the OT*, 252).

13. Beale goes so far as to claim, "it should not be astonishing to discover that eschatology is a dominant idea in the NT" (*New Testament Biblical Theology*, 129).

14. In Isa 40–66 the people of Israel are in exile. They are viewed as already having been sent out of the land. Isa 40–66 then predicts the eschatological return of the people. (Note: Isaiah employs an abundance of exodus imagery to depict the return of the people to the land.)

15. In Malachi the coming of the messenger clears the way and the "Lord, whom you seek, will suddenly come into His temple" (3:1). Thus, Malachi associates the future restoration of God's people with the exodus of the past and looks forward to the restoration of God's presence among his people. See ch. 7 for a look at the temple in

Jesus, the End Times, and the Arrival of the Kingdom

able to associate the coming of John the Baptist, and ultimately of Christ himself, with the theme of exodus and the return of the people of Israel from the exile. In fact, the coming of Christ and the return from the exile is itself the beginning of a new exodus.

That the new exodus in Mark 1:2–3 is focused on the end times derives from the fact that Mark presents the story of Jesus in terms of bringing to a climax the story of Scripture. Hence, Mark introduces Jesus as the one who proclaims, "The time is fulfilled; the kingdom of God is at hand" (Mark 1:15). Such an event is best described as "eschatological." In light of this, we are justified in reading the Gospels, and the entire NT for that matter, from the perspective that Jesus is ushering in the eschaton (end times).

We must understand that the prophecies of the OT regarding the restoration of the people are inherently tied to what we tend to call the end times. To somehow separate the work of Christ in his first coming and the return of Christ to the extent that in his return he ushers in the end is to insert a break that the writers of the NT and the Jewish world at the time of Jesus would never have understood. That is, the prophecies that Jesus fulfills are part and parcel of the prophecies of the end times. It is true, as we see from the rest of the NT and the pages of history, that Jesus did not completely bring about the New Creation in totality—for sin and death remain. But to say that Jesus did not inaugurate the end times is to seriously misunderstand his mission. To say that the Gospels are eschatological and that they present the inauguration of the climax of the OT story does not mean that they are marking the completion of the end also. For we realize that evil, suffering, and death still exist. It is this tension between the continuing presence of evil and the present reign of Christ that has led to much confusion among many Christians in regard to eschatology and the end times.

Furthermore, many are hindered from understanding Jesus as the fulfillment of the OT promises by the fact that some of the prophesies of the OT incorporate a finality or totality to them; that is, the effect is eternal or catastrophic, perhaps even resulting in the destruction of the cosmos. Naturally, many conclude that since this aspect of a given prophecy has yet to occur, then the prophecy has clearly not yet been fulfilled. Thus, they look to the second coming of Jesus as the fulfillment of a given prophecy. This is a very Western (either/or) way of thinking. For example, it is assumed that since the result of a given prophecy is the dissolution of

---

the NT.

the heavens, and since such has not occurred, then the fulfillment of the prophecy must await the future. Such thinking is not inherently wrong.

But what if the fulfillment of prophecy is more complex than this? Is it not possible that the fulfillment of a prophecy may happen over time? Might not the fulfillment of a prophecy have already begun in Christ, and continue in the life of God's people today, and climax in the New Jerusalem? That is, do we necessarily have to view a prophecy as being fulfilled at only one point in time? For, as I will contend in chapters 6 and 7, the NT identifies Jesus as the temple of God in fulfillment of the OT promises of the restoration of God's presence among his people. Yet, we also find that the NT people of God are the temple of God in continuity with the OT and Jesus as the temple. Finally, we see that the New Jerusalem is the climax of the promises of the temple. Thus, the promises of the restoration of the temple begin to find their fulfillment in Jesus, they continue to find their fulfillment in the NT people of God, and they are ultimately fulfilled in the New Jerusalem.

Jesus' Ministry in an End Times Context

It is necessary at this point to continue our investigation into the nature of the NT and the end times by looking at three arguments that the NT presents the person and ministry of Jesus in an end times or "eschatological" context.

The NT Presents the Teachings of Jesus in an End Times Context by Using Apocalyptic Language

First, understanding the NT in an end times context makes sense of the apocalyptic language used to describe the events in the life of Jesus and the coming of the Spirit. Thus, the first coming of Christ was an eschatological event for which the best language to depict was apocalyptic. What the prophets had looked forward to now finds its consummation in Jesus.

What is apocalyptic language? To put it simply, I prefer to define apocalyptic language as "the use of 'cosmic upheaval' language and imagery to describe events of 'covenantal significance.'"[16] By "cosmic up-

16. The more technical answer as to the nature of apocalyptic itself is that it is "A genre of revelatory literature with a narrative framework, in which a revelation is mediated by an otherworldly being to a human recipient, disclosing a transcendent reality which is both temporal, insofar as it envisages eschatological salvation, and spatial

heaval" language I am referring to such things as the stars falling from heaven,[17] the sun becoming darkened,[18] the moon turning into blood,[19] and earthquakes.[20] By events of "covenantal significance" I mean that the events themselves are in the context of the fulfillment of God's covenantal promises of redemption and restoration.

Now, for many of us who have read the Gospel stories depicting the events of the cross, resurrection, and the coming of the Spirit at Pentecost, this language has failed to conjure the tremendous significance of these events. We have simply concluded, often not even recognizing the apocalyptic nature of the language, that some supernatural phenomena occurred at the cross and at the pouring out of the Spirit at Pentecost.[21]

A problem at this point is that many readers may feel a bit uneasy at the notion that Jesus and the NT writers employed apocalyptic language. It is important that we understand that ancient writers employed this genre because it allowed them an avenue to move their readers/hearers emotionally as well as intellectually. Plain narration, as in most stories, may well persuade some, but if writers truly want to impact their readers/hearers, they must also learn to tell their stories in a manner that moves people emotionally.

---

insofar as it involves another, supernatural world" (Collins, "Introduction," 5). David Aune proposed a change that omits mediation by an otherworldly being, and adds "in autobiographical form" and "revelatory visions . . . so structured that the central revelatory message constitutes a literary climax" (Aune, "Apocalypse," 86–87). Apocalyptic language is just language used to describe such a worldview. The difficulty in defining the genre is that no one work displays all the characteristics set forth as apocalyptic.

17. Mark 13:25; cf. also Luke 21:25; Rev 8:12.
18. Matt 24:29; Mark 13:24.
19. Acts 2:20; Rev 6:12.
20. Matt 27:54; 28:2; Rev 11:3.
21. The events at the cross that may be viewed as apocalyptic include: darkness (Mark 15:33; Luke 23:44), an earthquake (Matt 27:51), tearing of the temple veil (Matt 27:51; Luke 23:45), and the bodies of the dead walking around town (Matt 27:52). The apocalyptic like events at Pentecost include: the presence of a violent wind, tongues of fire coming upon the people, and people speaking in foreign tongues (Acts 2:2–4). See below for further discussion.

Understanding the New Testament and the End Times

NT's Use of Apocalyptic Catchphrase "He Who Has Ears, Let Him Hear"

That we are to read portions of the NT within an apocalyptic framework is apparent from the use of the phrase "he who has ears let him hear."[22] For some readers, this phrase may resonate from the seven letters written in the book of Revelation. Indeed, each of seven letters incorporates this phrase.[23] By use of this apocalyptic catchphrase, John warns his readers/hearers to listen carefully to what is said. In addition to warning the readers/hearers to pay attention, this phrase also serves as an apocalyptic warning to listen carefully because the words are difficult to understand and only those with ears to hear will comprehend.[24]

This phrase also appears in the prophets of the OT. In Ezekiel the phrase is used in conjunction with a prophetic message from a prophet to the house of Israel. It serves as a stern warning. For example, Ezekiel is told, "Thus says the Lord God. 'He who hears, let him hear; and he who refuses, let him refuse'" (3:27).

The NT, however, most likely utilizes this phrase in light of the commissioning of Isaiah.[25] Isaiah is told go and prophesy to the people, "Keep on listening, but do not perceive; Keep on looking, but do not understand. Render the hearts of this people insensitive, their ears dull, and their eyes dim, lest they see with their eyes, hear with their ears, understand with their hearts, and return and be healed" (6:9–10). "He who has ears to hear" thus suggests that the prophetic message will not be heard by all, but only by those with "ears to hear."[26]

The apocalyptic aspect of this phrase then incorporates the notion that the prophets' messages were not easily understood. The relative obscurity of their messages allowed them to further harden the hearts of those without ears and eyes,[27] and to exhort those with ears and eyes to

---

22. Rev 2:7, 11, 17, 29; 3:6, 13, 22; 13:9; Matt 11:15; 13:9, 43; Mark 4:9, 23; Luke 8:8; 14:35.

23. Rev 2:7, 11, 17, 29; 3:6, 13, 22.

24. This is why Jesus used this phrase with reference to his parables. Cf. Mark 4:9, 23; Matt 11:15; 13:9, 43.

25. Cf. Isa 6; cf also, Jer 5:21; 17:23.

26. Note that Jesus was explaining all of his parables to his disciples privately (Mark 4:34). Thus, even the disciples did not understand the parable, but since they have "ears to hear" Jesus explained things to them.

27. Cf. Isa 6:9–10; Jer 5:21; 17:23.

respond.[28] It is this dual sense that stands behind the use of this phrase in the commands of Revelation 2–3. The apocalyptic vision of John and his message to the seven churches will only be heard by some. Those who hear must also "heed" and do the things "written in it" (Rev 1:3). Thus, this phrase served as a prophetic indication that the apocalyptic message of the prophets must be obeyed. Those without ears and eyes will only be further hardened in their unbelief and idolatry.

Jesus Uses "He Who Has, Ears Let Him Hear"

The importance of this discussion is that this catchphrase also appears in the words of Jesus. In fact, each of the Synoptics record that Jesus uttered this phrase.[29] The most significant use of this phrase occurs in the parable of the Sower.[30] This parable, which is one of only two parables in the Gospel of Mark, serves to lay a foundation for understanding the teachings of Jesus: "Do you understand this parable? And how will you understand all the parables?" (4:13). Thus, Jesus employed this apocalyptic catchphrase both to associate his message with that of the prophets and to mark his coming within an apocalyptic context.

Therefore, in accord with Isaiah, Jeremiah, and Ezekiel, Jesus arrives as an eschatological prophet who announces, by means of apocalyptic language, a message to the people of God. The difference between Jesus and the prophets is that, whereas the prophets announced that the kingdom of God was coming, Jesus announced that it was present in himself.[31]

The NT Uses Apocalyptic Language for Numerous Events In the Life of Jesus

Secondly, it is important to note that in several places the events of the life, death, and resurrection of Jesus, as well as the coming of the Spirit at Pentecost, are depicted by means of apocalyptic imagery.[32] The depiction

---

28. Cf. Ezek 3:25.

29. Cf. Matt 11:15; 13:9, 43; Mark 4:9, 23; Luke 8:8; 14:35.

30. Note that Mark clearly associates this phrase with the prophetic commissioning of Isaiah 6 (cf. Mark 4:10–12; Isa 6:9–11).

31. Cf. Mark 1:15; Luke 17:21.

32. It is superfluous for our purposes to debate the historicity of such events. That is, many wish to reject the historicity of these events because they are depicted in apocalyptic terms. Others will deny that the language is apocalyptic because they fear

of these events in apocalyptic language suggests that the biblical writers understood Christ's first coming in terms of the arrival of the eschaton.

For example, Matthew records that while Jesus was on the cross, "And behold, the veil of the temple was torn in two from top to bottom, and the earth shook; and the rocks were split, and the tombs were opened; and many bodies of the saints who had fallen asleep were raised; and coming out of the tombs after His resurrection they entered the holy city and appeared to many" (27:51–52). Matthew, Mark, and Luke all note, "And when the sixth hour had come, darkness fell over the whole land until the ninth hour" (Matt 27:45; Mark 15:33; Luke 23:44). And in Acts 2, at the descent of the Holy Spirit at Pentecost, Peter cites Joel 2 to explain the significance of what has transpired: "'And it shall be in the last days,' God says, 'That I will pour forth of My Spirit upon all humankind; . . . And I will grant wonders in the sky above, and signs on the earth beneath, blood, and fire, and vapor of smoke. The sun shall be turned into darkness, And the moon into blood, Before the great and glorious day of the Lord shall come'" (Acts 2:17, 19–20).[33]

The use of such apocalyptic imagery—of stars falling, the sky darkening, and earthquakes opening the tombs of the dead—clearly places these events in an end times context. The problem for many at this point is that they associate the end times with the end. And indeed this is true. What, then, is the significance in pointing out that such language is also used of these key events in the life of Christ and the coming of the Spirit? This must mean that in Christ the end has begun![34]

Thus, we should begin to view the entirety of the NT within an end times context. This explains why Jesus incorporated the language of the apocalyptic prophets. Moreover, the NT clearly places the life, death, and resurrection of Jesus and the coming of the Spirit in an apocalyptic context. In doing so, they relate these events to the inauguration of the fulfillment of the covenant promises of Scripture. With the coming of Christ and his baptism, the kingdom of God has begun and the kingdom of this world is coming to an end.

Any view, then, that presents the end times as something primarily future fails to account for the presence of apocalyptic language throughout

---

that by doing so the historicity of the events will be questioned. The proper response is to recognize the clear use of apocalyptic language and then to determine how that may or may not affect the historicity of the events.

33. Cf. Joel 2:30–31.

34. Now, one may ask, end of what? This will be explored more fully in ch. 7. For now, let us note that the end of the kingdom of this world has begun!

the Gospels and the importance of such for the proclamation that in Jesus the kingdom of God has come.

Jesus as the End Times Prophet Who Announced the Coming of the Kingdom of God in His Presence and His Summons to Follow Him

The OT story ends with the people of God in a state of exile; or, more accurately as slaves on the land God gave them: "Behold, we are slaves today, and as to the land which You gave to our fathers to eat of its fruit and its bounty, behold, we are slaves in it" (Neh 9:36).[35] The promise of land is perhaps the key theme of the OT covenant. The OT promises that if Israel obeys the covenant then they will enjoy peace and prosperity on the land.[36] But their failure to obey meant that they would be sent from the land into exile.[37] Exile, however, meant not only their removal from the land, but also their loss of the presence of Yahweh.[38] God himself would leave them. After all of this occurred, more prophets arose and announced that if the people repent God would restore them to the land.[39] But it is not merely the people of Israel that would be restored to the land; God himself would also return to the land.

It is this context in which we must read John the Baptist's proclamation, citing Isaiah 40:3, that he is the one who will "clear the way for the LORD in the wilderness; Make smooth in the desert a highway for our God" (Mark 1:2–3; Luke 3:4). The coming of Christ is indeed the fulfillment of Yahweh returning to the land. This is central to understanding the NT and the inauguration of the end times in Christ. Jesus was much more

---

35. Cf. Ezra 9:9. This significant thesis has been worked out thoroughly in the work of NT Wright. See his *The New Testament and the People of God* and *Jesus and the Victory of God*.

36. Cf. Deut 28:3–6; Lev 26:3–10.

37. This is clearly set forth in the covenant. If the Israelites disobey and break the covenant with God, then they will be uprooted from the land (cf. Deut 28:32–37, 49, 64). Leviticus uses even more graphic language when it says that the land will "spew you out" (Lev 18:28; ESV, NET, NKJ all say "vomit").

38. *Yahweh* (often spelled without the vowels YHWH) is the covenant name for God in Hebrew (cf. Exod 3:14–15). The English equivalent is "Lord," but one must be careful because "Lord" translates both *Yahweh* and *Adonai*. The Greek uses *Kurios*.

39. The prophets do so in accord with Deut 30:1–6. This is clear in 2 Chr 6:37–39; 7:14.

than God in the flesh who was sent to die on the cross and pay for our sins. Jesus was God in the flesh who was returning to be among his people![40]

Thus, it was Jesus himself, the very presence of God among humankind, that established the beginning of the kingdom of God. This is the significance of Jesus' proclamation that "The time is fulfilled, and the kingdom of God is at hand. Repent and believe the gospel" (Mark 1:15).[41] This is also why Jesus proclaimed that "the kingdom of God is in your midst" (Luke 17:21). And in Luke 11:20 Jesus announces, "But if I cast out demons by the finger of God, then the kingdom of God has come upon you." The presence of Christ is the fulfillment of the presence of the kingdom of God. And this entails the restoration of God among his people! Thus, what is announced in the opening of the Gospels serves to place the incarnation in the context of the inauguration of the kingdom of God.

Thus, the NT uses apocalyptic language to describe the life, death, and resurrection of Jesus, and the coming of the Holy Spirit. This apocalyptic language associates the events in the life of Christ and the coming of the Spirit in the context of the end. Jesus, also, employed apocalyptic language in his teaching. As a result, we see that in Christ himself the kingdom of God is now present. The end has come—though not fully, for death, sin, and suffering remain.

The Kingdom of God That Jesus Announced Is the Fulfillment of All God's Promises: The Eschaton Has Begun to Arrive

That the kingdom of God is already present throughout the entire NT era is further evidenced by the consistent use of end times designations for the present in the NT. First, we find that throughout the NT the term "last days" is consistently utilized to refer to the present. In Acts 2:17, Peter cites Joel 2 to explain the significance of the events that transpired with the pouring out of the Spirit and he concludes, "'And it shall be in the last days,' God says, 'that I will pour forth of My Spirit upon all humankind'" (Acts 2:17). The epistles also use the term "last days" and apply it to the

---

40. This is the significance of the temple in Scripture, as we will examine in chs. 6–7.

41. Though the NIV and NET translate the verse by saying that the kingdom of God "is near," we must note that the Greek *engiken* commonly expresses a spatial nearness more than a temporal one. That is, the nearness is not one of time, in the sense that it will come soon. Instead, the nearness is to be found spatially in the nearness of the person of Christ himself. See Edwards, *Gospel according to Mark*, 46–47.

present. Paul does so in 2 Timothy 3:1.[42] Peter, likewise, warns his readers about men in the last days.[43] The author of Hebrews similarly states, "God, after He spoke long ago to the fathers in the prophets in many portions and in many ways, in these last days has spoken to us in *His* Son, whom He appointed heir of all things, through whom also He made the world" (1:1–2). And, 1 John goes so far as to claim that these are not only the last days, but it is the "last hour" (2:18).

Conclusion

So, how does all of this relate to the opening questions?: Why then was Jesus baptized? Why was Jesus named Immanuel? Why does Matthew begin his Gospel with a genealogy? Why does the Gospel of John begin with "In the beginning"?

In all of these we find that the Gospel writers were linking the events of the coming of Christ, from his incarnation to his death and resurrection, with the fulfillment of the covenant promises of God and the coming of the kingdom of God. Jesus is baptized with a baptism of repentance on behalf of the nation because he knew that repentance must precede the restoration of Israel.[44] So, he repents for the nation.[45] Thus, in his repentance and baptism the "kingdom of God is at hand" (Mark 1:15).

Jesus is Immanuel (Matt 1:25) because he is himself the embodiment of YHWH returning to the land and the end of the exile. Hence, Mark's opening citation: "The voice of one crying in the wilderness, 'Make ready the way of the Lord, Make His paths straight'" (1:3). Mark sees, in John the Baptist's cry, Jesus as the "Lord" who is returning from the wilderness! Thus, the baby is named Jesus. But it must be understood that Immanuel is *who* he is.

---

42. Though some suggest that Paul was informing Timothy about what it will be like (future) in the last days, the use of the present imperatives ("realize this" in 2 Tim 3:1; and "avoid such men" in 3:5) strongly suggests that Paul was informing Timothy of a present crisis for which he needed to be prepared. This understanding accords with the rest of 2 Timothy, which focuses on Paul's appeals to Timothy to maintain his ministry.

43. Cf. 2 Pet 3:3.

44. This is especially clear in the covenant itself (cf. Deut 30:1–6). That repentance must precede the restoration is also evident in Daniel's prayer in Daniel 9.

45. This does not negate repentance on the part of the people, hence John the Baptist's message of repentance and the continued focus of the NT on the need to repent and be saved (cf. Acts 2:38; 3:19; 8:22; 17:30; 26:20).

Understanding the New Testament and the End Times

Matthew's Gospel commences with a genealogy (1:2–17) because it serves to identify Jesus with the completion of the story of the OT. The story, as Matthew frames it, begins with Abraham and runs to David, then from David to the exile, then from the exile to Jesus: "Therefore all the generations from Abraham to David are fourteen generations; and from David to the deportation to Babylon fourteen generations; and from the deportation to Babylon to *the time of* Christ fourteen generations" (1:17). Matthew, therefore, is announcing in Jesus that the era of the exile is over and the story of Israel has come to its fulfillment in Jesus.

Why does John 1:1 begin with a clear allusion to Genesis 1:1? The Gospel of John begins by quoting Genesis because John wishes for us to see in the coming of Christ the beginning of the New Creation. Thus, for John the "beginning" is a new beginning in Jesus.

What might this mean for us? First, it means that in Jesus we have the fulfillment of God's covenant promises and that we must read the Bible in this light. Secondly, it means that the eschaton (end times) has begun in Jesus. We live in the "last days." The "last days" then are not something to query about as though they are future and potentially not important. Instead, they are something for us to presently endure.[46] Finally, the inauguration of the New Creation in Jesus means that our mission as God's people entails the bringing in of the New Creation.[47]

One of the difficulties that many have at this juncture relates to the problem of the future of the kingdom. Many of us have become so accustomed to thinking of the end times as something wholly in the future that we have trouble grasping the present reality of the kingdom. Some, perhaps, are concerned with how this might affect our view of the return of Christ. Though this is understandable, we must warn against the urge to hold so tightly to one perspective that we neglect other truths simply because they are problematic for us. We must find room in our convictions for the whole counsel of God.

The end has begun in Christ, and yet we also affirm that Christ will return to consummate his kingdom.

---

46. We will explore this facet of the eschaton in ch. 8.
47. This we will explore more fully in ch. 12.

5

Understanding Prophecy and the End Times

Prophecy, in the biblical tradition, is not exclusively or even primarily about making pronouncements and predictions concerning the future. Rather, prophecy is speaking words of comfort and/or challenge, on behalf of God, to the people of God in their concrete historical situation.[1]

In my classes over the years when teaching this great book, I make a final plea in the opening lecture regarding *the necessity of exegesis* as the proper way—indeed the *only* way—that leads to understanding. . . . The unfortunate reality is that almost all of the popular stuff written on Revelation, which tends to be well known by many of these students, has scarcely a shred of exegetical basis to it. Such interpreters usually begin with a previously worked out eschatological scheme that they bring to the text, a scheme into which they tend to spend an extraordinary amount of energy trying to make everything in the text fit, and which they then attempt to defend, but with very little success.[2]

Introduction

THE FAILURE TO UNDERSTAND prophecy, both the purpose of prophecy and the nature of prophetic language, is a significant factor in much of the contemporary misunderstandings related to the end times. A popular conception of the prophets is that they were primarily prognosticators of things to come. In particular, the OT prophets were seen as those who had divine insight into the coming of the Christ and the end of the world. A common popular assumption among many Christians is that one of the

---

1. Gorman, *Reading Revelation Responsibly*, 23.
2. Fee, *Revelation*, xx.

main objectives of prophecy relates to the "last generation"[3]—which is then assumed to be either our present generation or a near future one. From this point, the biblical interpreter then filters both contemporary events and the biblical text in such a way that reinforces these convictions. Furthermore, it is often asserted that the prophets used language in a "literal" fashion. Therefore, if a prophet says that "stars will fall from the sky," then it is assumed that a literal event in which stars fall from the sky will take place. As we will see, the nature and purpose of prophecy was much more concerned with the prophets' own present world. The prophets spoke to the people of their day in the language of their day.

Understanding the Nature and Purpose of Prophecy

To properly understand biblical prophecy we must first ask, what is the primary purpose of prophecy? To do this, we must also come to understand the language of the prophets. That is, how did they go about describing the things that they were prophesying? Did they use language in a woodenly literal manner or did they employ imagery? And, how might we know when they are using language literally or figuratively?

We must also inquire as to the nature of prophecy and its fulfillment. That is, when prophecy is fulfilled does it tend to take on a more literal, one-to-one correspondence, or does the fulfillment occur in a manner that transcends the initial expectations? For this we have the advantage of the NT. The NT consistently cites the OT in terms of promise-fulfillment. So, as we examine the fulfillment of prophecy in the NT, we may observe the manner in which the prophesies of the OT are fulfilled. Then, we must determine whether or not this provides a pattern for our understanding of prophecy as a whole and what to expect in the future.

Prophecy Had Meaning to Its Original Audience

We must understand several factors with regard to the purpose of prophecy in general. First, and foremost, is that fact that all prophecy—in fact, all Scripture—had meaning to its original audience. In fact, we can go so

---

3. The term "last days" will be addressed in ch. 8. We will observe there that it does not have in view some final generation immediately prior to the return of Christ, but that throughout the NT it points to both the current generation of the writer and the entire era from the cross and resurrection of Christ, or even Pentecost, to the return of Christ.

far as to assert that the prophets were centrally concerned with the people whom they were addressing.[4]

A reading of the prophets consistently demonstrates that their primary concern was the generation to whom they were speaking.[5] For example, Isaiah begins his prophecy with the proclamation of the Lord: ". . . Sons I have reared and brought up, but they have revolted against Me" (Isa 1:2). The prophet then exhorts them to repent and to "Wash yourselves, make yourselves clean; remove the evil of your deeds from My sight. Cease to do evil, learn to do good; seek justice, reprove the ruthless; defend the orphan, plead for the widow" (Isa 1:16–17). These opening words of Isaiah set the context for the entire book of Isaiah. Isaiah was proclaiming a message to the people of his day who had strayed from the covenant with God by doing evil and neglecting justice. This does not mean that Isaiah does not prophesy things that were fulfilled hundreds of years later. Indeed he did, as the rest of Scripture makes clear. What this does mean is that even in conveying a message to his people, parts of which finds their fulfillment generations later, the focus of the message of Isaiah was relevant to the generation of Isaiah's time.

This is further evident from looking at the famed prophecy of Isaiah 7, which many today often assume refers only to the birth of Christ. The entire passage, however, speaks words of exhortation (7:3–8) and then judgment (7:9–16) directly to Ahaz, the king of Judah. Thus, the original setting and purpose of this prophecy was directed to Ahaz. The question then becomes: Since the prophecy finds its ultimate fulfillment in Jesus, should we run first to the NT[6] to determine the meaning of Isaiah 7 as a whole, or do we need to first determine the context and setting of Isaiah 7? Since it is apparent that the prophecy of Isaiah 7 is directed to Ahaz and the events of the eight century BC, I suggest that it is this context with which we must begin.

What is true for the book of Isaiah is universally true for the prophets. They proclaimed a message first and foremost to the people of their

---

4. The *Dictionary of Biblical Prophecy and the End Times* notes that in the ancient world prophets "functioned as intermediaries between the pagan gods and the respective kings" (Hays, Duvall, and Pate, *Dictionary of Biblical Prophecy*, 353). Thus, the primary focus of the prophets was not only the people of their day, but in particular the king. The biblical prophets of the OT generally fit quite well with this description.

5. Gordon Fee notes, "The primary meaning of any text, including apocalyptic texts, is that which John himself intended, which in turn must be something the original readers would have been capable of understanding" (*Revelation*, xxi).

6. Many popular prophecy writers might even suggest that we run to the contemporary events first.

own generation. Overall, the prophets are best characterized as "covenant enforcers." That is, they were concerned with whether or not the people of God were faithful to the covenant that the Lord had established with his people; specifically, the covenant as stipulated in Deuteronomy. That is, the prophets were primarily concerned with the people to whom they were speaking and their faithfulness, or lack thereof, to the covenant God had made with Israel. Therefore, when it comes to understanding the language and imagery of the prophets, we must not only examine the context and setting of that time, but also how the people of that day would have understood the earlier books.

The Language of Prophecy Looks Backwards before It Looks Forward

A second factor that is central to a proper understanding and interpretation of the prophets is the fact that the language of the prophets looks backwards before it looks forwards. This is very important for how one reads prophecy. For many of the popular prophecy writers today propose that the biblical prophets were miraculously given insights into events of the distant future and were describing future events in the language of their day. They propose that only when we look at these events in light of our current events can the words of the prophets and biblical writers be made known. This is famously argued by Hal Lindsey, who suggests that in the book of Revelation John was given a preview of twentieth-century nuclear warfare, which he then described in language of the first century.[7] The problems here, which are too numerous to detail,[8] include the fact that if this approach were true, the book of Revelation would have had little to no relevance to John's readers. But one of the main interpretive principles accepted by most commentators of the book of Revelation is that the language and images in the book of Revelation derive not from the future, but from the past. That is, John is viewing Jesus through the lens of the OT! The images of dragons and lions and lambs all derive from the OT, not the future.[9]

---

7. See Lindsey, *There's a New World Coming*, 12–13. Lindsey suggests, "You might say that John was put into a 'divine time machine' and transported nineteen centuries into the future."

8. For a response to the writings of Hal Lindsey, see Boersma, *Is the Bible a Jigsaw Puzzle*, 1979.

9. See especially Bauckham, *Climax of Prophecy*, 174–98. Also, this does not

In this regard, one may consider the prophets in the same way that one might view a present-day pastor or church leader. Consider a situation in which a beloved pastor went to preach during a typical weekend church service. Suppose the pastor shared with his church that, though he was prepared to preach his weekly sermon, instead he felt led by the Lord to share what the Lord had recently shown him. He then explained, in great humility, how God appeared to him in a dream. He recounted for the duration of his message the details in which God revealed to him the events that would close human history in the year 4078. After the service, the congregation was exuberant over the message. They knew their pastor was a man of God. But who would have thought that God would show him this wonderful message of his plan for the end of history? Such talk may have continued among the congregation over lunch and throughout the evening as word spread through the town and even among neighboring churches.

At one such get together, however, one of the elders, being a devoted follower of Christ and a zealous mentor of the younger generations, began to discern the relevance of the message for discipleship. After pondering things for a short bit, he began to realize that the message, as wonderful as it was in so many ways, had no practical relevance. In fact, since the "prophecy" would not find its fulfillment for more than two thousand years, it was not even something that he needed to make his children and grandchildren aware of since it relates to only a very distant generation.

Now if this pastor were enrolled in a seminary course on preaching, his sermon would be given a failing grade. For, a message that has no relevance or practical application for the people to whom it is addressed is not a good message. The application of his message is vacant. As far as affecting life transformation in the people to whom God has called him to serve, he has failed. Even supposing for a moment that the vision were true, perhaps the pastor should have called a special Sunday night session to announce to everyone what God had shown him. But as far as a weekend sermon is concerned, the message was meaningless and it has no place in the weekly preaching. For, it does not effectively relate to his people in any way. Therefore, the sermon was a waste.

---

mean that Revelation has no application or reference to the future. It does! I fully affirm that the return of Christ is a future event. But, the primary focus of Revelation is the significance of Jesus as the fulfillment of the OT and the implications for the people of God—both the people of God to whom John was writing and our generation as well.

Thus, the original context of prophecy is that the prophet himself was concerned with the people of his generation. When reading the prophets, then, one must first determine what the prophet was saying to his people. One must not assume that the original intent of the prophet relates to a fulfillment in our present generation. It may well have. But this is not where we start.

Again, this does not intend to suggest that prophecy has no relevance to us. Of course it does. All Scripture has bearing to all generations, especially in terms of its application—see 2 Timothy 3:16–17. What I am suggesting is that we must first look to the original context to determine the meaning of the passage. That original context includes a message to the people of that day. That message was relevant and understood by them—for if it was not relevant to them or understood by them, then how could they ever have been expected to apply it?

When Will These Things Be Fulfilled?

Another important distinction among various interpreters relates to the question of when. That is, when are the prophecies going to find their fulfillment? The difficulty in even laying out the various views with regard to the time of fulfillment is that many of the popular prophecy writers do not agree with much of the scholarly world on which prophecies are awaiting future fulfillment.[10] This is crucial. For, as we will see, some suggest that Malachi 4:5 predicts that Elijah will return before the second coming of Christ, while others view this verse as already fulfilled by John the Baptist.

The view presented here suggests that we are to first look at the prophecy in its original context and what it would have meant to the people of that day. But, we must also recognize that prophecy also looks forward to its ultimate fulfillment in Christ—by means of his life, death, and resurrection. For indeed, we have already established that all God's promises are "yes" in Christ (2 Cor 1:20). A given prophecy may also look beyond Christ to the work of the Spirit among the people of God, and ultimately to the great consummation in the New Jerusalem.[11]

---

10. I do not intend to suggest that among the popular prophecy writers there are no scholars. Certainly, there are some scholars who tend to affirm many of the conceptions advocated by the popular writers. But, I do believe that they represent a minority among the scholarly world.

11. It is beyond our objectives here to fully flesh out this point. One may understandably object that not every prophecy is absolutely fulfilled by Christ. Though I might wish to affirm that such is true, I will have to settle for now with the contention

Prophecy and God's Grand Design

Many of the popular conceptions regarding prophecy are essentially what one might call a "flat" interpretation. For example, a prophet describes the rebuilding/restoration of a temple, and so it is flatly expected that a physical temple will be rebuilt/restored. When we turn to the pages of the NT, however, we see that Jesus himself claims to be the temple of God. So we must ask, is Jesus the fulfillment of the OT promises of the rebuilding/restoration of the temple? I realize that for many the answer seems quite apparently "no." After all, the prophet predicted a rebuilt temple and Jesus is not such a building. But, this conclusion assumes that the language of the prophets is to be understood flatly; it assumes that when the prophet predicted the rebuilding/restoration of the temple, he meant a physical building.

But, what if the prophecies regarding the rebuilding/restoration of the temple looked beyond a physical temple and pointed to the presence of God among his people? Since Jesus is indeed the presence of God among his people, then might we come to understand that he is indeed the rebuilt/restored temple in complete fulfillment of all that God has promised. After all, was the prophet looking forward to the rebuilding of a physical building or to the restoration of God's presence among his people?[12] The answer must reside in the determination of the purpose of the prophecy and not merely in a "flat" or "wooden" interpretation of the language that the prophet employed.

By raising such questions I am intending to point out the fact that many of our differences regarding the interpretation of fulfillment of prophecy are the result of differing assumptions as to the language of the prophets and the nature and purpose of prophecy. In my opinion, these are the two most significant issues in understanding prophecy. Consequently,

---

that all prophecy in general is fulfilled by Christ (2 Cor 1:20). A more complete answer would have to delve deeply into the correspondence with Christ and the nature of the NT people of God and the New Jerusalem—e.g., Jesus is the temple, the NT people of God are the temple, and the New Jerusalem is the temple. Note that Peter appears to affirm such: "As to this salvation, the prophets who prophesied of the grace that would come to you made careful searches and inquiries, seeking to know what person or time the Spirit of Christ within them was indicating as He predicted the sufferings of Christ and the glories to follow. It was revealed to them that they were not serving themselves, but you, in these things which now have been announced to you through those who preached the gospel to you by the Holy Spirit sent from heaven—things into which angels long to look" (1 Pet 1:10–12).

12. I will examine these questions in more detail in chs. 6 and 7.

when it comes to understanding prophecy and its fulfillment, we must read the Scriptures carefully to determine the major concern of the prophet himself in uttering a given prophecy, and how we are to understand the language that he used. From there we must then discern if/how the prophecy points to Christ as its fulfillment.

It is my personal experience, as an earnest Christian growing up in a conservative evangelical environment, and as a scholar and teacher in both the academy and the church for more than twenty-eight years, that many Christians have a poor grasp of the nature and purpose of prophecy. The failure to grasp the role of prophecy—particularly the consideration of the original audience and their circumstances that brought about the prophecy, as well as what the prophet himself was intending to convey to them—is a root cause of much of the contemporary confusion regarding prophecy. These problems are compounded by the lack of understanding of the biblical story and how God is working out his plan in a manner that transcends our limited conceptions. That is, we see from the NT that the fulfillment of a given prophecy often points to something far more grand than the prophet himself likely realized. That something grander is Jesus! In fact, the key assumption presented here is that all Scripture, including prophecy, points to Christ.[13]

The Nature of the Language of Scripture in General and Prophecy in Particular

One of the more common mistakes made by the popular interpreters of biblical prophecy is to impose on the biblical writers various assumptions as to the nature of the prophetic language that contravene the worldview of the prophets and the biblical world. One of the major assumptions is that the biblical writers used language in a "literal" way to describe their prophecies. Now, in one sense, we may all agree with this statement. Especially because "literal" is often used as a synonym for "true." Certainly, we evangelicals, and many non-evangelicals, believe that the words of the Bible are true (hence "literal"). Beyond this, however, the meaning of "literal" is actually quite vague.[14]

---

13. This will be the primary point in our examination of the temple in chs. 6 and 7.

14. For an excellent discussion of "literal" see Poythress, *Understanding Dispensationalists*.

If by "literal" one means "normal," that is understandable. That is, the argument might suggest that we should understand the language of the prophets in particular and Scripture in general as one normally understands a typical communication. And such would be fine. The difficulty here is that one is often unsure even in our own casual conversations as to whether one is using language in a direct, normal sense or in a figurative manner, until either time or circumstances make it clear. This is also true of the biblical world. For example, in John 11, Jesus tells his disciples that "our friend Lazarus has fallen asleep" (11:11). The disciples, taking Jesus' words in the normal sense of "fallen asleep," respond, "Lord, if he has fallen asleep, he will recover" (11:12). John then clarifies for his readers, "Now Jesus had spoken of his death, but they thought that he was speaking of literal sleep" (11:13).

The same type of misunderstanding occurs in a prophetic context in John 2. There Jesus, in response to the demand for a sign, replies, "Destroy this temple, and in three days I will raise it up" (2:19). The Jews, however, misunderstanding Jesus, assert, "It took forty-six years to build this temple, and You will raise it up in three days?"(2:20). It is again only when John provides clarification that his readers understand: "But He was speaking of the temple of His body" (2:20).

If these misunderstandings can occur in an historical narrative such as the Gospels, how much more shall we expect such to occur in the prophetic literature? How can we navigate our way through the prophets? What might direct us to understand the language of the prophets and the purpose of prophecy? The answer is Jesus. All Scripture, including prophecy, points us to Christ (1 Cor 1:20).

The New Testament and the Fulfillment of Prophecy in Christ

What is most puzzling regarding the popular conceptions of prophecy and its interpretation is that there is often little regard for the nature of fulfillment as found in the NT. Should we not look at the NT to determine how prior prophesies were interpreted and/or fulfilled? If, in doing so, we find a consistent pattern of interpretation with regard to prophecy—e.g., they have a consistent christological, or Christ-centered, focus—then are we not justified to conclude that this is a central focus of prophecy? Should we not strive to determine the manner in which prophecy points us to Christ? Unfortunately, many of the popular prophecy writers do not look to the

NT to determine how a given prophecy points us to Christ. Instead, of assuming Christ as the center of all prophecy, a wooden definition of "literal" is assumed to be the only means by which prophecy may be interpreted.

For example, Malachi 4:5 predicts, "Behold, I am going to send you Elijah the prophet before the coming of the great and terrible day of the LORD." We may suppose that many readers, including some even at the time of Malachi, may have drawn the conclusion that in some manner Elijah himself would return before "the day of the LORD." At face value, such an interpretation makes good sense.[15] In the NT, however, Jesus affirms that John the Baptist was the fulfillment of "Elijah, who was to come" (Matt 11:14). The question then becomes: Does Jesus' interpretation—that John the Baptist fulfills the prophecy of Malachi 4:5—constitute the totality of the fulfillment predicted by Malachi, or must there be some "literal" fulfillment of the prophecy?

It is here that we find that some present-day interpreters claim that John the Baptist was not the totality of the fulfillment of Malachi 4:5, despite the words of Jesus.[16] They contend that since John the Baptist was not *literally* Elijah, then he could not have fulfilled the prophecy of Malachi 4:5.[17] At what point, however, do we allow the NT to determine the meaning of a prior revelation? Certainly, it is feasible that there will be a future fulfillment of Malachi 4:5. But this is a question of interpretation. After all, we must determine if Jesus meant for us to conclude that Malachi 4:5 has been fulfilled completely through John the Baptist. The answer cannot lie with the assumption as to what "literal" means.

Instead, the answer must reside with how Jesus and the NT writers understood this prophecy. That is, what did the disciples think Jesus meant? Or, more particularly, what did Matthew, who recorded this event for us, think Jesus meant? As for what the disciples understood Jesus to have meant, we must note that the context of Matthew, the Gospels, and the NT as a whole, strongly suggests that indeed John the Baptist was the complete fulfillment of Malachi 4:5. For, as I argued previously, Matthew

15. Whether or not the people of Malachi's time would have thought such must be addressed. See Taylor and Clendenen, *Haggai, Malachi*, and also Block, "My Servant David."

16. "The Jews always understood it of the literal Elijah. Their saying is, 'Messiah must be anointed by Elijah'" (Jamieson et al., *Commentary, Critical and Explanatory*, n.p.).

17. Some of these proponents will further suggest that Elijah is one of the two witnesses who will literally return in the three and a half years before the return of Jesus (see Rev 11:1–14). For a thorough look at the account of the two witnesses in Rev 11:1–14, see my *Revelation and the Two Witnesses*.

Understanding Prophecy and the End Times

presents the story of Jesus as the fulfillment of the story of Israel and God's covenant with his people. Now, one may see how some of the early Jewish Christians (or perhaps some of the Jewish opponents of the church) queried as to how Jesus could have been the Messiah and fulfiller of God's promises when Malachi clearly predicts that Elijah would come first! Matthew then narrates for us, in response to this suggestion, the fact that Jesus noted that John the Baptist was the fulfillment of this prophecy.[18]

Furthermore, we see that the NT affirms that key prophecies in Malachi are fulfilled in Jesus and the NT people of God. These prophecies relate to the coming of the kingdom in Christ. For example, in Mark 1:2, John the Baptist cites Malachi 3:1 in his proclamation that Jesus is the promised coming one.[19] Mark 11:11 also references Malachi 3:1. And Paul cites Malachi 3 when he describes the NT people of God in terms of the temple of God.[20] But, Malachi 4:5 indicates that these prophecies will not happen until Elijah comes first. Thus, it would have been important for the early Christians to be assured that the prophecy regarding the coming of Elijah had been fulfilled. This is why it is vital for Matthew to note that Jesus declared that the prophecy of Elijah coming was fulfilled in the coming of John the Baptist.

How then was the prophecy of Elijah coming fulfilled in John the Baptist? It is here that we turn to the Gospel of Luke. For, Luke informs us that John the Baptist will go forth "in the spirit and power of Elijah" (1:17). That is, John the Baptist will not actually be the person of Elijah. Instead, he will fulfill the ministry of Elijah. As a result of a careful reading of the NT, we can see that the prophecy of Malachi 4:5 does not refer to the reincarnation of Elijah, but to the ministry of John the Baptist, who came in the "spirit and power of Elijah."

Now many readers may be naturally apprehensive at the suggestion that prophecy may be fulfilled in a manner that transcends the literal. This is understandable. For at this point the Scriptures appear vulnerable. For, who is to say what actually constitutes the fulfillment of a prophecy? And

---

18. Such an argument would have been more likely to be believed by the Christian community. Hence the suggestion that Matthew was written to Christians.

19. Mark 1:2–3 is a composite of Exod 23:20; Mal 3:1; and Isa 40:3. Mark may have introduced the citation with a reference to Isaiah (and omitting the prophet Malachi) because 1:3 is a clear citation of Isa 40. Since Isaiah was a more prominent prophet, Mark may have chosen Isaiah as the prophet upon which to introduce the citations. That Mark 1:2 is a citation of Mal 3:1 is quite evident, and that it is not from Isaiah is confirmed by the fact that the citation in Mark 1:2 has no parallel in Isaiah.

20. Cf. Mal 3:2 and 1 Cor 3:13–15.

how do we know if this is what the Bible meant? Therefore, many conclude that the wisest approach is to put safeguards on the Bible in order that it will not be abused. But, such apprehensions may well serve as a negative and inhibit us from understanding the Bible as it was meant. For, in attempting to safeguard Scripture from abuse, we may well place such restrictions on the text that we fail to let the Scriptures speak for themselves. The result is that the Scriptures come to mean only what we allow them to mean. Of course, such persons are convinced that what they have allowed the Bible to mean is only what it in fact means. But, I must ask, in our effort to safeguard the Bible from misinterpretation, have we ourselves misinterpreted the Bible?

As mentioned at the outset of this chapter, the justification for placing such limitations on the meaning of a prophecy is bound up with the assumption that the Bible is to be interpreted "literally." But, if this is not how the NT consistently interprets the OT, then on what basis do we devise a system that ultimately arrives at conclusions contrary to the very practice of the NT?[21] We should be cautious about developing a system of interpretation that forces an absolute meaning on a word or phrase without regard to how that word or phrase was understood by later writers.

For, no one wonders why Jesus did not restore the temple three days after its destruction (which occurred in AD 70), when he clearly said that he would.[22] We know that he was talking about his body. And in this light we acknowledge that he indeed raised the temple three days after its destruction, just as he said! There is no question here. Everyone agrees

---

21. It is not appropriate at this juncture to label the first group "conservative" and the second "liberal," for these terms are too often highly polemicized—especially the latter term. That is, we should not throw out the term "liberal" every time someone sees a deeper meaning within a passage. Using polemicized language tends not only to affirm our preconceived boxes, which may inhibit our understanding of Scripture, but also to erect barriers between one another so that we fail to respect one another and our differences. For, even among those scholars who prefer a "literal" hermeneutic we find the acknowledgement that the fulfillment of prophecy often transcends the "literal" meaning of the prophecy. For example, that prophecies regarding the temple find some level of fulfillment in Jesus is universally recognized. Those scholars who suggest that since Jesus is the fulfillment of the prophecies regarding the temple (see chs. 6–7), then we must be prepared to discern how other such prophecies may also find their fulfillment in a manner that transcends the "literal," are not unilaterally to be dismissed as "liberal." As fellow members of the body of Christ we must overcome such petty divisiveness. Many honest, genuine, Bible-believing brothers and sisters have come to various conclusions regarding the nature of prophecy, its manner of fulfillment, and its implications for the end times.

22. John 2:19.

that "He was speaking of the temple of His body" (John 2:21). But, if this prophecy was fulfilled in a manner that transcended the literal temple building (about which, it must be noted, everyone who heard him assumed he was speaking), then might not Ezekiel's prophecy of the rebuilt/restored temple likewise refer to Jesus?[23]

Fulfillment That Transcends Our Initial Expectations

One of the primary features of prophecy relates to the nature of the fulfillment of prophecy. Namely, that prophecy, as evidenced by the fulfillment in the NT, often transcends what might have been originally expected. In fact, we might affirm that God always outdoes what was expected.

What might this mean? The most obvious example at this juncture is the prophecies of the temple. Though we will explore this question more completely in the next two chapters, it should be noted that if the fulfillment were restricted to a physical building in Jerusalem, then God's presence would be just that: restricted! God's presence on the earth would be located in one place—a place, in fact, in which only one person was permitted, and only once per year! But, if we see Jesus as the fulfillment of all the prophesies of the temple, and if Christ is present, by means of his Spirit in and with all those who believe, then we come to see that God's presence is indeed far more pervasive than if it were limited to a building. All of this, as we will see, looks forward to the absolute, pervasive presence of God and Christ throughout the entirety of the New Jerusalem![24]

Conclusion

The interpretation of prophecy is no simple task. I have hopefully provided several insights into the interpretation of prophecy. First, we have noted that prophecy is primarily directed to the people of its day. For, the prophet was concerned with the character and conduct of his contemporaries. And it is here that we must begin. What might the prophecy have meant to the prophet and his original audience?

Secondly, I have noted that we must also look to the NT to determine the nature of fulfillment. We will look at this point more deeply with regard to the temple in chapters 6 and 7. At this juncture, I have suggested

---

23. This point will be developed in the next two chapters.
24. See Rev 21:3–4, 7, 22.

that all prophecy points to Christ and the NT people of God, as Peter notes in 1 Peter 1:10–12. When we examine the nature of fulfillment in the NT, we can see that often the fulfillment transcends the original context of the OT prophecy. Thus, we have seen that in the NT John the Baptist fulfilled the ministry of Elijah. Thus, despite the fact that a simple reading of Malachi 4:5 might warrant the suggestion that Elijah will someday reappear, the NT has made it clear that John the Baptist was the fulfillment of this prophecy—much to the surprise of everyone! Therefore, we can discern that the nature of the fulfillment of prophecy often points to something greater than what was originally expected. This we will observe in the next two chapters as we examine what Scripture says regarding the rebuilding/restoration of the temple and how the fulfillment in Jesus transcends the flat meaning of the OT prophecies.

6

The End Times and the Temple

My thesis is that the Old Testament tabernacle and temples were symbolically designed to point to the cosmic eschatological reality that God's tabernacling presence, formerly limited to the holy of holies, was to be extended throughout the whole earth.[1]

But if the Temple was always the sign and the means of the true theocracy, then the Temple-in-person, that is, Jesus himself, is now that sign.[2]

[The temple] is not spiritualization in our usual sense of the word, but the very opposite. In Christ is realization. It is not so much that Christ fulfills what the temple means; rather Christ is the meaning for which the temple existed.[3]

Moreover, I will make My dwelling among you, and My soul will not reject you. I will also walk among you and be your God, and you shall be My people. (Lev 26:11–12)

The Jews therefore answered and said to Him, "What sign do You show to us, seeing that You do these things?" Jesus answered and said to them, "Destroy this temple, and in three days I will raise it up." The Jews therefore said, "It took forty-six years to build this temple, and will You raise it up in three days?" But He was speaking of the temple of His body. When therefore He was raised from the dead, His disciples remembered that He said this; and they believed the Scripture, and the word which Jesus had spoken. (John 2:18–22)

---

1. Beale, *Temple and the Church's Mission*, 25.
2. Wright, *How God Became King*, 247.
3. Clowney, "Final Temple," 177.

Introduction: Jesus Is the Temple of God

JESUS IS THE TEMPLE! This is something pretty basic for most Christians. I do not know of any Christian who would deny that Jesus is the temple of God. At the same time, however, I suspect that many have not really thought about the implications of what Jesus was saying. What does it mean to say that Jesus is the temple? In what sense is Jesus the temple? And, does Jesus' claim to be the temple of God have any bearing on the OT prophecies of the restored temple?

It is in part the failure to ask such questions that allows many to adhere to a theology that contends that the OT prophecies regarding the rebuilding of the temple are awaiting a future fulfillment in the rebuilding of a physical temple in Jerusalem and that the rebuilding of this temple is a key sign of the coming of our Lord. One such voice proclaims: "The practical preparations to build the Third Temple are the clearest signs yet that we are rapidly approaching the time when the Messiah will return to set up His holy kingdom on earth. We are living in the generation that will witness the Second Coming."[4] This understanding that a physical temple building will be rebuilt in Jerusalem as a sign of the imminent return of Christ is commonplace among many evangelicals. The problem here as I see it derives in part from a failure to grasp the nature and purpose of the temple and its fulfillment in Jesus.

What I will set forth in this chapter is that the nature of the temple of God is intimately tied to the presence of God among his people and not to a building. I will also contend that the primary purpose of the temple is for the presence of God both to dwell throughout the entirety of the Earth and among all of humankind.[5] Consequently, as we will see, the prophesies of the OT related to the temple and its restoration were never intended to be fulfilled by a physical structure.

I will also contend that a physical building cannot provide the fulfillment of the ultimate objective of God's intent to dwell among all humankind and throughout the entirety of creation. This derives from the fact that a physical building inherently limits God's presence both to one place (e.g., the temple mount in Jerusalem) and to one person (namely, the High

---

4. Jeffrey, *New Temple and the Second Coming*, vii.

5. This contention corresponds well with the theme of Beale's *The Temple and the Church's Mission*. Beale states, "my thesis is that the Old Testament tabernacle and temples were symbolically designed to point to the cosmic eschatological reality that God's tabernacling presence, formerly limited to the holy of holies, was to be extended throughout the whole earth" (25).

Priest, who, himself, was permitted access to God's presence only once per year). As a result, it becomes apparent that the ultimate fulfillment of the promise of God to dwell among his people, must transcend a physical building. Now it is worth noting that physical structures, such as the temple of Solomon, indeed served a purpose for a time. But, as we will observe, they were never intended to suffice as the permanent place of God's dwelling among his people—only Christ and the Spirit could provide that!

I will also argue that those who propose that a still future temple will be rebuilt in Jerusalem in supposed fulfillment of the OT prophecies have failed to grasp both the nature and purpose of the temple and how such were fulfilled by the tabernacling presence of Christ.[6] That such prophecies looked forward to Christ is crucial for understanding the NT and the fulfillment of the OT. Furthermore, as we shall see, this fulfillment in Christ carries forward into the NT people of God, who are themselves the temple of God by means of the indwelling of the Spirit. And all of this will find its consummation in the New Jerusalem where God dwells among all people and throughout the entirety of the New Creation!

Nature and Purpose of the Temple

To begin our discussion on the significance of Jesus as the temple and the relevance to the prophesies of the restoration of the temple, as well as the importance of such for the people of God today, it is important first to determine the nature and purpose of the temple in Scripture. In sum, throughout the Bible the temple is the place where God dwells.[7] This is evident in the prophecy of Ezekiel 40–48, which is often cited as a prediction of the future restored temple in Jerusalem.[8] The depiction of the city/temple closes with this statement: "and the name of the city from *that* day *shall be*, 'The LORD is there'" (Ezek 48:35). The description of the New Jerusalem similarly includes the statement, "And I saw no temple in it, for the Lord God, the Almighty, and the Lamb, are its temple" (Rev 21:22). There is no temple in the New Jerusalem because the entire city is a temple! This is the heart of the meaning and purpose of the temple: it is the place where God is!

---

6. Cf. John 1:14. I will argue this at length in ch. 7.

7. Cf. the *Dictionary of Biblical Imagery*: "The temple in its most basic sense symbolizes the dwelling place of God" (849).

8. For example, Schmitt and Laney, *Messiah's Coming Temple*.

Understanding the New Testament and the End Times

One of the central texts in Scripture relating to the promise of God to dwell among his people is that of Leviticus 26:11–12. In Leviticus 26, the covenant promises of blessing for obedience and curses for disobedience are set forth.[9] The promises of blessing in Leviticus 26:4–13 include "rain" (26:4), "peace" (26:6), and that the people will be "fruitful and multiply" (26:9).[10] The climax of these promises is found in verses 11 and 12: "Moreover, I will make My dwelling among you, and My soul will not reject you. I will also walk among you and be your God, and you shall be My people." Notice that the list of blessings for obedience climaxes in the promise that YHWH[11] himself will be among them and be their God![12] Of all the covenant promises of Yahweh to his people, the highpoint is that God himself will be among them.

Now, understandably, some may attempt to comprehend this promise in terms of the prediction of the construction of a physical temple. It is my contention, however, and an examination of the rest of Scripture will bear this out, that the most prominent feature of the temple even here in the Leviticus passage is that of the unhindered presence of God among his people. As we shall see, the rest of Scripture, which builds on this promise, affirms that the fulfillment of this promise transcends a physical building. At the same time, there are several important indications in the text of Leviticus that affirm that God will indeed dwell among his people in a manner that transcends a building.

First, in looking at the text of Leviticus 26:12 more carefully, we observe that the passage promises that God will "walk" (Heb: *halak*) among his people. This connotes an intimate relationship of God among his people. This intimacy is closely tied to the dwelling of God among Adam and Eve in the garden.[13] Leviticus connects the promised restoration of God's presence with the garden by use of the verb "walk" (*halak*). For, the

---

9. A covenant is an agreement between two parties, usually between a greater (king) and a lesser (the people). The king promises to protect and bless his subjects, while the people promise to obey the king's laws. If the people obey, they are blessed. If they disobey, they are cursed (cf. Lev 26; Deut 27–28).

10. Note the allusion to Genesis here. This will be an important point to remember.

11. "Yahweh" is the covenant name for God in the OT. Hebrew is often written without vowels; hence "YHWH." When the vowels are added, this name is typically rendered "Yahweh."

12. I will discuss as we proceed the importance of Lev 26:3–13 (esp. vv. 11–12). For now, it should be noted that the significance of Lev 26:3–13 is evident from the fact that key prophetic passages referring to the temple (e.g., Ezek 37:24–28; 2 Cor 6:14–18; Rev 21:3–4) all either cite or allude to this promise.

13. See Wenham, *Book of Leviticus*, 330.

term used in Leviticus 26:12 is the same as that of Genesis 3:8, where God was "walking" among Adam and Eve.[14] The link with Genesis is further supported by the promise of blessing that the people will be "fruitful and multiply" (Lev 26:9) in accord with the promise in Genesis 1:28. As I will note below, it is of great importance to observe that the covenant promise of God again dwelling among his people in Leviticus 26:11–12 alludes to the garden![15] For this suggests that the future presence of God among his people entails the restoration of Eden.

Now, in Eden God dwelt among Adam and Eve in a far more transcendent manner than the confines of a physical temple. For the presence of God in Eden was not hindered by a building. As G. K. Beale concludes, "his special revelatory presence dwelt in a limited manner in human-made structures. But when he fully redeems the world and recreates it, he will fill the entire creation with his presence and dwell in it in a fuller way than ever before."[16]

That the dwelling of God among all humankind embodies the goal of Scripture and is fundamental to the nature and purpose of the temple may be more clearly evident by examining the consummation in the New Jerusalem. For, as his presence in the garden was not restricted to a building, so also in the consummation God will dwell with humankind throughout the entirety of the New Creation.[17] As John notes, referring to the New Jerusalem, "And I saw no temple in it, for the Lord God, the Almighty, and the Lamb, are its temple" (Rev 21:22).

Central to developing a biblical theology of the temple, then, is the understanding that the primary significance of the temple lies in the presence of God among his people. We see in the great covenant promise of Leviticus that the climax of the covenant is when God will again dwell among his people. We also see an indication in this promise that links the future dwelling of God among his people with the dwelling of God in Eden.[18]

---

14. The verb "walk" (*mithallek*) has the exact same form in Lev 26:12 and Gen 3:8.

15. This phenomenon, whereby the description of God residing in a temple in a manner corresponding to God's dwelling among humanity in the garden, is not limited to Leviticus. The famous promise to David of the construction of a temple also uses the same verb (2 Sam 7:6–7). See Collins, *Genesis 1–4*, 185.

16. Beale, *Temple and the Church's Mission*, 227. Beale's work is a wonderful look at the theme of temple in Scripture. Much of the overall thrust of this chapter is indebted to Beale's work.

17. See Rev 21–22.

18. To say that the fulfillment of the temple will occur when God again dwells

The Garden of Eden as a Temple

It is important for an understanding of the nature and purpose of the temple to understand the garden of Eden[19] in terms of a temple.[20] Though Genesis does not explicitly identify Eden as a temple, this was, in fact, the understanding espoused by both the later writers of Scripture and much of the Second Temple Jewish literature.[21] The Genesis narrative does, of course, possess implicit features from which the prophets and the Second Temple writers derived their conviction that Eden was a temple.

Eden Was the Place of God's Presence

Among the evidences that Eden was a temple is first and foremost the fact that the Genesis narrative affirms that Eden was the place of God's presence. As noted above, this is indicated from the statement in Genesis 3:8: "And they heard the sound of the LORD God walking in the garden in the cool of the day." Kiel observes that "The 'garden' was therefore the first place on earth where the Shekinah dwelt."[22] The presence of God among Adam and Eve was a fundamental component of the garden and of the temple. Beale notes, "Israel's temple was the place where the priest experienced God's unique presence, and Eden was the place where Adam walked and talked with God."[23] Gordon Wenham adds, "the description of Eden with its trees, rivers, gold, and so on emphasized God's presence there."[24]

---

among his people, and that this fulfillment links back to Genesis, conforms greatly to the thesis of ch. 5. Namely, that prophecy ultimately points us to Christ and that the imagery of the prophets, especially in the book of Revelation, points backwards to earlier texts.

19. I am using "Eden" and the "garden" as synonymous. The Genesis account does suggest that there was a distinction (cf. Gen 2:8, 10). But to parse out the distinction is not significant for our objectives.

20. For a thorough analysis of Eden as a temple, see Stordalen, *Echoes of Eden*; see also Beale, *Temple and the Church's Mission*, 66–76.

21. In referencing Second Temple Jewish writers, I am referencing Jewish writings not included in the OT from the end of the sixth century BC (when the second temple was constructed) through the first century AD (when the temple was destroyed) and perhaps into the second century. These writings are relevant because, along with portions of the OT itself, they help to inform us as to the common perspectives that circulated within the Jewish world during this time.

22. Kiel, *First Book of Moses*, cited in Collins, *Genesis 1–4*, 185.

23. Beale, *Temple and the Church's Mission*, 66.

24. Wenham, *Genesis 1–15*, 76.

The End Times and the Temple

That this justifies viewing the garden as a temple derives simply from the fact that the very nature of a temple is such that it represents the dwelling place of God. If God dwelt there, and he did, then it must be understood in terms of a temple.

Eden the Mountain of God

That the later biblical writers depict Eden as a temple also derives from the fact that they assert that Eden was on a mountain. Though this detail is not given in the Genesis account, it is affirmed in the prophets. Thus, Ezekiel notes, "You were in Eden, the garden of God; . . . And I placed you there. You were on the holy mountain of God; You walked in the midst of the stones of fire. You were blameless in your ways from the day you were created, until unrighteousness was found in you. . . . And you sinned; Therefore I have cast you as profane from the mountain of God" (28:13–16).[25]

Why is it significant that Eden was located on a mountain? Well, "mountain" has multiple associations in Scripture.[26] One of which is the association of mountains with kingdoms. This derives from the fact that the capital of an ancient kingdom always resided at the top of a mountain. But, the use of "mountain" is also associated with a temple.[27] For, every temple in the OT dedicated to YHWH is on a mountain—including the end times temple of Ezekiel 40–48.[28] Furthermore, Isaiah, in his great prophetic reference to the end times temple, notes, "Now it will come about that in the last days, the mountain of the house of the LORD will be established as the chief of the mountains, and will be raised above the hills; and all the nations will stream to it. And many peoples will come and say, 'Come, let us go up to the mountain of the LORD, to the house of the God of Jacob'" (2:2–3).[29] Notice that the people come not only to the "moun-

---

25. It is irrelevant for our sake whom the prophet is addressing. Of importance here is that the garden of Eden is directly equated with the "mountain of God." Cf. also Exod 15:17; Rev 21:10.

26. The *Dictionary of Biblical Imagery* notes that "biblical meanings of the mountain are paradoxical and even contradictory. Mountains are sometimes a symbol of refuge and security and sometimes a threatening place of military slaughter" (572).

27. The *Dictionary of Biblical Imagery* adds, "almost from the beginning of the Bible, mountains are sites of transcendent spiritual experiences, encounters with God or appearances by God" (573).

28. E.g., Isa 2:2–3; 66:20; Jer 26:18; 31:23; Mic 4:1; Ps 15:1; 24:3; 43:3. Cf. Ezek 40:2; 43:12.

29. Cf. Isa 66:20; Mic 4:1.

tain," but to the "house of the Lord," which clearly alludes to the temple.[30] The presence of temples on mountains was a fundamental feature of all temples in the ancient Near East. Consequently, Beale concludes, "a close link between mountain and temple is made throughout the OT, so that Mount Zion is sometimes merely referred to as 'mountain', 'hill' or other like image."[31] Therefore, we may conclude that Eden was understood by the prophets to have been on a mountain in accord with the association of it with a temple.

Furniture of the Temple Reflects Eden as a Temple

Further justification that Eden was depicted in terms of a temple is evidenced by the fact that the furniture of the temple was understood to represent elements of the garden. Thus, the lampstand directly outside the Holy of Holies represented the Tree of Life.[32] The temple of Solomon was depicted with plant and arboreal imagery so that it had a garden like appearance.[33] The presence of precious stones in Eden also associated it with the garden temples in the OT.[34] This may well explain why Ezekiel explicitly equates the garden with a sanctuary.[35] All of this finds its parallel in the New Jerusalem, where the Tree of Life reappears.[36]

Adam as a Priest in the Garden

Perhaps even more indicative that Eden was understood as a garden-temple is the fact that Adam is depicted in the Genesis account in terms of a priest fulfilling his sacred duties. For, Gen 2:15 states, "Then the LORD God took the man and put him into the garden of Eden to cultivate [*abad*] it and keep [*samar*] it." The significance is that the terms used

---

30. Beale adds, "the patriarchal small-scale temples were all on mountains, and Mount Sinai appears to have been conceived of as a temple" (*Temple and the Church's Mission*, 146).

31. Ibid., 145. Beale also notes the use of "mountain of the house" (Jer 26:18; Mic 4:1) and "holy mountain" or "holy hill" (e.g., Pss 15:1; 43:3; 99:9). On occasions the terms are explicitly connected with the use of "temple" (e.g., Isa 66:20; Pss 24:3; 43:3).

32. See *Dictionary of Biblical Imagery*, 486.

33. Cf. 1 Kgs 6:18, 29, 32, 35.

34. Cf. Gen 2:12; Ezek 28:13.

35. Cf. Ezek 28:18.

36. Rev 22:2. See discussion in ch. 7.

for "cultivate" (*abad*) and "keep" (*samar*) often depict the activities of the priest in exercising his temple duties.[37] Now, though these verbs may also be translated as "serve" and "guard," it is also true that when they are employed together they relate either to the Israelites "serving" God and "guarding" his word, or to the priests who "keep" the "service" of the tabernacle.[38] Furthermore, the priestly responsibilities related to the temple included the duty of "guarding" unclean things from entering. As a result the priests were even called "guards" on occasion.[39] These verbs employed to depict Adam's role in caring for the garden are used consistently for the caring of, or the guarding of, sacred space.

Adam, therefore, is not merely described as working in the garden, but as a caretaker of that which is holy. Ironically, after the fall and Adam and Eve's expulsion from the garden, Cherubim are appointed to "guard" Eden (Gen 3:24). That is, they are commissioned to do what Adam failed to do! In light of all this, Beale concludes that in Genesis 2 Adam is portrayed "against the later portrait of Israel's priests, and that he was the archetypal priest who served in or guarded God's first temple."[40]

Eden the Expanding, Earth-Filling Temple

I have noted that the nature of the temple is such that it represents the place of God's presence and that the goal is for God to dwell among his people throughout the entirety of the earth. That the prophets allude to the restoration of the temple in terms of Eden raises the question as to whether or not Eden was itself intended to fill the Earth. For, if the final restoration of the temple is depicted in terms of the garden of Eden, and if the New Jerusalem is ultimately that earth-encompassing temple,[41] then

---

37. See Wenham, *Genesis*, 67. He cites Num 3:7–8; 4:23–24, 26, etc. for *abad*; and Num 1:53; 3:7–8 for *samar*. We might also add 1 Chr 23:32; Ezek 44:14. Wenham concludes, "It is striking that here and in the priestly law these two terms are juxtaposed (Num 3:7–8; 8:26; 18:5–6), another pointer to the interplay of tabernacle and Eden symbolism" (67).

38. Beale, *Temple and the Church's Mission*, 67. Wenham notes regarding *samar*, "it is even more commonly used in legal texts of observing religious commands and duties (17:9; Lev 18:5) and particularly of the Levitical responsibility for guarding the tabernacle from intruders" (*Genesis*, 67).

39. Cf. 1 Chr 9:23

40. Beale, *Temple and the Church's Mission*, 68.

41. See ch. 7 for a discussion on the New Jerusalem as a temple.

one might suspect that Eden was, at least conceptually, intended to expand and fill the earth.

Now, admittedly, the Genesis account does not provide any explicit help at this juncture. Of course, we might note that perhaps we will never know if Eden would have eventually filled the earth since, with the expulsion of Adam and Eve, the narrative of Genesis takes us in another direction. Nonetheless, I will suggest that the notion of the expansion of the garden-temple, Eden, may be inferred from the Genesis narrative and, more particularly, from the depiction of Eden and the temple throughout the OT and Second Temple literature.

First, the conception of Eden as an expanding, earth-filling sanctuary is suggested from the command to Adam and Eve to "be fruitful and multiply, and fill the earth" (Gen 1:28). It is important to note that they were given this command before they sinned. Since, as we have observed, one of the goals of creation is for God to dwell with humanity, the inference is that the place of God's presence would also "fill the earth" as they were fruitful and filled the earth. This is further suggested by the fact that Adam and Eve were to "fill" and "subdue" the entire earth (Gen 1:28). Thus, assuming that humankind was to dwell eternally in the garden with God, this suggests that the garden would have expanded as humankind filled the earth. Now, admittedly, this is quite speculative. But, these suggestions gain a level of credence from the fact that we see later biblical writers and extra-biblical writers making some of the same considerations of Eden and the temple.

In looking at the OT, there appears a general thought that the presence of God would indeed fill the whole earth.[42] For instance, Numbers 14:21 states, "As I live, all the earth will be filled with the glory of the Lord." Isaiah likewise affirms, "They will not hurt or destroy in all My holy mountain, for the earth will be full of the knowledge of the LORD as the waters cover the sea" (11:9). As noted previously, mountains were commonly associated with temples. Thus, the reference to "My holy mountain" assuredly refers to the temple. Thus, again we see hints that within the OT there existed a conception that the temple will cover the entire earth.

Furthermore, we also see in the OT the notion that the eschatological temple would expand beyond the limits of the temple mount proper, and even the city of Jerusalem. For example, in Zechariah 1:16 the prophet notes, "I will return to Jerusalem with compassion; My house will be built

---

42. Beale develops this point in detail. I will only present some of the key points. See Beale, *Temple and the Church's Mission*, 123–67. Beale cites Num 24:5–9; Ezek 31:3–16;Isa 54; 66; Jer 3; Zech 1, 2; Dan 2.

in it." The prophet then observes that Jerusalem was to be measured.[43] The prophet is then told that because Jerusalem is going to have many nations that will have come to dwell in it,[44] the city was not to be measured. For, the city will be "inhabited without walls, because of the multitude of men and cattle within it" (Zech 2:4). Thus, according to Zechariah, Jerusalem will become so expansive, as a result of the influx of the nations, that it will expand beyond measure. Zechariah concludes, "'For I,' declares the Lord, 'will be a wall of fire around her, and I will be the glory in her midst'" (2:5).[45] Zechariah then appears to affirm the tradition of Jerusalem as an expanding, earth-covering temple.[46]

In addition to the biblical evidences, an array of Second Temple works pick up this theme of an expanding Eden. Beale examines a number of these writings and observes, "There are indications elsewhere in the Old Testament, which are developed later by Jewish commentators, that Eden and the temple signified a divine mandate to enlarge the boundaries of the temple until they formed the borders around the whole earth."[47] He surveys examples in the Dead Sea Scrolls, *Sirach*, *1 Enoch*, *Philo*, the *Sibylline Oracles*, and the *Testament of Benjamin* as instances of non-biblical Jewish writings that espouse the notion of an expanding temple, "based on the original intention that Eden was to expand."[48] All of this suggests that the notion of an expanding Eden was well circulated among the ancient Jewish interpreters.

In all, there are good indications within the OT itself that Eden was to expand and fill the earth with the presence of God. This theme is then captured by Second Temple Judaism. The analysis of chapter 7 will further contend that the New Jerusalem constitutes the climax of the fulfillment of the temple and that it is portrayed as encompassing the entire earth and as Eden fulfilled.

---

43. Cf. Zech 1:16; 2:2.

44. Cf. Zech 2:11. For a detailed look at Zechariah and the expanding temple, see Kline, *Glory in Our Midst*, 71–94; also Beale, *Temple and the Church's Mission*, 142–44.

45. See Smith, *Micah–Malachi*, 196.

46. I will develop the thought in ch. 7 that the eschatological temple will be an earth-filling temple. For now it is worth noting that if indeed the eschatological temple corresponds to Eden, and that temple expands, as Zechariah seems to indicate, then perhaps one may deduce that Eden was intended to expand.

47. Beale, *Temple and the Church's Mission*, 123.

48. Ibid., 154–66, 167.

Conclusion: Eden as a Temple

This preliminary look into Eden suggests that Eden was viewed as a garden-temple throughout the OT and into Second Temple literature. It was the place of God's presence among humankind, it was located on a mountain, the furniture of later temples was associated with Eden, and Adam is depicted as serving in it in accord with the roles and responsibilities of the priests in the OT sanctuary. Furthermore, there is reason to believe that Eden was intended to be an ever-expanding and all-encompassing garden-temple that brought the presence of God to the whole earth.

OT Temple and the Promise of Restoration

It does not take long into the Genesis narrative until we arrive at the sin of Adam and Eve and their expulsion from the garden-temple.[49] What was lost in the fall was far more than humankind's "innocence." Adam and Eve were expelled from the garden and, consequently, from God's presence! As a result, we find in the Scriptures a longing for a time when God's glory is again restored among his people.

In the interim, however, temporary structures were erected to suffice as the place of God's dwelling among humankind. The first of these was the tabernacle of Moses / tent of meeting. This actual tent was not only a temporary structure, but also a portable one. Eventually, the tabernacle was replaced by a more permanent building known as the temple of Solomon. Contained within the promise to David that his son would build this temple is the suggestion that perhaps this more permanent building might provide the fulfillment of the restoration of God's glory among his people. For David is told, "When your days are complete and you lie down with your fathers, I will raise up your descendant after you, who will come forth from you, and I will establish his kingdom. He shall build a house for My name, and I will establish the throne of his kingdom forever" (2 Sam 7:12–13). It is of vital importance, however, to recognize that the temple of Solomon, and, by nature, any physical temple structure,[50] was only temporary and could not in itself have been the fulfillment of the promises that God would dwell among his people.[51]

---

49. See Gen 3.

50. In saying "physical structure" I mean something that is part of the "present age." See the discussion of the "present age" and the "age to come" in ch. 8.

51. E.g., Lev 26:11–12.

On what basis might one say that the temple of Solomon and all such physical structures were only temporary and unable to fulfill the promises of God's dwelling among his people? First, as noted above, such physical buildings by their very nature place two inherent limitations on the presence of God. As a result of these limitations they are necessarily excluded from fulfilling the ultimate purposes of God to dwell among his people.

First, every physical structure limits God's presence to one particular place. Since, however, the presence of God was intended to dwell throughout the entire earth, no purely physical temple could provide the fulfillment of such! Secondly, a physical temple not only limits God's presence to only one place, but also to only one person (the high priest)—and even for him, only one time per year! This again strongly suggests that, though the temple indeed temporarily housed the presence of God, it could not have sufficed as the fulfillment of the place where God would "walk" among his people.

Secondly, the assertion that the tabernacle of Moses, the temple of Solomon, or any physical structure could not have fulfilled the promise of God that he would dwell among his people also derives from the inherent insufficiency of any physical structure to be the eternal dwelling place of God. This is noted by Solomon at the dedication of his temple: "Behold, heaven and the highest heaven cannot contain you, how much less this house which I have built!" (1 Kgs 8:27).[52] This is also affirmed by the apostle Paul, who notes that "The God who made the world and all things in it, since He is Lord of heaven and earth, does not dwell in temples made with hands" (Acts 17:24). Stephen, the first martyr, similarly notes, "the Most High does not dwell in houses made by human hands" (Acts 7:48).[53]

Now it is important at this juncture to observe the full force of Paul and Stephen's claims. For, their assertions incorporate an apologetic thrust arising against the Jewish leadership and their views of the temple. The Jewish leadership's desire to cling to a physical structure, in denial of Jesus as the true temple, provides an important basis for the NT's indictment of Judaism. For, to deny Jesus as the temple of God, in favor of another temple, is idolatrous. That the NT understands the rejection of Jesus in favor of a physical temple in such strong terms is supported by the fact that Herod's temple[54] is referred to as a building "made with hands" (Mark

---

52. Cf. Isa 66:1.

53. Beale affirms, "Stephen proclaims that since Israel's physical temples were 'handmade' (Acts 7:44–47), they could never be a permanent dwelling place for God" (*Temple and the Church's Mission*, 137).

54. I.e., the second temple, which was built c. 516 BC and stood until AD 70.

14:58).⁵⁵ The significance of the use of "made with hands" is that with every instance of this term throughout the NT, and even the Greek version of the OT,⁵⁶ it designates either idols themselves, or items that are deemed idolatrous. For example, this term is used in the Greek version of Isaiah to refer to a pagan temple.⁵⁷ In other places the term is used to designate idols themselves.⁵⁸ The only exception, which is not really an exception, is that this term is used by the author of Hebrews in the negative sense in order to contrast the physical temple and the temple through which Jesus entered. Thus, Hebrews emphatically declares, "He entered through the greater and more perfect tabernacle, *not* made with hands" (Heb 9:11).⁵⁹

Now, we must note that the problem the NT is addressing is not that the temples of Solomon or Herod were absolutely and inherently corrupt. For indeed, they sufficed for a time as the place of God's dwelling.⁶⁰ The problem arose when the temple itself, and not the presence of God within it, became the focal point. At that moment, it became as idolatrous as the pagan temples and idols. The temple, instead, was to point to a greater temple. That greater temple is Jesus. Thus, with the coming of Christ the genuine temple has arrived. Consequently, the former temple, which had served its purpose, was no longer necessary.

Therefore, to suggest that any physical temple might accomplish God's ultimate purpose of dwelling among his people throughout the entirety of creation derives from a failure both to grasp the nature and purpose of the temple in Scripture and from the inability of any physical building to accomplish this purpose. For, no physical temple is able to suffice as the ultimate fulfillment of God's promises, since such buildings

---

This was the temple structure that stood at the time of the NT. Though originally constructed five hundred years before Herod, the elaborate additions and beautification of Herod, beginning in 20 BC and lasting through the time of the NT—the construction was not completed until 63 AD—earned it the name "Herod's temple." Note the Jewish response to Jesus that it has taken "forty-six years to build this temple" (John 2:20) refers to the construction that was still underway.

55. The Greek is *cheiropoietos*.

56. The Greek version of the OT is called the Septuagint (literally, "the seventy"; hence, it is sometimes designated by LXX).

57. Cf. Isa 16:12.

58. In the LXX the term is used occasionally either to designate "idols" or in association with idols; e.g., Lev 26:30; Isa 2:18; 10:11; 21:9; 31:7; Dan 5:4, 23; 6:28.

59. Cf. Heb 9:24.

60. There is reason to suggest that the presence of God never returned from exile into the second temple, but such a debate is well beyond our purpose here. For a discussion of this, see Wright, *New Testament*, 268–72.

have the inherent problem of limiting God's presence to one location and to one person. The question then becomes, how does the promise of an eternal temple find its fulfillment? The answer must lie within the understanding of the temple as the presence of God among his people and not in a physical building—which is the essence of the New Jerusalem.[61]

The Restoration of God's Presence among His People in Terms of a New Eden

Introduction

One of the more significant events in the life of the nation of Israel is the tragic conquest and exile of the Southern Kingdom by the Babylonians (605 BC) and the subsequent destruction of both Jerusalem and the temple of Solomon (586 BC). It is not the place here to detail the significance of these conquests for the nation of Israel. Suffice it to say, they were catastrophic. Following these events, a number of prophets arose and promised the people that God would not only bring them back to the land, but that he would also restore his presence among his people.[62]

Consequently, especially after the destruction of Solomon's temple, the prophets longed for the day when God's presence would again dwell among his people.[63] What is of great importance to note is that when these prophets looked forward to the time when God would restore his presence among his people—i.e., the temple would be restored—they did so in language that was more fitting of God's dwelling in Eden than in terms of Solomon's temple, or any physical structure. That is, the prophets declared

---

61. Cf. Rev 21:3–4, 22. Now, this does not intend to diminish the role of the tabernacle of Moses and the temple of Solomon. They indeed sufficed temporarily as the place of God's presence among his people. They were not, however—for they could not have been—the fulfillment of God's covenant promises related to his eternal dwelling among his people. They had inherent limitations that barred them from even possibly fulfilling this role. As such, they were necessarily temporary structures. What we will now proceed to demonstrate is that after the destruction of the temple of Solomon, a number of the prophets then declared that God would restore his presence among his people. In doing so, they looked beyond the restoration of a physical structure such as the temple of Solomon to an eternal dwelling of God in fulfillment of the purpose of the temple. These prophets, however, describe the glorious fulfillment in language befitting a glorified Eden and not a restored physical structure.

62. Most importantly among these "prophets of restoration," as I like to call them, are Ezekiel, Daniel, Joel, Micah, Zechariah, and Malachi.

63. E.g., Ezek 36–37; 40–48; Dan 2; Mic 4.

that God would again dwell among his people. But they announced, as we will see, that God would dwell among all his people and throughout the entire creation in a manner that transcends the physical temple and is more in accord with Eden.

The prophets, then, did not look forward to a physically reconstructed temple as though that would actually accomplish all that God intended. For, they knew and understood that a temple building was limited in scope and in its ability to accomplish the utmost goal of God's dwelling among his people. Instead, they looked beyond the tabernacle of Moses and the temple of Solomon to a glorious fulfillment in the New Creation where the glory of Eden would be restored. The prophet Haggai thus proclaims, "The latter glory of this house will be greater than the former" (2:9).

The fact that when the prophets looked forward to the restoration of God's presence among his people they did so more in terms of Eden than Solomon's temple is crucial for understanding the prophecies in the OT regarding the temple and their fulfillment in the NT, as well as the implications for our understanding of the NT, the end times, and the present.

The Stone of Daniel as an Edenic Earth-Filling Temple

That the prophets conceived of the restoration of God's presence in terms of an Edenic temple is further supported by the narrative of Daniel 2. In Daniel 2, King Nebuchadnezzar has a dream, which only Daniel is able to interpret. In the dream itself Nebuchadnezzar sees a huge statue with four distinct parts.[64] This statue is then destroyed by a "stone" that is cut "without hands."[65] That the stone represents a kingdom in opposition to the four kingdoms represented by the statue is stated explicitly: "The God of Heaven will set up a kingdom" (2:44).[66] But, this stone also becomes a "great mountain," which, as I have already noted, is often symbolic of both a kingdom and a temple.[67] What is significant for our purposes is that the description of the dream and its interpretation employ a consistent use of temple imagery in relation to the stone.

---

64. Cf. Dan 2:31–33, 37–43. Note: Dan 2 is paralleled by Dan 7, which describes a vision with four beasts. These beasts are also representative of four kings/kingdoms (7:17). See Goldingay, *Daniel*, 173–78.

65. Cf. Dan 2:34–35, 44–45.

66. For the four parts of the statue representing kingdoms, see Dan 2:36–43. For the stone as a kingdom, see Dan 2:44–45.

67. Cf. Dan 2:35.

The End Times and the Temple

First, that the stone of Daniel 2 corresponds to an Edenic temple derives from the fact that the stone is said to have been "cut without hands" (Dan 2:34, 45). In addition to the implication that this stone's kingdom will be of divine origin, the indication that it was made 'without hands' surely associates this stone with the temple.[68] This corresponds to the references in Exodus, Deuteronomy, and Joshua in which the stones used for the construction of the altar were "uncut".[69] Consequently, the interpretation of the dream in Daniel 2 fits well with the thesis that the prophets looked forward to a time in which God's presence was restored among his people in an Edenic temple.

That the Genesis account and an Edenic temple resides in the background of Daniel 2 gains support from the fact that Nebuchadnezzar is said to rule over the "beasts of the field" and over "the birds of the air" (2:38). This language parallels very closely to the Greek version of Genesis 1:28. Furthermore, it should be noted that this language corresponds to the temple imagery used in both Stephen and Paul's assertions that God "does not dwell in houses made by *human* hands"[70] (Acts 7:48; 17:24–25). In fact, the NT consistently refers to the eschatological temple as "made without hands." In Mark's account, for example, it appears in the accusation against Jesus himself, namely, "We heard Him say, 'I will destroy this temple made with hands, and in three days I will build another made without hands'" (Mark 14:58). This alludes directly to Daniel 2:44–45.[71]

In making the assertion that Christ is himself the temple and that the Jerusalem temple is no longer of significance, it is important to note that both Stephen and Paul allude to the text of Daniel 2. Thus, not only did Stephen and Paul affirm that Daniel 2 was referencing a temple, but we also realize that the Jews must have thought so as well. For, if the Jewish world did not adhere to this understanding of Daniel 2, then the force of Stephen and Paul's argumentation is missing.[72] This strongly suggests

---

68. Lacocque has asserted that the "stone cut without human hands" "represents Mount Zion, the Temple not built by human hands" (*Book of Daniel*, 124).

69. Cf. Exod 20:25; Deut 27:6; Josh 8:31. See Beale, *Temple and the Church's Mission*, 153.

70. Cf. Mark 14:58; 2 Cor 5:1; Heb 9:11, 24.

71. See Evans, *Mark*, 445.

72. Had this interpretation not been prevalent, it would have been doubtful that Stephen and Paul would have alluded to it. For, one must assume that for their argument to have had any force among the Jewish listeners they would have needed to offer interpretations of Scripture that conformed to commonly held assumptions. It would have done them no good to base their already wild propositions about Jesus on some obscure reading of Daniel.

that the understanding of Daniel 2 in association with the temple was a prevalent interpretation at the time of the first century.

Secondly, Daniel describes the stone in language that corresponds to an Edenic temple, for the stone is said to have "filled the whole earth" (2:35). This is a clear allusion to Eden and the Edenic traditions referenced in the previous section.[73] In light of the eschatological nature of Daniel, it appears that this stone will bring about the climax of all of God's covenant promises, including the establishing of God's kingdom. That the imagery contains Edenic allusions suggests that this is the final kingdom that restores Eden-like conditions.

Thirdly, the almost passing reference to the "threshing floors" (2:35) suggests that the stone of Daniel 2 has allusions to the establishing of God's end times temple.[74] Such a reference associates the stone of Daniel 2 with the temple of Solomon. For, it is well known that the temple of Solomon was built "on the threshing floor of Ornan" (2 Chr 3.1).[75] The inclusion of 'threshing floors' appears to have significance in that it serves to alert the reader to the association with the temple.

Fourthly, that this kingdom "will never be destroyed" (Dan 2:44) also suggests that it serves as the fulfillment of the promise to David that his kingdom will be forever.[76] There appears here a connection with 2 Samuel 7 and the promise to David that his son would build the temple. In 2 Samuel 7, however, David is told that not only would his kingdom be forever, but also the temple would be forever. Therefore, the fact that the stone establishes a kingdom that "will never be destroyed" associates this eternal kingdom with the eternal temple.

Finally, Daniel notes that this stone will become a "great mountain" (2:35, 44). As noted above, mountains are commonly associated with both kingdoms and temples. That the stone's becoming a "great mountain" also relates to its function as a temple derives from the abundant association of mountains with temples. For, every temple in the OT associated with the worship of YHWH was on a mountain. This, added to the fact that the stone "filled the Earth," that it was "cut without hands," that it was associated with the "threshing floors," and that it "will never be destroyed"

---

73. Cf. Gen 1:26, 28; cf. Isa 2:2–3; 6:3; 11:9.

74. Cf. Mic 4:12.

75. Note the repeated references to the "threshing floor of Ornan" (5x) in the account of David's attempt to purchase the area for the building of a temple in 1 Chr 21:15–28. See Beale, *Temple and the Church's Mission*, 147–48.

76. Cf. 2 Sam 7:12–14.

increases the likelihood that the use of "mountain" in Daniel 2 relates to the imagery of a temple.

The stone of Daniel 2, then, is deeply entrenched in a context of temple imagery. That this stone represents God's end times kingdom hardly needs comment. Daniel, however, has combined the imagery of a kingdom with that of the temple. This accords with the overarching eschatological thrust of Scripture that associates kings and priests. For it was Israel's role to be both kings and priests.[77] Furthermore, the NT affirms that Jesus is our king[78] and priest[79] and that the people of God have indeed become kings and priests in Christ.[80]

The End Times Temple of Ezekiel and Eden

Many of the popular suggestions that the physical temple in Jerusalem will be rebuilt before the coming of Christ propose that the eschatological temple of Ezekiel 40–48 will be built in Jerusalem before the return of Christ.[81] This temple in Ezekiel, however, as will be noted, does not look forward to a physical building, but instead to the presence of God among his people in a manner that transcends the restrictions of a physical building. Moreover, as I will demonstrate in the next chapter, the NT clearly affirms that this temple finds its fulfillment in Jesus and, through the Spirit, in the NT people of God, and ultimately in the New Jerusalem!

The book of Ezekiel was written to the nation in exile.[82] They had been driven from the land and appeared to have been forsaken by the Lord. Nonetheless, Ezekiel promises the people that God will restore them and fulfill his covenant promises. Ezekiel states that God will "multiply men on you. . . . And I will multiply on you man and beast; and they will increase and be fruitful" (36:10–11). Later he notes that God promises to "multiply" their harvests (36:29–30).[83] In doing so, we observe that Eze-

---

77. Exod 19:6.
78. Rev 17:14; 19:16.
79. Cf. Heb 7–10; esp. 7:17; 10:21.
80. Cf. especially Rev 5:10; see also 1 Pet 2:9; Rev 1:6.
81. See for example Schmitt and Laney, *Messiah's Coming Temple*.
82. The exile refers to the time in which the people of Israel were captured and taken from the land. The Northern Kingdom of Israel was taken into exile by the Assyrians in 721 BC. The Southern Kingdom of Judah was taken into exile by the Babylonians in 605 BC.
83. See also Ezek 37:26.

kiel too is immersed in the language of Genesis.[84] This accords with our earlier observation that the prophets employ the language of Genesis and Eden in depicting the restoration of Israel and the temple.

Ezekiel further notes that the land itself looks forward to a restoration. In describing the restoration of the land, however, he emphatically depicts it in terms of Eden: "And they will say, 'This desolate land has become like the garden of Eden; and the waste, desolate, and ruined cities are fortified and inhabited.' Then the nations that are left round about you will know that I, the LORD, have rebuilt the ruined places and planted that which was desolate; I, the LORD, have spoken and will do it" (36:35–36). Here again we see that the prophets are not looking for a restoration of Israel purely in terms of the physical land, but also in terms of Eden.

Ezekiel, then, continues this theme when he describes the outcome of God's restoration of his covenant with his people:

> And they will be My people, and I will be their God. And My servant David will be king over them, and they will all have one shepherd; and they will walk in My ordinances, and keep My statutes, and observe them. And they shall live on the land that I gave to Jacob My servant, in which your fathers lived; and they will live on it, they, and their sons, and their sons' sons, forever; and David My servant shall be their prince forever. And I will make a covenant of peace with them; it will be an everlasting covenant with them. And I will place them and multiply them, and will set My sanctuary in their midst forever. My dwelling place also will be with them; and I will be their God, and they will be My people. And the nations will know that I am the LORD who sanctifies Israel, when My sanctuary is in their midst forever. (37:24–28)

Again, the repeated use of "multiply" places this promise in the context of the Genesis narrative.

Of even greater significance is the fact that both in Ezekiel 37:23 and in 37:26 the promise of Ezekiel directly cites God's covenant assurance in Leviticus 26:11–12: that he will dwell among his people. As noted earlier, the covenant promise of Leviticus 26 itself alludes to Genesis 3:8 by means of the use of "walking." Therefore, Ezekiel's prophecy of the restoration of both God's presence among his people and of the land are eschatological

---

84. Cf. Gen 1:22, 28.

in nature, and are best interpreted in terms befitting the restoration of Eden and not a physical temple made by "human hands."[85]

This prophecy, then, should be read primarily in light of Eden and not the temple of Solomon, nor any such physical structure. To suggest that this prophecy is to be taken in terms of a future temple building is to miss both the clear indications of Ezekiel—that he is looking beyond a physical house for God to the Edenic restoration of God's presence among his people—as well as the fulfillment in the New Creation through Jesus, the NT people of God, and the New Jerusalem.

Restoration of the Temple and the Nations

As we look further, the prophets inform us that one of the key features of the restored temple is that it is for the nations as well. Thus, Isaiah says, "Now it will come about that in the last days, the mountain of the house of the LORD will be established as the chief of the mountains, and will be raised above the hills; and all the nations will stream to it. And many peoples will come and say, 'Come, let us go up to the mountain of the LORD, to the house of the God of Jacob'" (2:2–3). Later Isaiah notes, "For My house will be called a house of prayer for all the peoples" (56:7).[86]

The role of the nations in regard to the fulfillment of the temple was central to Jesus' understanding of the temple. In fact, the failure of the leadership of Israel at the time of Christ to incorporate the nations was one of the primary reasons behind Jesus' rejection of the temple and the temple establishment. Thus, while overturning the money changers' tables in the temple courts, Jesus cites Isaiah 56:7: "And He *began* to teach and say to them, 'Is it not written, 'My house shall be called a house of prayer for all the nations'? But you have made it a robbers' den'" (Mark 11:17).[87] Therefore, as I will contend in chapter 7, the temple at the time of Christ was not fulfilling its ultimate purpose of being a sanctuary for the nations—for no temple made by human hands could do so.

---

85. In ch. 7 I will contend that this is indeed how the NT read Ezek 37 and Lev 26! For now, the reader may want to reference 2 Cor 6:16 and Rev 21:3, 7. Note that in both passages Ezek 37 is being cited; the former text cites it as fulfilled in the life of the NT people of God, the latter as fulfilled in the New Jerusalem.

86. Cf. Jer 3:16–18. The association of the "mountain of the Lord" and the "house of the God of Jacob" further supports the previous argument in Dan 2 that the stone is a temple.

87. Matt 21:13; Luke 19:46.

Conclusion

This all-too-brief survey of the nature and purpose of the temple in the OT has revealed several key features of the temple. First, the temple is by nature the place of God's dwelling. Secondly, the purpose of the temple is for God to dwell among his people. Finally, Eden was understood throughout the OT and the literature of the Second Temple period as a temple.

After the expulsion of Adam and Eve from the garden-temple, the promise of God's restored presence is reiterated in Leviticus 26:11–12: God will again "walk" among his people. In the interim, temporary structures (the tabernacle of Moses and the temple of Solomon) were permitted to house the presence of God. Such structures, though serving a temporary purpose, could not fulfill the goal of restoring the presence of God among all people and throughout the earth because all such dwellings were by their very nature restrictions on the presence of God—God's presence became limited to both one person and to one place.

With the destruction of the temple of Solomon, a number of prophets arose reaffirming God's promise that he would restore his presence among his people. These prophets, however, proclaimed that God would not merely rebuild his temple and restore his presence, but that he would do so in a manner that fulfills what was intended in Eden. Namely, that God's presence would be among all people—hence the inclusion of the nations—and throughout the entire earth.

In the next chapter, we will look at the NT and see that the goal of God's dwelling among all humankind and throughout the entire creation finds its fulfillment in Jesus. The NT writers, in fact, cite the key promises of Leviticus 26:11–12; Ezekiel 37:23–27; and Daniel 2 to affirm that in Jesus, the NT people of God, and the New Jerusalem these promises are fulfilled. And it is to this that we now turn.

7

The End Times, the Temple, and the New Testament

For a new theocracy to be inaugurated, a new Temple is necessary, so that the living God may there receive the worship of the world and from there administer his wise rule over creation.[1]

God's intention as the Creator is one day to fill every part of his creation with his presence, God's holy presence could not dwell fully in the old creation because it was a sin-tainted and idolatrous world. . . . Hence, his special revelatory presence dwelt in a limited and temporary manner in human-made structures. But when he would fully redeem the world and recreate it (so Rom 8:18–25), he would dwell in it in a fuller way than ever before.[2]

And My servant David will be king over them, and they will all have one shepherd; and they will walk in My ordinances, and keep My statutes, and observe them. And they shall live on the land that I gave to Jacob My servant, in which your fathers lived; and they will live on it, they, and their sons, and their sons' sons, forever; and David My servant shall be their prince forever. And I will make a covenant of peace with them; it will be an everlasting covenant with them. And I will place them and multiply them, and will set My sanctuary in their midst forever. My dwelling place also will be with them; and I will be their God, and they will be My people. And the nations will know that I am the LORD who sanctifies Israel, when My sanctuary is in their midst forever. (Ezek 37:24–28)

The latter glory of this house will be greater than the former. (Hag 2:9)

---

1. Wright, *How God Became King*, 239.
2. Beale, *Temple and the Church's Mission*, 152–53.

Understanding the New Testament and the End Times

Introduction

WE HAVE SEEN THUS far that the significance of the temple lay in the presence of God and not in a building. This is the nature of the temple. It is the place where God dwells. Thus, the purpose of the temple is for God to dwell among all his people throughout the entirety of creation. This, I have argued, is the essence of the prophecies of the restored temple. This is why, as noted in the previous chapter, the Scriptures, when they speak of the rebuilding of the temple, do so more often in terms of the garden and the restoration of Edenic conditions than in terms of the restoration of the temple of Solomon.

Now we must venture into the NT to determine the manner in which these prophecies were read by the writers of the NT.[3] Those who have followed the thesis presented here may already know where I am headed: namely, that the promises related to the temple and its restoration find its initial fulfillment in Jesus; this fulfillment continues, by means of the Spirit, in the life of the NT people of God; and finally the ultimate fulfillment of the promises of God's eternal dwelling among his people is the New Jerusalem—the eternal dwelling place of God among his people.

Jesus as the Fulfillment of the Very Purpose of the Temple

I began this study by observing the words of Paul to the Corinthians: "For as many are the promises of God, in Him they are yes" (2 Cor 1:20). With that in mind it is not surprising to see in the NT that the promises of the temple find their fulfillment in Jesus—the true temple of God. This is not simply rhetoric. Jesus is not the temple of God in some abstract sense. He

---

3. It is at this juncture that some have attempted to skip immediately to current events. Those who do so often contend that the OT says *x* about the temple (they usually point to the prophecies of the restoration of the temple, or they note that the major promises of the temple have not been fulfilled) and then they suggest that these promises must be fulfilled in the future (which usually means our lifetime). Hence, the obsession with current events and the notion that the Jews are about to rebuild the temple. The major problem with this line of reasoning is that the proponents of this thinking have skipped the NT entirely. There is not even an attempt to determine what the NT might say about the temple. Advocates of such thinking will usually concede that Jesus is the temple, but they fail to consider at all what it means to say that Jesus is the temple of God and whether or not it has any bearing on the OT promises of restoration, let alone why the NT constantly affirms that we are the temple of God. It is not at all responsible for Christians to read the OT and simply jump over the NT and proceed to the modern world. The question we must ask is, how do Jesus, Paul, and the whole NT understand the OT and the promises of the restoration of the temple?

is the fulfillment of all that God has promised, including what God has promised with regard to establishing his presence among humankind and throughout the earth. Thus, the fulfillment of the nature and purpose of the temple is found in Jesus!

I asked at the opening of the last chapter what it means to say that Jesus is the temple. I realized that many have not even pondered this question. It is my contention that the answer is everything! That is, everything that God intended to accomplish by means of the temple, namely, his abiding presence among us, finds its fulfillment in Jesus!

I contended in chapter 6 that the temple is the place of God's presence. And, of course, Jesus is the "tabernacling" presence of God among us (John 1:14).[4] Furthermore, the temple was the place where God's glory dwelt. And, of course, Jesus is the glory of God among us; as John affirms, "We beheld His glory" (John 1:14).[5] It was also demonstrated that the goal of the temple was for God to dwell among humankind forever. And, of course, we find from Jesus the affirmation, "I am with you always" (Matt 28:20).

Finally, it was noted that the ultimate goal of the temple was for God not only to dwell among all humankind, but to do so throughout the entirety of the creation. And, of course, we catch a glimpse of this in the Great Commission, in which Jesus commands us to "go" and "make disciples of all nations" (Matt 28:19). The implication is that, since we are the temple of God, as we go into all nations we bring the temple of God to the ends of the earth. And as we make disciples of nations, we bring the nations into the presence of God. Of course, all of this will climax in the New Jerusalem, where God dwells eternally throughout the entirety of the new creation and among all his people.

That in Jesus we see the fulfillment of the nature and purpose of the temple demonstrates clearly that the prophecies related to the temple find their fulfillment in Jesus.[6] And it is from this perspective that the writers of the NT present Jesus as the temple of God.

---

4. The Greek of John 1:14 says literally that he "tabernacle" among us. The version note for the NET Bible states, "The Greek word translated *took up residence* (*skenoo*) alludes to the OT tabernacle, where the Shekinah, the visible glory of God's presence, resided. The author is suggesting that this glory can now be seen in Jesus (note the following verse). The verb used here may imply that the Shekinah glory that once was found in the tabernacle has taken up residence in the person of Jesus."

5. Note that John 1:14 first says that Jesus "tabernacle" among us, and then, in the very next clause, affirms that "we beheld His glory." This confirms for us that the reference to "tabernacle" is to be read in light of the temple.

6. If, then, Jesus is in fact the fulfillment of the nature and purpose of the temple,

Now it remains to be seen that the prophecies of the restoration of the temple in the OT find their fulfillment in Jesus.

Jesus as the Fulfillment of the OT Prophesies Regarding the Temple

I noted from the outset that all Christians affirm that Jesus is the temple of God. This is a matter of consensus. In light of John 2:19–21, it is hardly objectionable. The proclamation that Jesus is the fulfillment of the temple, however, is not limited to John 2. For, this theme pervades the Gospels and is taught abundantly by Paul and the letters of the NT. What is often overlooked, however, is how the NT writers make abundant use of the OT in their affirmations that Jesus is the temple of God. In many ways, one might reasonably declare that the underlying fabric of the NT's affirmation that Jesus is the temple of God is the OT and the promises of the restoration of the temple.

Jesus as the Temple in the Gospels

The theme of Jesus as the temple of God is abundant in the Gospel of John.[7] I have already noted that John opens his Gospel by referencing Jesus as the tabernacling presence of God whose "glory" has been manifested.[8] Furthermore, we have the clearest pronouncement in the NT in John 2:19–21: "Jesus answered and said to them, 'Destroy this temple, and in three days I will raise it up.' The Jews therefore said, 'It took forty-six years to build this temple, and will You raise it up in three days?' But He was speaking of the temple of His body."

The temple theme runs very deep in the Gospel of John. What is most significant for our purposes is that Jesus is not merely the temple in some abstract manner. Instead, he is the temple in the fullest sense and in

---

there appears to be no basis left for anyone to claim that the prophecies of the OT must find their fulfillment in a rebuilt third temple in Jerusalem. To claim such is to deny that the nature and purpose of the temple finds its fulfillment in Jesus.

7. See Walker, *Jesus and the Holy City*, 161–200; Davies, *Gospel and the Land*, 288–96. N. T. Wright notes, "John describes Jesus not only as the Temple in person, but as the one in whom everything that would normally happen in the Temple is fulfilled, completed, accomplished. . . . All the functions of the Temple—festival, presence, priesthood, and now sacrifice—have devolved onto Jesus" (*How God Became King*, 103–4).

8. Cf. John 1:14.

The End Times, the Temple, and the New Testament

accord with all that God has promised throughout the OT. As one proceeds through the Gospel of John we see a growing understanding that the eschatological temple has arrived and that the physical structure in Jerusalem (or even in Gerizim for the Samaritans) has been fulfilled, and "an hour is coming, *and now is*, when the true worshipers shall worship the Father in spirit and truth" (4:23). In John, however, the fulfillment of this theme is ultimately at the cross and the subsequent giving of the Spirit.[9] For the promise to the woman in Samaria was that Jesus would give "living water" to her (4:10). Later John notes that the "living water" refers to the "Spirit, whom those who believed in Him were to receive; for the Spirit was not yet *given*, because Jesus was not yet glorified" (7:39).

How does this relate to the fulfillment of the OT prophecies of the restoration of the temple? The answer is found in Jesus' dialogue with the Samaritan woman. As the narrative proceeds, Jesus informs her that the "living water" that he gives "shall become in him a well of water springing up to eternal life" (4:14). The term translated "springing up"[10] alludes to Joel 3:18, which states, "And a *spring* will go out from the house of the LORD."[11] The importance of the citation from Joel is that it is a prophecy relating to the final restoration of Israel and the temple. Joel 3:1 says, "For behold, in those days and at that time, When I restore the fortunes of Judah and Jerusalem. . . ." Also, it should be noted that the water in Joel flows from the house of the Lord—i.e., the temple![12] The use of water imagery flowing from the temple during the time of restoration is quite significant. Therefore, the promise of the Spirit and the living water is in accord with promise of Joel and the final restoration of the temple.

The Gospel of Mark also places tremendous stress on Jesus as the temple of God in fulfillment of the OT. Mark, in fact, begins with a citation of Malachi 3:1: "Behold, I send My messenger before Your face, who will prepare your way."[13] The verse in Malachi continues, ". . . And the Lord, whom you seek, will suddenly come to His temple . . ." (3:1b). Thus, Mark, by beginning his Gospel with a clear and emphatic declaration that in Jesus the fulfillment of Malachi 3:1 has come, clearly establishes that in Jesus the restoration has come and God has returned to his temple!

---

9. The hour of Jesus' glorification in John is clearly the cross. See John 12:23.

10. Greek: *pege*.

11. The LXX of Joel 3:18 uses *pege* for "fountain." Cf. Zech 14:8.

12. Surely the "house of the Lord" in Joel is the temple.

13. Mark 1:2–3 is actually a composite citation of Mal 3:1 and Isa 40:3. Mark attributes both references to Isaiah. This is probably the result of the prominence of Isaiah.

Now, it is also significant to note that the coming of the Lord to his temple in Malachi is in accord with the Lord returning to the land in order to bring judgment: "But who can endure the day of His coming? And who can stand when He appears? For He is like a refiner's fire and like fullers' soap" (Mal 3:2). What is the significance of Mark's citation of Malachi? For this we must turn to Paul to observe the manner in which he uses the same passage from Malachi.

It is of great significance that Paul cites Malachi 3:2 in 1 Corinthians 3 when he informs the church in Corinth that God will judge the quality of each man's work.[14] This work to which Paul alludes is the building of God's temple.[15] Paul's argument in this section of 1 Corinthians relates to the validation of his apostleship over against those leaders who were claiming superiority to him. Paul explains that each leader in the church has been entrusted with the building of the temple of God—which is the people of God ("For we are God's fellow workers. You are God's field, God's building"; 1 Cor 3:9). The foundation of this temple is none other than Christ himself: "For no man can lay a foundation other than the one which is laid, which is Jesus Christ" (3:11). Paul then explains that the quality of each man's work (referring to the leaders who are responsible for building the temple) will be "revealed with fire; and the fire itself will test the quality of each man's work" (3:13; citing Mal 3:2). The significance of this argumentation is that Paul appears to set forth that the prophesy of Malachi 3 finds its fulfillment in his present ministry of building the temple of God. That Paul views his work as building the temple through the lives of the Corinthian Christians is confirmed by the fact that Paul concludes his argument by stating, "Do you not know that you are a temple of God, and *that* the Spirit of God dwells in you? If any man destroys the temple of God, God will destroy him, for the temple of God is holy, and that is what you are" (3:16–17). Paul then affirms that anyone who presents himself as a leader among the people of God will be held liable for building up God's temple—which is the church.

What is the importance of this for our understanding of Jesus as the temple in the Gospel of Mark? First, that Mark begins his Gospel with reference to Malachi 3 suggests that he understood the entire ministry of Jesus as bringing to fulfillment the promises of God returning to his temple.[16] Secondly, Paul's use of Malachi 3 demonstrates that the writers

---

14. Cf. 1 Cor 3:13–15.
15. Cf. 1 Cor 3:8, 16.
16. I must inquire, why else would Mark open his Gospel with a citation of Mal 3?

of the NT saw the fulfillment of Malachi in the present life of the church. What is the relationship between Mark's use and Paul's?

To answer this we must first note that the context of Malachi 3 is one of judgment.[17] And it is this theme of judgment on the temple that surrounds Mark's presentation of Jesus.[18] For, Jesus' references to the Jerusalem temple in the Gospel of Mark are mostly in the negative.[19] Mark, however, does seem to indicate that Jesus is the fulfillment of the temple. This is found most notably in the accusation against Jesus at his trial. Jesus is accused of claiming, "destroy this temple made with hands, and in three days I will build another made without hands" (14:58).[20] Since this charge appears at the end of Mark, it is sufficient to note that the Gospel of Mark also appears to be framed with references to the temple. Mark begins by citing Malachi 3 and the coming of the Lord to his temple as fulfilled in Jesus.[21] This coming, however, will include the judgment of the temple establishment.

But, if the temple is to be destroyed because of its lack of fruit,[22] then what will take its place? For Mark the answer is clear: Jesus. Jesus, after all, is the one who will build a temple not made with human hands![23] This understanding is confirmed by the rest of the NT, in which Jesus is the temple.

Also, the Gospel of Matthew is framed with the theme that Jesus is himself the presence of God among his people. The narrative portion of the Gospel of Matthew opens with a citation of Isaiah 7:14, which affirms that the child shall be called, "Immanuel" (Matt 1:23), which means "God with us."[24] The Gospel of Matthew then closes with Jesus' affirmation that "I am present with you always" (28:20), which is a hallmark of the restored

---

17. Cf. Mal 3:5.

18. Space will not allow me to explore this theme at this juncture. I note here that the fulfillment of the Lord coming to his temple (Mal 3:1; Mark 1:2) appears in Mark 11:11! Beginning at Mark 11:11 he then narrates Jesus' judgment on the temple establishment through Mark 13. See Walker, *Jesus and the Holy City*, 1–24.

19. This is because the temple establishment was commissioned to bring justice (See Mal 3:5; Jer 7:3–14) and they instead made it a den of robbers (Mark 11:17; cf. Jer 7:11).

20. That this is an allusion to the eschatological temple/kingdom of Daniel 2 will be discussed further below.

21. Paul adds that Mal 3 is also fulfilled in his present ministry.

22. Hence the significance of the cursing of the fig tree (Mark 11:12–14, 20–25).

23. Mark 14:58.

24. Matthew begins his Gospel with a genealogy (1:1–17). Thus, the encounter with Joseph and the angel is the beginning of the narrative portion of Matthew.

temple. Thus, the Gospel of Matthew begins and ends with this truth: Jesus is none other than the promised presence of God among his people! That is, the promise of the temple finds its fulfillment in Jesus!

Jesus as the Temple-Stone of Daniel 2

Jesus as the temple of God is an abundant theme in the NT. There are, in fact, numerous means by which we may establish the fact that Jesus is the fulfillment of the promises related to the restoration of the temple. Perhaps one of the most significant examples of this is that the NT declares that Jesus is the stone of Daniel 2. In the previous chapter I argued that the stone of Daniel 2 is associated with the restoration of the temple, in language befitting Eden.[25] The identification of Jesus as the fulfillment of the stone of Daniel 2 would then serve to link Jesus as the fulfillment of the temple of God.

That Jesus is the stone-temple of Daniel 2 is evident from the fact that during his trial Jesus explicitly declares himself to be the Son of Man in language tied to Daniel 7.[26] Though the title "Son of Man" is used by the prophets,[27] that Jesus used this title for himself in connection with Daniel 7 is clear from his declaration that "you shall see the Son of Man sitting at the right hand of Power, and coming with the clouds of heaven" (Mark 14:62; Matt 26:64), which is a citation of Daniel 7:13. The use of the Danielic title "Son of Man" throughout the Gospels is significant because it associates Jesus with the stone of Daniel 2. This is supported by the strong link between Daniel 2 and Daniel 7.[28] This link is both structural and thematic. Among the evidences that Daniel 2 and 7 are interrelated

---

25. In ch. 6 I argued that the stone of Dan 2 is associated with the restoration of the Edenic temple in light of the following: the Stone is "cut without hands"; it is said to "fill the earth"; it is associated with the "threshing floor"; it is to be established "forever"; and it becomes "a great mountain."

26. This title is used by Jesus of himself or applied to Jesus in: Matt 8:20; 9:6; 10:23; 11:19; 12:8, 23, 32, 40; 13:37, 41; 16:13, 27, 28; 17:9, 12, 22; 18:11; 19:28; 20:18, 28; 24:27, 30, 37, 39, 44; 25:31; 26:2, 24, 45, 64; Mark 2:28; 8:38; 9:9, 12, 31; 10:33, 45; 13:26; 14:21, 41, 62; Luke 5:24; 6:5, 22; 7:12, 34; 9:22, 26, 44, 56, 58; 11:30; 12:8, 10, 40; 17:22, 24, 26, 30; 18:8, 31; 19:10; 21:27, 36; 22:22, 48, 69; 24:7; John 1:51; 3:13, 14; 5:27; 6:27, 53, 62; 8:28; 9:35; 12:23, 34; 13:31; see also Acts 7:56.

27. Esp. Ezekiel, e.g., 2:1.

28. Space will not allow me to develop this point too deeply. See Lucas, *Daniel*; Lucas argues that chs. 2–7 form a cohesive unit that is chiastically arranged. In his proposal, which is widely acknowledged, chs. 2 and 7 are paired, chs. 3 and 6 are paired, and chs. 4 and 5 are paired (p. 68). See also Goldingay, *Daniel*, 158.

is the fact that both chapters relate dreams embodying four kingdoms. In each account the destruction of the fourth kingdom, which is the most terrifying, results in the coming of the Divine kingdom. The destruction of the four kingdoms in Daniel 2 is by means of the stone. Whereas, in Daniel 7 it is by means of the Son of Man. In light of the parallels between Daniel 2 and 7, it is widely recognized that the Son of Man in Daniel 7 is equated with the stone of Daniel 2. Therefore, Jesus' use of the title "Son of Man" in terms of Daniel 7 strongly suggests that he is indeed the stone of Daniel 2.

The writers of the NT clearly pick up on this as well. For, the imagery of Daniel 2 is applied to Jesus in his trials. In both Matthew and Mark, the primary charge against Jesus at his trial is that he proclaimed, "destroy this temple made with hands, and in three days I will build another made without hands" (Mark 14:58).[29] The use of "made without hands" is a clear allusion to Daniel 2:34, 45.[30] This suggests that the NT authors understood that Jesus is the stone of Daniel 2 and that God's end times temple is being built in him.

Further identification of Jesus as the stone of Daniel 2 is found in Jesus' proclamation that "he who falls on this stone will be broken to pieces" (Matt 21:44).[31] Of great significance is the fact that the term translated "broken to pieces" is the same term used in the Greek version of Dan 2:44.[32] Added to this is the fact that Jesus is also clearly identified as the "stone the builders rejected" (Matt 21:42; Luke 20:17; Mark 12:10).[33] Though the citation the "stone the builders rejected" is from Psalm 118:22, the use of "stone" here is also connected to Daniel 2. This is supported by the fact that Daniel 2:44 is cited one verse later in Luke 20:18 and two verses later in Matthew 21:44!

Finally, both the stone of Daniel 2 and the temple that Jesus builds are "made without hands (Mark 14:58)."[34] The description of the stone-

---

29. Cf. Matt 26:61. Technically, it is not Jesus speaking here but some who stood to testify against Jesus at his trial (cf. Mark 14:57–58). That Stephen and Paul affirm that the temple Jesus made is "without human hands" (Acts 7:48; 17:24), alluding to Dan 2, strongly suggests that the accusation against Jesus, or something like it, came from Jesus himself. That is, he probably did cite Dan 2 and apply it to himself.

30. Cf. Mark 14:55–64; Matt 26:61; 2 Cor 5:1; Heb 9:11, 24; and Acts 7:48; 17:24–25; with Dan 2:34, 45.

31. Cf. Luke 20:18.

32. The term is *likmao* and is translated as "crushed" in Dan 2:44 of the NAS. Nonetheless, it is the same term used in Matt 21:44.

33. Cf. Acts 4:11.

34. Cf. Dan 2:34, 45; cf. Mark 14:55–64; Matt 26:61; Acts 7:48; 17:24.

temple in Daniel 2 as "not made by human hands" serves to identify it as being divine in origin. That Jesus is the divine temple in the NT goes without saying. This is another reason why the NT writers associate Jesus as the temple with the stone of Daniel 2!

Therefore, the end-time stone imagery of Daniel 2 refers to Jesus. Not only is Jesus the stone-temple of Daniel 2, but it is the rejection of him as such that leads to the condemnation of the leadership of Israel. The important point too stress here is that the declaration of Jesus as the temple of God cannot be divorced from the OT. That is, Jesus' declaration to be the temple of God was not made in a vacuum. It is directly in fulfillment of key OT promises that God would restore his presence to all the nations and throughout the entire earth. To reject Jesus as the fulfillment of this is what led to his pronouncements of impending judgment on the leadership of Jerusalem and the physical temple structure.

Jesus as the Temple in Paul and the NT

In chapter 3 I argued that the fulfillment of the promises of the OT have their initial fulfillment in Jesus; the fulfillment then carries forward to the NT people of God; and, ultimately, it finds its consummation in the New Jerusalem. And as we venture into the epistles of the NT we begin to observe a transition along these lines with regard to the temple. Most notably, the NT writers, beginning from the assumption that the fulfillment of the temple is found in Jesus, now begin to equate the NT people of God with the temple. Jesus, though indeed the temple, is now viewed as the "cornerstone" of the building. The building is now represented by the people of God:

> So then you are no longer strangers and aliens, but you are fellow citizens with the saints, and are of God's household, having been built upon the foundation of the apostles and prophets, Christ Jesus Himself being the corner stone, in whom the whole building, being fitted together is growing into a holy temple in the Lord; in whom you also are being built together into a dwelling of God in the Spirit. (Eph 2:19–22)

Now, just as we earlier asked what it means to say that Jesus is the temple, so too we must ask, what does it mean to say that the people of God are the temple of God? Is there any relationship with the people of God being the temple of God and the prophecies of the OT regarding the restoration of the temple?

The answer again is unequivocally, yes! It is, in fact, foundational to the NT that the people of God are depicted as the temple of God in accord with the fulfillment of the OT prophecies of the restoration of the temple.[35]

The NT People of God as the Temple

The most significant aspect of the temple in the NT in relationship with the prophecies of the OT occurs in relation to the people of God as the temple. For, though it is clear that Jesus is the temple of God in the NT, the NT does not draw an unambiguous line from the OT to Jesus as the fulfillment—though making such a connection is not difficult, as we have seen. But when it comes to the declaration of the people of God as the temple, the NT makes it very clear that we are the temple of God in fulfillment of the prophecies of the restoration of the presence of God among his people!

That the NT people of God are depicted as the temple in relation to the promises of the OT temple is evident, first, by means of Paul's description of the people of God as the temple of God in accord with the OT tabernacle and temple. Paul refers to himself as a "wise master builder" (1 Cor 3:10), which corresponds to the skilled workman in the construction of the tabernacle in Exodus.[36] Furthermore, Paul depicts the people of God as being constructed of "gold, silver, precious stones, wood" (3:12)—all items used in the construction of the temple.[37] Even more emphatically, the NT affirms that God abides with us—making us the temple.[38] That the people of God are the temple is very clear in Paul's declaration, "Do you not know that you are a temple of God, and that the Spirit of God dwells in you? If any man destroys the temple of God, God will destroy him, for the temple of God is holy, and that is what you are" (3:17). Paul also affirms,

---

35. This is summed up in Christopher Wright's observation that Paul's "argument in Ephesians 2:11–22 is saturated with Old Testament imagery" (Wright, "Christian Approach to Old Testament Prophecy," 8). It is worth noting that immediately prior to his depiction of the people of God as the temple in Eph 2, Paul cites Isa 57:19 (cf. Eph 2:17), which is a prophecy of the return of Israel from exile. Thus, Paul associates the people of God as the temple with the OT promises of the restoration of Israel. This, of course, should not be surprising if the fulfillment has already come in Jesus.

36. Cf. Exod 31:4; note that this echoes Exod 35:31–32.

37. That the wood is to be included with the gold, silver, and precious stones derives from the fact that these four items are only found together in connection with the construction of the temple (cf. 1 Kgs 5:17; 6:20–21, 28–30; also 2 Chr 3–4; cf. 1 Chr 29:2 LXX with 1 Cor 3:12)

38. Cf. 1 Cor 3:16–17; 6:19; 2 Cor 6:16; Eph 2:20–22; 1 Pet 2:5; Rev 3:12.

"or do you not know that your body is a temple of the Holy Spirit who is in you, whom you have from God, and that you are not your own?" (6:19).

What must be stressed is the fact that the NT not only explicitly identifies the people of God with the temple, but it consistently does so in accord with the OT promises of restoration. This is evident in Paul's affirmation that "we are the temple of the living God" (2 Cor 6:16). In order to buttress his contention that the church is the temple of God, Paul references the OT promise, "Just as God said, 'I will dwell in them and walk among them; And I will be their God, and they shall be My people'" (2 Cor 6:16). Paul's citation of the OT here is itself a composite of two verses: Leviticus 26:11–12 and Ezekiel 37:26–27! Now I have already noted that these two verses are central to all the prophecies relating to the future temple.[39] Thus, the primary OT prophecies referring to the goal of God's dwelling among his people—Leviticus 26:11–12—and the promise of his restored presence among his people—Ezekiel 37:26–27—are applied by Paul to the NT people of God in the context in which these prophesies are presently being fulfilled!

This is of the utmost significance. For, any claims that certain biblical prophecies regarding the rebuilding of the temple still have a future fulfillment have overlooked the fact that Paul cites these prophecies as fulfilled. Yes, Jesus is the fulfillment of these! And, now it might be added, so too are the NT people of God. That is, by means of the Holy Spirit dwelling among the people of God today, the promise that God will "walk" among his people is presently being fulfilled!

Furthermore, we not only find that the central passages of the restoration of the temple are fulfilled in the presence of God, by means of the Spirit, among the NT people of God, but we also see that Paul depicts the NT people of God as a temple in language that is more appropriate to the garden of Eden than to Solomon's temple. This is seen in Paul's use of garden imagery in his description the NT people of God as temples. For, in his introduction to the depiction of the people of God as temples, he states,

> I planted, Apollos watered, but God was causing the growth. So then neither the one who plants nor the one who waters is anything, but God who causes the growth. Now he who plants and he who waters are one; but each will receive his own reward according to his own labor. For we are God's fellow workers; you are God's field, God's building. (1 Cor 3:6–9)

39. See ch. 6.

The New Jerusalem as the Temple

Though the fulfillment of the promises of the restoration of God's presence has begun in Christ and continues by means of the Spirit in the life of the people of God today, it is also true that the entirety of the end times promises in Scripture climax in the New Jerusalem.[40] The New Jerusalem, thus, represents the consummation of the dwelling of God among his people. In fact, there is a close connection between the description of the New Jerusalem in Revelation 21–22 and the end-times temple of Ezekiel 40–48. What is even more essential to observe is that the key promises of Leviticus 26 and Ezekiel 37 relating to the promise of the restoration of God's presence among his people are also cited in Revelation 21–22 as fulfilled in the New Jerusalem.

The description of the New Jerusalem, in fact, opens with the declaration:

> And I saw a new heaven and a new earth; for the first heaven and the first earth passed away, and there is no longer any sea. And I saw the holy city, New Jerusalem, coming down out of heaven from God, made ready as a bride adorned for her husband. And I heard a loud voice from the throne, saying, 'Behold, the tabernacle of God is among men, and He shall dwell among them, and they shall be His people, and God Himself shall be among them. . . . He who overcomes shall inherit these things, and I will be his God and he will be My son. (Rev 21:1–3, 7)

This, too, alongside Paul's reference to the present dwelling of the Spirit among the NT people of God, is a citation of both Leviticus 26:11–12 and Ezekiel 37:26–27! Thus, these key covenantal promises of the restoration of the presence of God among his people are cited as fulfilled in the depiction of the New Jerusalem in Revelation 21:1–3, 7.[41] The New Jerusalem, then, represents the climax of the intimacy of God among his people.

In addition to the explicit identification of the New Jerusalem with the promise of Leviticus 26 and Ezekiel 37, the entire account of the New Jerusalem in Revelation 21–22 is filled with descriptions that the city is indeed a temple. First, we see that John is taken to a mountain to view the holy city.[42] The close association with mountains and temples was noted

---

40. Cf. Rev 21–22.
41. Just as Paul cited these verses as fulfilled in the present indwelling of the Spirit.
42. Cf. Rev 21:10.

in chapter 6.⁴³ We are also told that nothing unclean enters this city, which suggests that the entire city is sacred space.⁴⁴ Furthermore, in accord with the holy of holies in the OT temple we find that the dimensions of this city are a perfect cube: "and he measured the city with the rod, fifteen hundred miles; its length and width and height are equal" (Rev 21:16).⁴⁵ This suggests that the New Jerusalem is not only a temple, which incorporates the presence of God and the Lamb, but that the entirety of it is the holy of holies (21:22)! This accords well with the stress on the fact that the end times restoration includes the presence of God among all people and throughout the entirety of the creation. For God to dwell in such a manner would indeed render the entire creation the holy of holies.

Therefore, the depiction of the New Jerusalem is one in which the end times temple fills the entire cosmos of the new creation. Revelation collapses the temple, city, and land into one end times picture depicting the climax of God's communion with his people.

Furthermore, the description of the New Jerusalem corresponds more closely to the restoration of an Eden-like garden, more than the temple of Solomon. For, John notes,

> And he showed me a river of the water of life, clear as crystal, coming from the throne of God and of the Lamb, in the middle of its street. And on either side of the river was the tree of life, bearing twelve kinds of fruit, yielding its fruit every month; and the leaves of the tree were for the healing of the nations (Rev 22:1–2).

The depiction of the New Jerusalem in terms of Eden is further evidenced by reference to the Tree of Life⁴⁶ and the river of life.⁴⁷ This again affirms the thesis that the prophecies of the temple find their fulfillment in an Eden-like garden. Thus, though John sees a New Heaven and New Earth (21:1), what he goes on to describe is the people of God enjoying the presence of God in a garden-like city, which itself constitutes the temple (21:2–3, 10—22:3). But this is no ordinary temple. This is the Edenic garden-temple in fulfillment of God's purpose in creation.

That the New Jerusalem represents the ultimate fulfillment of the restoration of God's presence among his people is further evidenced by the

---

43. See ch. 6.
44. Rev 21:27; 22:15; cf. 2 Chr 23:19; 29:16; 30:1–20.
45. Cf. 2 Chr 3:4, 8.
46. Cf. Gen 2:9.
47. Cf. Gen 2:10.

close relationship between the account of the New Jerusalem in Revelation 21–22 and the end-times city/temple of Ezekiel 40–48.[48] For one, in both the vision of Ezekiel 40–48 and the depiction of the New Jerusalem in Revelation 21–22, the corresponding temples are similarly described as cities/temples. The temple in Ezekiel 40–48 is introduced as "like a city" (Ezek 40:2). Similarly, the New Jerusalem is deemed "the holy city" (Rev 21:10). Also, the prophets Ezekiel and John are taken to a "high mountain" to view the respective city/temples.[49] In both accounts, the gates of the city/temple have the names of the tribes of Israel.[50] Also, the description of each city/temple includes a river that flows from the inner sanctum, or the throne of God himself.[51] Finally, both city/temples have the trees that bear fruit that is for the healing of the nations (Ezek 47:12; Rev 22:2).[52]

This is crucial for our understanding. For one of the key passages proposed by those who believe that a physical temple must be rebuilt in Jerusalem is the prophecy of Ezekiel 40–48. Yet, in the introduction to this prophecy Ezekiel cites the great promise of Lev 26:11–12.[53] And it is this promise that Paul cites and applies to the NT people of God in 2 Cor 6:16. And now John cites these same promises in Rev 21:3, 7 as fulfilled in the New Jerusalem!

Consequently, the NT clearly affirms that the promises of the restoration of God's presence in an end-times temple find their initial fulfillment

48. There is in fact much evidence that the entire narrative of Rev 19–22 corresponds with Ezek 37–48. That the climaxes of both are closely interwoven then comes as no surprise. See Beale, *Revelation*, 1070–21. Beale notes, "the primary reason that John throughout [Rev] 21:9–22:5 excludes most of the detailed descriptions of the Ezekiel 40–48 temple and its ordinances is because he understands it as fulfilled in God and Christ's presence and not in a physical structure" (*Revelation*, 1091).

49. Cf. Ezek 40:2; Rev 21:10.

50. Cf. Ezek 48:31–34; Rev 21:12–13.

51. Cf. Ezek 47:1–12; Rev 22:1–5.

52. We could delve much further here—though space eludes us—in drawing out the connections between the prophecy of the restored temple in Ezek 36–48 and the New Jerusalem in Rev 21–22. There are numerous parallels in Ezek 36–48 to the narrative of Rev 19–22. For example, both have a summons to the birds to gorge themselves; both use "Gog and Magog"; fire comes down from heaven and destroys Gog and his followers; both John and Ezekiel are taken to a high place where they are shown a vision of a new city; both see a figure with a measuring rod who is to measure; the city/temple is a square with gates, walls, and foundations, and with three gates on each side; both depict God's tabernacling; both refer to God's glory; both have waters flowing out of the city/temple from the throne; and both have a tree with fruit that is for healing.

53. Ezek 36–39 are transitional and serve to introduce the means by which God will bring about the restoration of his people and his temple. Chapters 40–48 then depict the final state of this restoration.

in Jesus, are presently being fulfilled in the life of the NT people of God, and will be ultimately fulfilled in the New Jerusalem.

The Restoration of the Temple and the Present

All of this suggests that the end times temple of Ezekiel 40–48 is not fulfilled by some physical rebuilt temple in Jerusalem immediately prior to the return of Christ. Instead, the fulfillment is Jesus, the NT people of God, and ultimately the New Jerusalem. At this point one may note that it does not appear that the present existence of the temple by means of the Spirit's abiding through the people of God is greater than the former as predicted in Haggai 2:9; let alone that we have Eden-like conditions in the present. Indeed, this is true. This is a perfect example of the tension created by the already/not yet aspect of eschatology.[54] For, in fact, Jesus is the temple and his resurrection was the beginning of the New Creation! This New Creation has already begun in Christ, continues through his people, and climaxes in the New Jerusalem. Hence, Paul affirms, "Therefore if any man is in Christ, he is a new creature; the old things passed away; behold, new things have come" (2 Cor 5:17).[55] We also observe that Paul directly relates the concept of the New Creation to the end times temple. For, the entire context of 2 Cor 3–5 is one of new creation and temple![56] But in what sense can we say that the "latter glory" is "greater than the former"?

There are several points that need to be made at this juncture. First, it was noted that in Christ the presence of God is no longer restricted to one person. Hence, John concludes, "we beheld His glory" (John 1:14). That is, in Christ the presence of God was experienced by more than one person. This makes the temple of Christ superior to the physical temple in Jerusalem, and the "latter glory" is already surpassing that of the former temple. Furthermore, by means of the Spirit's indwelling of the people of God, God's presence continues to be experienced by more and more people.

---

54. The notion of an "already/not yet" eschatology will be discussed in more detail in ch. 8. For now I will simply note that the NT indicates that in one sense prophecies regarding the restoration of God's presence have *already* begun to be fulfilled in Jesus, and through the Spirit in the life of the people of God today. At the same time, there is a dimension in which these same prophecies have *not yet* been fulfilled—in the sense that these same prophecies indicate a glorious restoration in which there is no more suffering or death. Thus, the fulfillment is in one sense *already* here and in another sense the consummation of God's promises have *not yet* come.

55. Cf. 2 Cor 5:17; Gal 6:15–16; Col 1:18; Rev 3:14.

56. See Beale, *Temple and the Church's Mission*, 253–59.

Therefore, in light of the fact that the presence of God is experienced by more than one person, the "latter glory" is greater than the former.

Finally, as the people of God disperse to the ends of the earth, so too God's presence, which indwells every believer, now transcends beyond the one place of the physical temple to the ends of the earth. This is the significance of the Great Commission. For, in carrying forth the gospel to the ends of the earth, we are also extending the presence of God throughout the entire earth. Therefore, in light of the fact that the presence of God is beginning to encompass the entire earth rather than one particular location, indeed the "latter glory" is already greater than the former.

At the same time, it is true that though the kingdom of God has come in Christ, we still experience sin, death, and suffering in the present. Such will remain until the consummation when it is finally eliminated.[57] Christ, in fact, noted that the nature of the coming of his kingdom is such that it would start small, like a mustard seed, and yet when it grows fully it will be large enough for all the birds.[58] This means that the present time is one in which both the kingdom of God and the kingdom of the world coexist.[59] The "latter glory" is indeed greater than the former in the present, but only in part—as evidenced by the continued presence of evil. Thus, though the prophecies of the restoration of God's presence have come in Christ and the Spirit, there is still a future consummation for which we wait anxiously!

Excursus: Is the Ultimate Fulfillment of the Temple Literal or Symbolic?

The key to understanding the promises regarding the temple is that the Scriptures stress that the significance of the temple is found in the presence of God among his people, and not in a building. The temple is relational! Therefore, when the NT affirms that Jesus is the temple, we can immediately realize that we have the beginning of the fulfillment! Jesus is the temple! And as God with us, we have the inauguration of the fulfillment of the prophecies of the restored temple.

---

57. Cf. Rev 21:4.

58. Cf. Mark 4:30–32.

59. See ch. 8 for a more detailed discussion of the kingdom of God and the kingdom of this world.

Understanding the New Testament and the End Times

At this point some may continue to object because they assert that the prophecies of the Bible must be fulfilled literally.[60] Some, in fact, will prefer to designate my position as a "symbolic" or "spiritual" fulfillment as opposed to the "literal." Those who assume that all prophecy must be fulfilled "literally" will readily agree that Jesus is the "symbolic" fulfillment of the temple. They, however, will assert that there must also be a "literal" fulfillment—which for them takes the form of a physical temple in Jerusalem. This assumption, however, is unjustified.

First, the assertion that all prophecies must have a "literal" fulfillment is nowhere found in Scripture.[61] Not only that, but we have seen that often the fulfillment of prophecy transcends the literal (e.g., John the Baptist as Elijah, and Jesus as the temple). Thus, to contend that prophecy must have a literal fulfillment goes beyond what the Bible says and is contradicted by many of the fulfillments of prophecy in Scripture. Therefore, to assume that a literal temple must be built in fulfillment of the OT promises is an assumption that the Bible never supports. Furthermore, that the NT clearly indicates that Jesus is the fulfillment of the promises regarding the temple means that this assumption is indeed incorrect.

Secondly, to assert that there must also be a physical temple in Jerusalem is to fail to understand the nature and purpose of the temple and how this could only have been fulfilled in Christ. The Scriptures confirm that the ultimate purpose of the temple cannot be fulfilled by a physical building.[62] The fulfillment then must point us to Christ, the NT people of God, and the New Jerusalem, all of which transcend any physical structure.

---

60. But, to say that the fulfillment of the prophecies regarding the temple must be fulfilled in either a "literal" or a "symbolic" manner is to concede to modernist conceptions. The biblical world did not think in such a manner in which things could be so easily separated.

One of the problems with this perspective is the difficulty in defining what is meant by "literal." In a sense, one may well say that the position argued here is that the temple is "literally" fulfilled in Christ and his church. Now, we can say this because the definition of "literal" must be in accord with the nature and purpose of the temple. If the nature and purpose of the temple relates to the presence of God among his people, then it is easy to see that Jesus is the "literal" fulfillment of the temple!

61. This point is especially relevant because most who assert that prophecy must be fulfilled literally also advocate for a strong view of *sola Scriptura* (Scripture alone). That is, they argue vociferously that we must only believe in what the Bible says. Yet, here we see that they have devised rules to determine what the Bible means that are themselves not found in Scripture.

62. There is an analogy here with the first coming of Christ (which I hesitate to use, for fear of being misunderstood). The analogy is that the Jewish leadership at the time of Christ was reading the OT in a manner that led them to believe that the

Consequently, we find that the fulfillment of prophecy is far more glorious than what might have been expected from the prophecy itself. As a result, I suggest that this is the "literal" fulfillment. It is not literal in terms of a physical building of wood and costly stones; but the eternal temple was never intended to be a physical building. It is the literal fulfillment in that this is what the prophecies were pointing to all along! Edmund Clowney affirms that the temple "is not spiritualization in our usual sense of the word, but the very opposite. In Christ is realization. It is not so much that Christ fulfills what the temple means; rather Christ is the meaning for which the temple existed."[63] G. K. Beale, likewise, concludes, "our contention has been that the presence of God filling the whole new creation is the 'literal' reality to which Israel's first two temples pointed."[64]

Conclusion

Consequently, all that God has purposed in the temple is fulfilled first in the person of Christ, then in the NT people of God, and it climaxes in the eternal abiding of God with his people in the New Jerusalem. This understanding accords well with the emphasis in Scripture on the temple as the presence of God among his people. Since buildings made by human hands were merely temporary structures that limited God's presence to one place and to one person, the prophets looked forward to the fulfillment of God's renewed presence among all his people throughout the entire earth. This is evident in the key text of Ezekiel 37:24–27, which itself is citing Leviticus 26:11–12. But we have observed that Paul cites these passages in 2 Corinthians 6:16 and applies them to the current life of the people of God. And John cites them in Revelation 21:3, 7 as fulfilled in the New Jerusalem!

That such prophecies find their fulfillment in the presence of God among the people of God today, and ultimately in his presence in the New Jerusalem, fits precisely with everything we have seen regarding the temple in Scripture. For one, God does not dwell in buildings made by human

---

Messiah was to be a certain type of leader; namely, a political ruler who would free them from Roman occupation and establish his messianic kingdom. Jesus, however, transcended this conception. He was indeed the Messiah who established his kingdom. But, he did so in a manner that transcended the kingdoms of the world. In a similar manner, those who suggest that the prophecies regarding the temple must be fulfilled literally are failing to see that in Christ the prophecies of the temple have been fulfilled—but in a manner that transcends what might otherwise have been expected.

63. Clowney, "Final Temple," 177.
64. Beale, *Temple and the Church's Mission*, 352

hands. Consequently, neither Jesus nor his church nor the New Jerusalem can be described as made by human hands. Secondly, the presence of the Holy Spirit in the life of the people of God today ("your body is a temple of the Holy Spirit who is in you"; 1 Cor 6:19) and the presence of the Father and the Son in the New Jerusalem (Rev 21:22) constitute them both as temples—the presence of God among his people. Also, the people of God in the NT are commanded to go to the ends of the earth. The command of Jesus for his disciples to "Go therefore and make disciples of all nations" (Matt 28:18) must be viewed in terms of the end times fulfillment of the command to Adam and Eve to fill the earth. Thus, the New Jerusalem encompasses the whole earth, which serves to confirm that God's goal of dwelling among his people is fulfilled.

The significance of this for our understanding of the temple is that it confirms both the nature and the intent of the temple. For, God desires to dwell throughout his entire creation and among all humankind. As the people of God fulfill the command to go to the ends of the earth and makes disciples, the presence of God begins to dwell throughout his creation and among all those who receive him. The consummation of this is clearly in the New Jerusalem, in which God dwells among all people and throughout the entire New Creation.

The conclusion that I have reached here, then, is that the prophecies of the temple have found their fulfillment in Jesus, and, through the Spirit, in the NT people of God, and ultimately in the New Jerusalem. If this is true—and I am convinced that it is not only true, but central to the message of Jesus—then to suggest that a temple will be rebuilt in Jerusalem in fulfillment of prophecy is to deny the centrality of Jesus and the message of the NT.[65] The notion that a literal temple in Jerusalem will be rebuilt in fulfillment of prophecy is not simply an exegetical question—literal or symbolic—it is a Jesus question.[66] I suggest that many have simply failed to understand the Scriptures on such matters because they do not have a high enough view of Jesus.

To contend that a third temple is about to be constructed in fulfillment of prophecy suggests that Jesus was not the fulfillment of those prophecies. To simply assert that Jesus could not be the fulfillment of

---

65. I am not suggesting that the Jews will never build another temple. Perhaps they will. What I am contending is that any such temple has no bearing on the fulfillment of any prophecy in Scripture. All such prophecies are fulfilled in Christ, the NT people of God, and the New Jerusalem.

66. Technically, it is a hermeneutical question. But I have contended that Jesus should be the center of our hermeneutics. Thus, for me, it is a Jesus question.

all the OT prophecies about the temple because he is not a building and because the prophecies must find a literal fulfillment (i.e., in a building) fails to understand the nature and purpose of the temple, and the NT message of the person and work of Jesus. This claim also assumes that a literal hermeneutic (or, method of interpretation) must be imposed on the Bible, contrary to all that we have noted in relation to the biblical view of the temple. The Bible simply fails to affirm an absolutely literal hermeneutic. Thus, we can either assume that all prophecies must have a literal fulfillment, and that Jesus, the NT people of God, and the New Jerusalem do not fulfill all the OT prophecies regarding the temple, or we can observe throughout the pages of the NT that Jesus, the NT people of God, and the New Jerusalem fulfill all the OT prophecies relating the temple—and therefore, not all prophecies have a literal fulfillment![67]

Why does this all matter? First, it matters in that we are called to handle "accurately the word of truth" (2 Tim 2:15). Proper interpretation is essential. Secondly, we see the endless speculations and wild prognostications that abound in the popular Christian marketplace. Such works take our focus off our task as God's means by which he is bringing in his kingdom and focus them instead on wild speculations about the future. Thirdly, the theme of the temple speaks to the heart of the Christian life. Instead of looking to Jerusalem for some rebuilt temple as a key indication of the imminent return of Jesus, the Scriptures emphatically call us, as the temple of God, to live out the mission of God in holiness.[68] I will develop these thoughts more fully in chapter 12. For now, I will simply note that the implications of this look at the temple in Scripture affirm that we must have a high view of Jesus and that we must begin to consider the implications of what it means to be the temple of God—for that is what we are!

---

67. Of course, we could at this point debate the meaning of "literal." That is, if "literal" were defined in terms of the intent of the temple—that is, as the place of God's presence—then Jesus was the "literal" fulfillment of the temple prophecies! But I don't think such is necessary. My point here should be clear. We need to alter our insistence on an absolute literal hermeneutic, or at least clarify what is meant by "literal."

68. Cf. 2 Cor 6:14—7:1; 1 Cor 3:16–17.

8

The Tribulation and the People of God

The suffering and death of Jesus's people is not simply the dark path they must tread because of the world's continuing hostility toward Jesus and His message. It somehow has the more positive effect of carrying forward the redemptive effect of Jesus's own death, not by adding to it, but by sharing in it. . . . But if they are to bring his kingdom in his way, they will be people who share his suffering.[1]

It is at this precise point that believing that "the great tribulation" has partially begun should inspire believers to be even more on guard against sin and satanic deception.[2]

For just as the sufferings of Christ are ours in abundance, so also our comfort is abundant through Christ. (1 Cor 1:5)

Now I rejoice in my sufferings for your sake, and in my flesh I do my share on behalf of His body (which is the church) in filling up that which is lacking in Christ's afflictions. (Col 1:24)

Introduction

PERHAPS THE KEY TO the book of Revelation is found in the throne room scene in chapters 4–5.[3] In chapter 5, the One seated on the throne is

---

1. Wright, *How God Became King*, 201.
2. Beale, *New Testament Biblical Theology*, 224.
3. This is a somewhat ironic statement for someone like myself to say. For when I read Revelation early in my career from the popular eschatological approach, I used to skip chs. 4–5. The thinking was that ch. 1 was relevant as an introduction to the book. Chapters 2–3 were relevant to the churches at the time. Chapter 6 and following then began to narrate the events of the future tribulation that led to the coming of the Lord.

holding a scroll in his right hand, which is sealed with seven seals. John then begins to weep when he realizes that "no one was found worthy to open the book" (5:4). Suddenly a voice says to him, "stop weeping; behold, the Lion that is from the tribe of Judah, the root of David, has overcome so as to open the book" (5:6)! When John turned to look to see this lion we are surprised to find out that he saw not a lion, but "a lamb standing, as if slain" (5:6).

Now we know, of course, that the lion *is* the lamb. Jesus is both the "lion of the tribe of Judah" (5:5) and the "lamb that was slain" (5:12).[4] I suspect, however, that John is conveying to us something far more important than the mere truth that Jesus is both the lion and the lamb. John is telling us that the means by which Jesus became the lion is by his being the lamb! Craig Keener comments, "Here the central paradox of Revelation and of the Christian faith in general comes to the fore: Jesus conquered not by force but by death, not by violence but by martyrdom."[5]

What does this have to do with tribulation? Everything. For throughout the NT we see the people of God are depicted as imitators of Christ.[6] Therefore, as we venture to look at the concept of tribulation and the end times, I will contend that as Christ suffered and overcame so as to reign, so shall we. Paul, in fact, encourages the church in Thessalonica on this very point: "You also became imitators of us and of the Lord, having received the word in much tribulation with the joy of the Holy Spirit" (1 Thess 1:6). The *New Bible Dictionary*, under the entry "tribulation," affirms, "The tribulation of Christ is the pattern and norm for the experience of the Christian community. Thus, tribulation is inevitable and to be anticipated."[7] It is, in fact, through the suffering of Christ and the NT people of God that the kingdom of God comes to "earth as it is in heaven" (Matt 6:10).

Nonetheless, it has become commonplace among much of the popular Christian world to view the people of God as though they are exempt from tribulation and suffering, or at least from the "great tribulation,"

Chapters 4–5 were merely a nice introduction to all of this, but I honestly supposed that they were not necessary.

4. As noted earlier, it is very important to the interpretation of Revelation to understand that the imagery derives from the OT. E.g., the Lion of the tribe of Judah comes from Gen 49:9; the Lamb that was slain comes from Isa 52:13—53:12.

5. Keener, *Revelation*, 186.

6. The people of God in the NT are called to imitate Jesus, or to imitate their leaders who themselves imitate Jesus. See 1 Cor 4:16; 11:1; Eph 5:1; 1 Thess 1:6; 2:14; Heb 6:12; 13:7.

7. Marshall et al., *New Bible Dictionary*, 1028.

which, it is proposed, will descend upon the world in the days immediately prior to the return of Jesus. Many proponents of this view, in fact, claim that those Christians who are alive at the time of the "great tribulation" will be raptured (taken away) and spared from it.[8]

As one can see, we have two very different theological perspectives. On the one hand, some propose that tribulation is what awaits the wicked during the last days. When this tribulation arrives, the righteous are either exempt from suffering or they are altogether removed. Either way, the righteous are not affected. On the other hand, I am proposing that throughout Scripture, and especially in the NT, suffering and tribulation are the lot of the Christian life.[9]

Let's step back for a second and approach the matter this way. Certainly, all Christians will acknowledge that the goal of the Christian life is to attain to the resurrection from the dead—when we are united with Christ and experience the true reality in which there is no more suffering or mourning or pain or death. The question is, what must we do to attain such? For many Christians the answer is usually quite simple. We must accept Jesus into our heart as our Savior. Okay, fair enough. But is that all that one must do? I mean, is that really all that the Christian life boils down to—believing in Jesus and then awaiting the resurrection?

Would it not be nice if the Bible would just come out and say, "This is what you must do to attain to the resurrection"? Well it does! Philippians 3:10 says, "That I may know Him and the power of His resurrection and the fellowship of His sufferings, being conformed to His death; in order that I may attain to the resurrection from the dead." There it is: a recipe! If we "know him" and "the power of resurrection" and are "conformed to his death," then we will attain to "the resurrection from the dead"![10]

The often overlooked element here is that attaining "to the resurrection from the dead" is via the way of suffering—"being conformed to his death." What I aim to demonstrate in this chapter is that suffering—cross

---

8. I will address the idea of a rapture below, and in more detail in ch. 10.

9. In the present chapter I will address the biblical text and what it says about tribulation. In ch. 12 I will discuss why I believe that this matters. For now, I will mention only that if tribulation is the lot of the Christian life, then we should prepare for it. This places an urgency and a necessity to spiritual formation. On the other hand, to suggest that tribulation is only for the wicked, and in the future, suggests to many Christians that they really have no need to grow in Christ in order to be prepared to endure the war with the dragon of Revelation (cf. Rev 12).

10. Though the translations may differ here, they are all in effect capturing the Greek. The grammar here is what we call a "first-class conditional": these sentences are saying that if the first part is true, then the second will occur.

bearing—is in fact a necessary element for living in the kingdom of God and for maturing in Christian discipleship; with the result of eventually attaining to the resurrection! If we desire to reign with him, then we must suffer with him. For, if we aim to be lions, then we too must become lambs!

"Tribulation" in the NT

The fact that "tribulation" (*thlipsis*)[11] is the present lot of the Christian life is evident throughout Scripture[12] and the NT in particular. Thus, Jesus warned his disciples, "Then they will deliver you to tribulation [*thlipsis*], and will kill you, and you will be hated by all nations on account of My name" (Matt 24:9). Jesus also said, "In Me you may have peace. In the world you have tribulation [*thlipsis*], but take courage; I have overcome the world" (John 16:33).

A look at the book of Acts confirms that all three uses of *thlipsis* refer to direct tribulation or persecution for the people of God.[13] In Acts 11:19, persecution is the fate of the people of God: "So then those who were scattered because of the persecution [*thlipsis*] . . ." In Acts 14:22, Paul informs the churches of Lystra, Iconium, and Pisidian Antioch, "through many tribulations [*thlipsis*] we must enter the kingdom of God" (Acts 14:22). And, in Acts 20:23 Paul explains, "the Holy Spirit testifies to me in every city that imprisonment and afflictions [*thlipsis*] await me." Throughout the NT, then, *thlipsis* refers primarily to the present suffering of the people of God.[14]

This understanding holds true with the use of the verbal form *thlibo*.[15] In fact, the use of the verb *thlibo* in Matthew 7:14 is associated with

---

11. Greek: noun form is *thlipsis*, and the verbal form is *thlibo*. This word may also be translated "affliction" or "persecution." *Thlipsis* occurs forty-five times in the NT, whereas *thlibo* occurs ten times. There are three occurrences of compounds that derive from *thlibo*, but they provide nothing new to the discussion of this word.

12. In the OT (LXX), *thlipsis* is used consistently for the affliction of Israel and righteous individuals. *Thlipsis* is used more than thirty times in the LXX of the Psalms, e.g., 9:9. See Barnett, *Second Corinthians*, 72.

13. There are two other uses of *thlipsis* in Acts (7:10, 11), but these are irrelevant for our purposes since they occur in a historical narrative. In both instances, the term is used to describe either the affliction of Joseph himself or of the entire region.

14. E.g., 2 Cor 6:4; Phil 4:14; Col 1:24; 1 Thess 1:6; 3:3; 2 Thess 1:4; Heb 10:33; Rev 1:9; 2:9, 10.

15. E.g., Matt 7:14; 2 Cor 4:8; 7:5; 1 Thess 3:4; 1 Tim 5:10; Heb 11:37. There are, in fact, very few instances in which *thlipsis* refers to the suffering or persecution of those outside the body of Christ. One of these exceptions is in 2 Thess 1:6–7, where Paul

the "narrow path," which is "hard" (ESV), "difficult" (NET, NKJ), or "narrow" (NAS, NIV), and "leads to life."

Not only, then, is suffering the lot of the Christian life, but I would go so far as to suggest that it is the means by which the disciple of Christ enters into glory. Paul affirms this when he tells the Corinthians, "For momentary, light affliction[16] is producing for us an eternal weight of glory far beyond all comparison" (2 Cor 4:17).

In the NT, then, "tribulation" has a general meaning of suffering. And this suffering is primarily that of the people of God. In fact, for the people of God it is something that is to be expected, while at the same time it is also a source of blessing![17] As Paul Barnett notes, "'Afflictions' are the portion of the messianic people, but so too, is the divine 'comfort.'"[18]

Tribulation in Light of the Kingdom of God and the Kingdom of This World

Understanding the NT teaching regarding tribulation follows from a proper understanding of the nature of the kingdom of God and its relationship to the kingdom of this world.[19] One of the primary reasons why

---

notes, "For after all it is *only* just for God to repay with affliction those who afflict you, and *to give* relief to you who are afflicted." Even here we note that the primary context is the suffering of the people of God. Paul just notes that God will afflict those who afflict us.

Another instance in which *thlipsis* is used for the unbelieving is in Rev 2:22, where the church in Thyatira is warned that Jezebel and those who follow her ways will be afflicted: "Behold, I will cast her upon a bed *of sickness*, and those who commit adultery with her into great tribulation, unless they repent of her deeds." This verse, however, does not suggest a worldwide tribulation of the wicked. The addressees are those in the church in Thyatira. The tribulation that is coming is for those who are a part of the church but are following this false teacher.

Perhaps a final exception in which *thlipsis* is not directly applied to the people of God appears in Rom 2:9, where Paul states, "*There will be* tribulation and distress for every soul of man who does evil." As we look at this passage, we do not see in it a detailed description of a tribulation for the world. Paul, in fact, appears to be relating a general maxim: if you do evil, you will suffer for it. For a look at Matt 24:21, 29 and Rev 7:14, see below.

16. The Greek word translated "affliction" here is *thlipsis*.

17. Cf. Rom 5:3–5.

18. Barnett, *2 Corinthians*, 73.

19. Much of popular Christian thinking has been affected by various forms of dualism. For example, many think in terms of physical and spiritual, between earthly and heavenly, and between the present time and eternity. In many instances, this line of thinking is very misguided and derives from a secular view of the world. Biblical

The Tribulation and the People of God

I think that many have misunderstood what the Bible says about the end times is that they have failed to properly comprehend what the NT teaches in regards to the kingdom of God, its presence here and now, and that, for those who are members of God's kingdom, it entails suffering.

One of the obstacles related to the kingdom of God and the kingdom of the world regards the timing of these kingdoms: that is, when do they exist or come into being? The difficulty in understanding the nature of these kingdoms derives from the titles/phrases used in Scripture to express these dueling kingdoms. That is, the terminology, which was quite appropriate for the time in which it was first used, has not been properly translated for our generation.

The NT teaches that there are two ages, or two kingdoms.[20] There is "the present age," which corresponds to the kingdom of this world.[21] And there is "the age to come," which corresponds to the kingdom of God.[22] In Mark 10:30 we see Jesus referencing both ages: "but that he will receive a hundred times as much now in the *present age*, houses and brothers and sisters and mothers and children and farms, along with persecutions; and in the *age to come*, eternal life."

Now it is only natural for us to see the phrase "the age to come" and to think of it as something in the future—it is after all "the age to come." But the question we must ask is whether or not it is still the age to come. That is, at the time Jesus uttered the words "the age to come," it was still in the future; hence the designation "the age to come." But, might it be possible that in the coming of Christ and his death and resurrection "the age to come" has arrived? Thus, "the age to come" previously referred to a future time, but now the same phrase represents the present. It is the failure to grasp this which, I suggest, is one of the main sources of confusion.

"The Age to Come" Has Arrived

The present reality of "the age to come"/kingdom of God is evident in several passages in the NT. For example, Paul notes that "they were written

---

dualism distinguishes between the sphere of "the present age" and "the age to come." As will be uncovered as we proceed, the latter is not relegated to the merely spiritual world, nor is the former merely physical. For an excellent discussion see Pearcey, *Total Truth*.

20 Note the Greek word for "age" (*aion*) is sometimes translated as "world."
21. Cf. Mark 10:30; Gal 1:4; Titus 2:12.
22. Cf. Matt 12:32; Mark 10:30; Luke 18:30; Eph 1:21; Heb 6:5.

for our instruction, upon whom the ends of the ages have come" (1 Cor 10:11). The author of Hebrews confirms that the last days have arrived in Jesus: "God, after He spoke long ago to the fathers in the prophets in many portions and in many ways, in these last days has spoken to us in His Son" (1:1–2). This may also be seen, for example, in Hebrews 6:4–5: "For in the case of those who have once been enlightened and have tasted of the heavenly gift and have been made partakers of the Holy Spirit, and have tasted the good word of God and the powers of the age to come."[23] Paul, likewise, affirms that Christ presently rules over every name—both in "the present age" and in "the age to come":

> These are in accordance with the working of the strength of His might which He brought about in Christ, when He raised Him from the dead and seated Him at His right hand in the heavenly places, far above all rule and authority and power and dominion, and every name that is named, not only in this age but also in the one to come. (Eph 1:19–21)

The difficulty, however, is that though "the age to come" is now present, the NT writers continue to call it "the age to come." Thus, some modern readers, not understanding that the NT writers are using the same language to describe a present reality, simply assume that "the age to come" still refers to the future. A careful reading of the NT confirms that the writers of the NT, though still retaining the designation "the age to come," clearly believe that it has arrived in the present through Jesus.

The Overlapping Presence of Both "the Age to Come" and "the Present Age"

Another difficulty arises with regard to the NT teaching on these two kingdoms. Namely, that the NT clearly affirms that though "the age to come"/kingdom of God has begun, so also "the present age"/kingdom of this world continues to exist. That is, despite the fact that "the present age" may represent a defeated kingdom, it still remains a present reality. Oscar Cullman describes us as living between D-Day and V-Day.[24] D-day has come and we are presently awaiting V-Day in that, though the decisive victory over Satan and the kingdom of this world has been won, we are still looking forward to

---

23. Despite the overall difficulty of this passage, for reasons beyond our objectives, the text clearly affirms that these people have already tasted the "powers of the age to come."

24. See Cullman, *Christ and Time*.

The Tribulation and the People of God

V-Day, in which there will be a "new heaven and a new earth," for "the first heaven and the first earth passed away" (Rev 21:1).

Now it must be understood that by affirming the present arrival of "the age to come" I do not intend to negate in any sense the future climactic coming of the kingdom of God. Certainly, I affirm that there will be a day when "the present age"/kingdom of this world will be abolished and "the age to come"/ kingdom of God will arrive in fullness. However, until then "the age to come," or the kingdom of God, exists conterminously alongside the "present (evil) age" (Gal 1:4).

The present existence of both kingdoms creates a tremendous tension for the members of the kingdom of God. For, as the children of God, we live in two kingdoms—sort of. We remain in the kingdom of the world—as aliens (1 Pet 2:11)—and experience pain, suffering, and death.[25] Yet, at the same time we are members of God's kingdom ("citizens of heaven" as Paul says in Phil 3:20). Herein lies the tension.

A Biblical Worldview of Two Kingdoms

This results in a dualistic look at the world. This too needs clarification. For, in the popular Christian world, which itself is heavily influenced by modernist and even postmodernist thinking, the distinction between the two ages/kingdoms is spatial or ethical. That is, the kingdom of God (heaven) is one kingdom, while the kingdom of this world (earth) is another. The result is that many conceive of the two kingdoms in terms of the "world" (i.e., physical), which is bad, and the "heavenly" (i.e., spiritual), which is good. This is neither a biblical view of reality nor a proper conception of the end times. For, God does not exist "up there" while we exist "down here."[26] God dwells everywhere, as Psalm 139:7–8 affirms.

---

25. Jesus affirms that while we live in the world we are not members of the world and its kingdom: "I have given them Thy word; and the world has hated them, because they are not of the world, even as I am not of the world. I do not ask Thee to take them out of the world, but to keep them from the evil *one*. They are not of the world, even as I am not of the world. Sanctify them in the truth; Thy word is truth. As Thou didst send Me into the world, I also have sent them into the world" (John 17:14–18).

26. This line of thinking is more in line with a secular ideology. Thus, many in the secular arena in the science-vs.-faith debates contend, along the lines of a dualistic worldview, that belief in God is "religious" and not pertinent to the realm of science. The supposition that the kingdom of God is spiritual and the kingdom of this world is physical is actually the result of Enlightenment thinking, which has numerous adverse effects. Among them is the notion that the world may be divided into upper and lower spheres: the lower sphere contains that which is knowable through science, while the

Understanding the New Testament and the End Times

The dualism presented in Scripture that distinguishes these two kingdoms is instead an eschatological one. That is, the two kingdoms are temporally (i.e., related to time) distinct in that the kingdom of God lasts forever, while the kingdom of this world will cease to exist someday. Thus, the radical distinction between the two kingdoms relates to the fact that the kingdom of this world is passing away, while the kingdom of God lasts forever.[27]

It is important at this point to further distinguish the characteristics of "the present age" and "the age to come." For by doing so, I believe that we will see that tribulation is indeed one of the primary characteristics of the kingdom of God. That is, it is through tribulation and suffering that the kingdom of God is victorious.

"The Present Age" and "the Age to Come"

In the NT, "the present age"/kingdom of this world is characterized as temporary and destined to perish. In his epistle, John notes, "the world is passing away" (1 John 2:17). And Paul affirms, "Yet we do speak wisdom among those who are mature; a wisdom, however, not of this age, nor of the rulers of this age, who are passing away" (1 Cor 2:6). Furthermore, Jesus says that the present age will end at the final judgment: "and the harvest is the end of the age" (Matt 13:39).

"The present age"/kingdom of this world is, furthermore, that which contains sin and sinful people and is ruled by Satan himself.[28] Ultimately, the 'present age'/kingdom of this world relates to the world as it presently is. In this vein Paul describes it as, "the present evil age" (Gal 1:4).[29] Not only is the present age evil, but Paul adds that it has Satan as its ruler: "in whose case the god of this world has blinded the minds of the unbelieving" (2 Cor 4:4).[30]

"The present age"/kingdom of this world is also one of apparent prosperity, peace, and safety. But indulging in such now leads to condemnation for eternity.[31] This is the thrust of Jesus' parable of the man who built

---

upper sphere consists of that which is the object of religious belief. See Pearcey, *Total Truth*. Unfortunately, this secular distinction has worked its way into the church.

27. Cf. 1 John 2:17.

28. Cf. John 12:31; 14:30; 16:11; 2 Cor 4:4.

29. Cf. Eph 2:2: "age of this world."

30. Note: Instead of "world," as the NAS has it, the NIV, NKJ, and NET all read "age" here. Again, the Greek is *aion*.

31. See Ps. 73, esp. 73:17.

The Tribulation and the People of God

barns to store all of his crops.[32] The parable closes with "But God said to him, 'You fool! This *very* night your soul is required of you; and *now* who will own what you have prepared?'" (Luke 12:20).

In contrast, "the age to come"/kingdom of God is that which the Lord is building. As noted previously, the kingdom of God has already come by means of Christ's death and resurrection, and the coming of the Spirit.[33] But, unlike "the present age"/kingdom of this world, "the age to come"/kingdom of God offers suffering, persecution, and tribulation.[34] Members of "the age to come"/kingdom of God are indeed kings and priests.[35] But, their manner of ruling is akin to Jesus. That is, they rule as lions by being lambs! This is clear in the exhortation of Revelation 3:21: "He who overcomes, I will grant to him to sit down with Me on My throne, as I also overcame and sat down with My Father on His throne." This passage explicitly compares the ruling of the people of God with the ruling of Christ. And the means by which each rule is by "overcoming." But, we know that Jesus overcame by being the lamb.[36]

It is to the contrast of these two kingdoms that Jesus was referring in Luke's version of the Sermon of the Mount:

> And turning His gaze on His disciples, He *began* to say, 'Blessed *are* you *who are* poor, for yours is the kingdom of God. Blessed *are* you who hunger now, for you shall be satisfied. Blessed *are* you who weep now, for you shall laugh. Blessed are you when men hate you, and ostracize you, and cast insults at you, and spurn your name as evil, for the sake of the Son of Man. Be glad in that day, and leap *for joy*, for behold, your reward is great in heaven; for in the same way their fathers used to treat the prophets. But woe to you who are rich, for you are receiving your comfort in full. Woe to you who are well-fed now, for you shall be hungry. Woe *to you* who laugh now, for you shall mourn and weep. Woe *to you* when all men speak well of you, for in the same way their fathers used to treat the false prophets. (6:20–26)

In this passage, we see that Jesus clearly has two groups of persons in mind. The first group is blessed, while the latter is warned of impending judgment. The former suffer and do not enjoy (so to speak) the comforts

---

32. See Luke 12:16–21.
33. Cf. 1 Cor 10:11.
34. Cf. Acts 14:22; Rev 1:9.
35. Cf. 1 Pet 2:9; Rev 1:6; 5:10.
36. Cf. Rev 5:5–6.

of life in the present kingdom (age); while the latter presently live high on the hog (if such an idiom were appropriate for that time). In the eschaton, however, the former will be rewarded, while the latter will suffer.[37]

Implications for the People of God

How does all of this affect our understanding of tribulation? Very simple: the present existence of both ages/kingdoms means that the people of God, who are members of "the age to come"/kingdom of God, will suffer in the present. Tribulation is indeed the lot of the Christian life.

In fact, it may be said that membership in the kingdom of God entails suffering, persecution, and tribulation. For this reason, John refers to himself as, "I, John, your brother and fellow partaker in the tribulation and kingdom and perseverance *which are* in Jesus, was on the island called Patmos, because of the word of God and the testimony of Jesus" (Rev 1:9). Thus, John, while affirming that we are partakers of the "kingdom," also notes that it is one of "tribulation and perseverance." This concurs with Jesus' warning to his disciples cited earlier: "in Me you may have peace. In the world you have tribulation, but take courage; I have overcome the world" (John 16:33).

What does this all have to do with the end times? Everything! For it is against the backdrop of these two competing eschatological kingdoms (the kingdom of God and the kingdom of this world) that we must read Jesus' great call to discipleship:

> If anyone wishes to come after Me, he must deny himself, and take up his cross and follow Me. For whoever wishes to save his life will lose it, but whoever loses his life for My sake and the gospel's will save it. For what does it profit a man to gain the whole world, and forfeit his soul? For what will a man give in exchange for his soul? For whoever is ashamed of Me and My words in this adulterous and sinful generation, the Son of Man will also be ashamed of him when He comes in the glory of His Father with the holy angels. (Mark 8:34–38)

Therefore, those who seek his kingdom must take up their crosses and follow him. Just as Jesus established his kingdom by the way of the

---

37. Note: The former group, those in the kingdom of God, are blessed to have already begun, to some extent, to receive their blessings. For, Jesus states that they are blessed (note the present tense) and that their reward is great in heaven (Luke 6:23). In fact, the kingdom of God is presently theirs (Luke 6:20).

cross, so too shall we. This is precisely what the Lord was conveying to Ananias regarding Paul: "Go, for he is a chosen instrument of Mine, to bear My name before the Gentiles and kings and the sons of Israel; for I will show him how much he must suffer for My name's sake" (Acts 9:15–16). Paul himself later affirms that we are children of God: "and if children, heirs also, heirs of God and fellow heirs with Christ, if indeed we suffer with *Him* in order that we may also be glorified with *Him*" (Rom 8:17). Thus, tribulation is the lot of the Christian life and in some way a necessary corollary to being a child of God. Thus, Paul writes to the Thessalonians, "so that no one would be disturbed by these afflictions; we have been destined for this" (1 Thess 3:3–4).

It is in this vein also that Jesus explains to his disciples that he is giving them authority to rule over the nations: "you may eat and drink at My table in My kingdom, and you will sit on thrones judging the twelve tribes of Israel" (Luke 22:30). Yet, despite the fact that they are kings, their kingdom is one in which they will suffer! The very next verse in Luke 22 in fact states, "Simon, Simon, behold, Satan has demanded *permission* to sift you like wheat." That is, though they will rule over the nations, they are not to do so prosperously, but will be in constant conflict with the devil. Their kingship, in fact, will stand in direct contrast with the kings of "the present age." A few verses earlier Jesus explains: "And He said to them, 'The kings of the Gentiles lord it over them; and those who have authority over them are called "Benefactors." But not so with you, but let him who is the greatest among you become as the youngest, and the leader as the servant'" (Luke 22:25–26).

At this juncture someone may suggest that the NT does not affirm that all of the people of God experience suffering for the kingdom, but only those who have "been destined for it" (1 Thess 3:3). Well, Peter seems to understand that those who experience suffering do not constitute the exception, but the rule: "But resist him, firm in *your* faith, knowing that the same experiences of suffering are being accomplished by your brethren who are in the world" (1 Pet 5:9). That such is the lot of the Christian life for all of the people of God leads Peter to likewise affirm,

> Beloved, do not be surprised at the fiery ordeal among you, which comes upon you for your testing, as though some strange thing were happening to you; but to the degree that you share the sufferings of Christ, keep on rejoicing, so that also at the

revelation of His glory you may rejoice with exultation (1 Pet 4:12–13).[38]

In fact, the best reading of 1 Thessalonians 3:3 is that Paul is including the church in Thessalonica with those who have been destined for suffering.[39]

What is most often present, then, in the popular world of eschatology, is the failure not only to properly distinguish between these two kingdoms, but also to understand that they both presently exist. The present time is one in which both "the present age"/kingdom of this world, which is evil and ruled by the devil, and "the age to come"/kingdom of God, in which the people of God rule through suffering, exist simultaneously!

This does not intend to deny that there is indeed much within the kingdom of God that is still in the future. For, we are awaiting the coming of the New Heavens and the New Earth.[40] We are longing for the resurrection of our bodies.[41] And we are longing for the day when the New Jerusalem descends and "there shall be no longer any death; there shall no longer be any mourning, or crying, or pain" (Rev 21:4). But these features of the kingdom of God, which are awaiting the consummation, have also begun to break into the present![42] Thus, the kingdom of God has come, and is here, and yet we are longing for its climax.

When Is the "Great Tribulation" for the Wicked?

But what about the "great tribulation"? Many have proposed that a "great tribulation" will occur in the future immediately prior to the second coming of Christ. Thus, when talk of "tribulation" surfaces it is this notion of a future worldwide tribulation for the wicked, from which the people of God have been raptured away, that is most often being considered. According

---

38. We can go much further into the NT's establishing of this point. For now, it must suffice to add one more verse to the mix: "In this you greatly rejoice, even though now for a little while, if necessary, you have been distressed by various trials, so that the proof of your faith, *being* more precious than gold which is perishable, even though tested by fire, may be found to result in praise and glory and honor at the revelation of Jesus Christ" (1 Pet 1:6–7).

39. See Green, *Letters to the Thessalonians*, 161–62.

40. Cf. Rev 21:1–2.

41. Cf. Rom 8:23; 1 Cor 15:20–28.

42. As I noted in the previous chapter, Paul cites Ezek 37:24–27 and applies it to the present, while Rev 21:3 cites the same passage and applies it to the consummation. This makes great sense if we acknowledge the continuity between the kingdom of God in the present and the kingdom of God in the consummation.

The Tribulation and the People of God

to proponents of this view, the narrative of Revelation refers to events that take place during a "great tribulation" of the final three and a half years of human history.[43] What then does the Scripture teach in regard to the "great tribulation"?

The NT clearly teaches that those who have afflicted the people of God will themselves be afflicted by God: "For after all it is *only* just for God to repay with affliction those who afflict you" (2 Thess 1:6). So yes, there is a tribulation in which the world is repaid for how they have treated the people of God. There are, however, a couple of qualifications that must be noted before we can proceed.

First, the NT says very little of a "great tribulation." In fact, one of the difficulties in deriving any significant teaching about an end times "great tribulation" arises from the fact that the term "great tribulation" (*thlipsis* with the adjective "great," *megale*) occurs only four times in the NT.[44] And, in fact, we can limit our discussion of a "great tribulation" in the NT to three verses, since Acts 7:11 references a "great affliction" that arose during the time of Joseph.

The most common reference that is proposed to support the notion of a final "great tribulation" is that of Matthew 24:21. The context of this verse, however, suggests that Jesus is depicting the suffering of the people of God. For Jesus says, "for then there will be a great tribulation, such as has not occurred since the beginning of the world until now, nor ever shall."[45] This "great tribulation," in accord with everything we have learned about "tribulation" in the NT, appears to include the suffering of the people of God. For, in the next verse Jesus states that those days will be shortened "for the sake of the elect" (Matt 24:22). Furthermore, the use of "great tribulation" in Matthew 24:21 appears to directly allude to Daniel 12:1.[46] Both passages, in fact, contain the identical phrase "tribulation,

---

43. Some will suggest that the tribulation is seven years long. The use of three and a half or seven among popular eschatological thinking derives from their understanding of the time frames given in Revelation and Daniel. Those who refer to three and a half years note that this is the time frame given in Revelation (11:2, 3; 12:6, 14; 13:5), though Revelation itself derives its time frame from Daniel (see Dan 7:25; 9:27; 12:7, 11, 12). Those who advocate for a seven-year tribulation period derive their time frame from a particular interpretation of Dan 9:24–27.

44. Cf. Matt 24:21; Acts 7:11; Rev 2:22; 7:14.

45. We will address Matt 24 and Mark 13 more deeply in ch. 10. For now, we will reflect only on the understanding of the "great tribulation" of Matt 24:21.

46. See Beale, *Revelation*, 433: "Dan. 12:1 is acknowledged as the likely origin for the idea of 'the great tribulation.'"

such has never happened since."[47] The significance of the allusion is that the immediate context of Daniel 11:28—12:3 describes the suffering of the people of God as a result of their faithfulness to God. That is, Daniel is not setting forth a tribulation against the wicked, but one that the wicked sponsor against the people of God. The "tribulation" in Daniel 12, then, is that which the people of God suffer for their loyalty to God.[48] Thus, we have strong indications that the "great tribulation" of Matthew 24 is not a future tribulation for the wicked, but describes the fate of the people of God.[49]

The final two occurrences of the "great tribulation" are found in the book of Revelation. Revelation 2:22 says, "Behold, I will cast her upon a bed *of sickness*, and those who commit adultery with her into great tribulation, unless they repent of her deeds." Though it may appear at first sight that this is a threat to unbelievers that could possibly correspond to some conceived future time of distress upon the wicked, a closer examination of the "great tribulation" of 2:22 is that it contains an imminent threat to the false teachers of Thyatira, and not a reference to a future worldwide tribulation against the wicked. That is, the threat is not to the wicked throughout the world, but to those who profess to be in the community of God's people.

The final occurrence of "great tribulation" in the NT appears in Revelation 7:14. In 7:9, John sees a "great multitude." He is then told, "These are the ones who come out of the great tribulation" (7:14). Here also the "great multitude" who endures the "great tribulation" represents the people of God! For, this is evident from the description of them:

> they are before the throne of God; and they serve Him day and night in His temple; and He who sits on the throne shall spread His tabernacle over them. They shall hunger no more, neither thirst anymore; neither shall the sun beat down on them, nor any heat; for the Lamb in the center of the throne shall be their shepherd, and shall guide them to springs of the water of life; and God shall wipe every tear from their eyes. (7:15–17)

---

47. My own translation. Note: Matt 24:21 is apparently alluding to Theodotian's Greek text of Daniel. The Greek of both passages reads: *thlipsis hoia gegonen aph*— with the only exception being that Matthew adds the adjective *megale* ("great").

48. See Beale, *Revelation*, 433; Smalley, *Revelation*, 196.

49. In ch. 10, I will address the fact that this sermon of Jesus has a present relevance, both for the disciples to whom Jesus spoke and for us as well.

Further supporting the consideration that the "great tribulation" of Revelation 7:14 affects the people of God is the significance of Daniel 12:1. This relationship is suggested first by the fact that both verses represents the people of God enduring a "great tribulation." Secondly, Revelation 7:14 and its larger context of the seven seals of 6:1—8:1 is contextually tied to Matthew 24:5-28. That is, the account of the "great multitude" in Revelation 7:9-17 is in the midst of the description of the seven seals.[50] The depiction of the seven seals, however, especially the first four, is deeply indebted to Matthew 24:5-14.[51] This is evident in that the first four seals of Revelation 6 correspond very well with the descriptions of the events depicted by Jesus in Matthew 24:5-14. Therefore, in light of the explicit statement that the "great multitude" who endure the "great tribulation" are the people of God, and the connection of the "great tribulation" of Revelation 7:14 with that of Daniel 12:1, I conclude that in this passage also *thlipsis* refers to the suffering of the people of God.

So, in all, the NT does not appear to describe in any instance a future "great tribulation" of the world from which the people of God are exempt. On the contrary, the use of "tribulation" and the "great tribulation" refers to the suffering of the people of God.

Present or Future Tribulation for the Wicked?

Finally, the NT does not provide any explicit indication that a tribulation against the wicked will immediately precede the second coming of Christ.[52] The reason for stating this is that the few references to a tribulation that confronts the wicked may well be understood as something imminent. Thus, those passages that indicate that there will be a tribulation do not necessitate that it is something wholly in the future. Indeed, Paul tells Timothy, "that in the last days difficult times will come" (2 Tim 3:1).[53] But, as I noted earlier in the discussion of "the age to come," "the

---

50. Cf. Rev 6:1—8:1. For a discussion of the relationship of the accounts of the 144,000 (Rev 7:1-8) and the great multitude (Rev 7:9-17) to the seven seals, see my *Revelation and the Two Witnesses*, ch. 6.

51. Cf. Mark 13:5-13 and Luke 21:8-19.

52. To thoroughly defend this position would require me to delve too deeply afield into the interpretation of Revelation and Daniel. Thus, for now I will have to move forward with only a few passing comments, knowing full well that there is much more to discuss.

53. That the "last days" of 2 Tim 3:1 were present at the time of Paul's writing to Timothy is evident in that Paul tells him to "avoid" such men (2 Tim 3:5). That

last days" have already begun. As Stephen Smalley states, "We conclude that the 'great ordeal' survived by the redeemed does not occur exclusively at the end of history. The time of judgment has already been set in motion in John's day, and may overtake believers as well as unbelievers (cf. [Rev] 2:22) at any time, until the end of time."[54]

What About the Rapture?

Finally, in light of the abundance of NT evidence that "tribulation" is something that the people of God endure, why do some suggest that Christians will be raptured from the earth so that they do not have to face the tribulation?[55]

One of the reasons for suggesting that Christians will not have to face the tribulation is that the conception of a tribulation is often misdefined as God's wrath upon the wicked. The problem is that this notion of tribulation finds no real place in Scripture. Instead, "tribulation," as I have argued, primarily refers to the fate of the people of God. Now, it is true that God's wrath is never poured out on the faithful people of God. In fact, by its very nature the wrath of God is poured out on the wicked for what they have done to the people of God. Consequently, if it were such that a future tribulation of God's wrath on the wicked for how they have treated the people of God was to occur, then it would naturally and necessarily follow that the people of God would be exempted from such a tribulation. For, it is indeed true that God's wrath is never poured out on the righteous.

But even this exemption from God's wrath does not have to entail the removing of the people of God from the earth. The exodus is a prime example. For, during the plagues on Egypt the Israelites were not removed but preserved. This corresponds to Jesus' prayer in Gethsemane in which he asks the Father, "I do not ask Thee to take them out of the world, but to keep them from the evil *one*" (John 17:15). There is, in fact, nothing in Scripture that indicates that the people of God will be removed from the scene while God pours out his wrath on the wicked.[56]

---

is, the people whom Timothy is to realize are characteristic of the "last days" are the very people that he is to "avoid." This confirms that such people were already present; therefore, so too are the last days.

54. Smalley, *Revelation*, 196.

55. Many of those who propose that there will be a future "great tribulation" on the earth aimed at the wicked do not believe that the people of God will be raptured. The notion of a rapture is advocated by only a small number.

56. Matt 24:40–41 does not refer to a rapture either. For, in this passage the

The Tribulation and the People of God

God's wrath on the wicked, in fact, seemingly necessitates the presence of the people of God. For, when we look at the example in Egypt, we see that when God poured out his wrath on the Egyptians, the Egyptians responded by increasing the suffering of the Israelites. Thus, as we read the Exodus account, we find that as Moses approached Pharaoh with God's ultimatum to repent and release the Israelites, Pharaoh not only failed to repent, but he decided to increase the burden on the Israelites.[57] Thus, if we were to propose that a future tribulation against the wicked were to occur, it would not mean glad tidings for the people of God.

Conclusion

Throughout the NT, the term *thlipsis* primarily indicates the suffering of the people of God. In most cases, this suffering is at the hands of the wicked on account of the faithfulness of the people of God in their prophetic witness. The NT teaching on "tribulation" leads to the conclusion that tribulation/affliction/persecution is part and parcel of what it means to be a member of the kingdom of God. Even the "great tribulation" is one that the people of God endure at the hands of the world.[58] As G. K. Beale notes, "Whatever its nature, tribulation always comes because of believers' faithful witness to Jesus."[59]

Therefore, those who wish to be his disciples are in fact commanded to take up their crosses and follow him. To enter the kingdom of God, in fact, one must suffer. This was true for Jesus. This was true for Paul. And this is true for the people of God today.

What does this all mean for us today? We must understand that suffering for the kingdom of God is not only a necessary part of being in his kingdom, but is also a source of blessing and a cause of joy. Jesus noted that we are not only blessed, but that we should "Be glad in that day, and leap *for joy*, for behold, your reward is great in heaven" (Luke 6:23). "For to you it has been granted for Christ's sake, not only to believe in Him, but

---

"taking" of one and the remaining of the other is compared to that of the time of Noah (Matt 24:37). But those taken at the time of Noah were the wicked. It was Noah who was "left behind." Thus, it stands to reason that those taken in Matt 24:40–41 are likewise the wicked, while the people of God are "left behind."

57. Cf. Exod 5:5–9.

58. This is a major theme of the book of Revelation. Namely, that the people of God will suffer at the hands of the world, as masterminded by the devil, but that they are the ones who are redeemed.

59. Beale, *Revelation*, 434.

also to suffer for His sake" (Phil 1:29). The source of this blessing derives from the fact that our tribulations/afflictions (*thlipsis*) are the means by which we triumph: "And not only this, but we also exult in our tribulations, knowing that tribulation brings about perseverance; and perseverance, proven character; and proven character, hope; and hope does not disappoint, because the love of God has been poured out within our hearts through the Holy Spirit who was given to us" (Rom 5:3–5). Paul adds to this, "For momentary, light affliction is producing for us an eternal weight of glory far beyond all comparison" (2 Cor 4:17). In chapter 12, I will address more deeply why this matters. For now, it should already begin to be apparent: if suffering is the lot of the Christian life, then we must "be on the alert" (Mark 13:34, 35, 37)!

9

Understanding the Second Coming of Christ

But of that day or hour no one knows, not even the angels in heaven, nor the Son, but the Father alone. (Mark 13:32)

Repent therefore and return, that your sins may be wiped away, in order that times of refreshing may come from the presence of the Lord; and that He may send Jesus, the Christ appointed for you, whom heaven must receive until the period of restoration of all things about which God spoke by the mouth of His holy prophets from ancient time. (Acts 3:19–21)

However, when the Son of Man comes, will He find faith on the earth? (Luke 18:8)

Introduction

THROUGHOUT THE HISTORY OF the church there has been no shortage of spurious groups who have been preoccupied with the alleged "signs" of the times and the return of Christ—often to the neglect of the true mission of the church. Now, don't get me wrong here. The NT does give indications (or "signs" if you wish) as to what must transpire before the return of Christ. These signs, however, as we will see, relate directly to the mission of God's people in building the kingdom of God.

When it comes to the issue of the second coming of Christ, the focus of the NT is not the timing of Jesus' return, nor even the signs that indicate that his return is near. Instead, the NT is far more concerned with: "However, when the Son of Man comes, will He find faith on the earth?" (Luke 18:8). That is, will we be ready? So, we must ask ourselves: are we being faithful? That is, if Christ were to return at this moment, would he find us doing the work of the kingdom for which we have been assigned?

Understanding the New Testament and the End Times

In the next two chapters I will look at what the NT says about the second coming of Jesus. Are there any signs that warn us that Jesus' return is imminent? What does the NT say must take place before his return? Does not the NT warn us that Jesus' return will be marked by an increase in wars, famines, and false Christs? Did Jesus inform us that there will be a final generation that will witness all these things—so that, even if we do not know the precise time of Jesus' return, we will still know the "season"?

In this chapter I will contend that the NT is far more concerned with the mission of God's people in building his kingdom. In fact, I would say the message of the NT is clear: the return of Jesus is awaiting the faithfulness of God's people in accomplishing his mission on the earth. Once we have completed such, by his grace, then Christ will return. That's it. No indication of an increase in earthquakes, famines, wars, and false prophets.

In chapter 10, I will look at the NT in response to the popular eschatology that suggests that various signs will alert us to the timing of Jesus' return. I will examine in particular the Olivet Discourse in Mark 13 and its parallels in Matthew 24–25 and Luke 17, 21.[1] I will note now that this sermon of Jesus is not concerned with giving details as to the time of Jesus' return. Instead, there is something far more profound, far more important, and of far greater concern that Jesus was trying to convey.

Before proceeding, allow me to throw out one thought. The devil is very smart. He is cunning. He is clever. He is insidious. He knows, perhaps better than we, that the will of God is to bring his kingdom to the earth. Since God's kingdom is built through God's people, then does it not make sense for the devil to do all that he can to thwart the efforts of the people of God, which are intended to build the kingdom? Would it not make sense for the devil to divert the focus of the people of God to sitting idly by and reading their newspapers in order to "discern the signs of the times," when all along the "signs of the times" are interwoven with the people of God doing the work of God?

Now, this is not to say that all those who are engaged in prophetic speculations are also sitting idly by. However, my experience is that many Christians who get entrenched into the apocalyptic fervor also tend to become numb when it comes to social justice and peacemaking on the earth—which are two attributes that are to be characteristic of the people

---

1. The Olivet Discourse is the name for the sermon of Jesus recorded in Mark 13, Matt 24–25 (though an argument may be made that the sermon in Matthew begins in 23:1), and Luke 17, 21. It is so called because in Matthew and Mark the setting is specifically said to be the Mount of Olives (Matt 24:3; Mark 13:3). This sermon is commonly thought to be Jesus' definitive words on the end times.

of God. I have heard too many Christians say something to the effect of: "Why worry about peace? Peace will not come to the earth until Jesus returns." This line of thinking is fundamentally counter to the gospel and the mission of God's people. Are we not the ones who are blessed by God so that we receive the kingdom of heaven (Matt 5:3)? And does that not include being peacemakers (Matt 5:9)?

What Must Happen before Jesus Returns?

Many of us have been told that we are to look for specific events that are to occur before the return of Jesus. These proposed signs include the increase of war, famine, earthquakes, and the rise of a one-world government. We are then told that these purported signs can then be examined in order to determine a supposed increase, not only in the frequency of their occurrences, but in their intensity. This is one of the more common arguments that supposedly indicates that the coming of Christ is near. Hal Lindsey wrote, "To the skeptic who says that Christ is not coming soon, I would ask him to put the book of Revelation in one hand, and the daily newspaper in the other, and then sincerely ask God to show him where we are on His prophetic time-clock."[2] But, what does the NT really say about all this?

Interestingly, the NT does affirm that certain things must occur prior to the return of Christ. It is my suggestion, however, that the NT gives us three reasons for the delay in Jesus' return. These three factors are not in and of themselves "signs," but merely indicators as to why Jesus has not returned. Instead of inspiring a negative outlook, the delay in Christ's return relates directly to the overall thesis of this book: namely, that a proper understanding of the end times promotes a healthy understanding of the mission of God's people.

The Conversion of the Nations

First, the delay in the return of Christ derives from the mercy of God, who is waiting for all humankind to be saved.[3] In 2 Peter, Peter provides an explanation as to the delay in Christ's return. Apparently, some skeptics were mocking the Christians because Christ had not returned. Peter

---

2. Lindsey, *There's a New World Coming*.
3. Perhaps I might clarify this by saying that God is waiting for all those who are going to be saved to be saved. I have no interest at this point to enter into theological debates as to who the "all men" are.

replies, "The Lord is not slow about His promise, as some count slowness, but is patient toward you, not wishing for any to perish but for all to come to repentance" (2 Pet 3:9). Thus, in his infinite mercy, God has determined that the climax of the kingdom of God will occur when the nations have been redeemed.[4]

Acts 3:19–21 relates the coming of Christ with God's mercy upon the nations and his desire that they should know him. In the opening of Acts 3, Peter heals a crippled man at the temple gate. Peter then explains to the crowd that had gathered that it was not himself who healed the man, but it was "the name of Jesus" (Acts 3:16) that healed him. Peter then exhorts the people:

> Repent therefore and return, so that your sins may be wiped away, in order that times of refreshing may come from the presence of the Lord; and that He may send Jesus, the Christ appointed for you, whom heaven must receive until the period of restoration of all things about which God spoke by the mouth of his holy prophets from ancient time. (3:19–21).

Thus, Peter affirms that the repentance of the people is intended to accomplish three things—all of which are introduced by a term or phrase indicating purpose.[5] These three are "*so that* your sins may be wiped away," "*in order that* the times of refreshing may come," and "*that* he may send Jesus." Note that each of these point to the coming, or climax, of the kingdom of God. Looking more carefully at each of these demonstrates that the return of Christ is tied to the repentance of the nations.

First, Peter notes that they must repent *in order that* "your sins may be wiped away" (Acts 3:16).[6] Now, it is important to clarify that having

---

4. This point is not to be mistaken for the notion that the gospel must be preached to all the nations (Matt 24:14: "And this gospel of the kingdom shall be preached in the whole world for a witness to all the nations"). For, as I will contend in ch. 10, the context of this verse (Matt 24:14) does not even have the second coming in view.

   Also, it is worth noting here that we must inquire as to whether or not those who advocate the proclamation of the gospel to the ends of the earth are more concerned with fulfilling the supposed prerequisites for the return of Jesus, or with the nations coming into the kingdom of God.

5. The Greek uses three different expressions here but each of them declares the purpose of that which follows. A purpose clause indicates that an act took place with the intended result being such. It does not mean that the actual result took place—which in this instance is obvious because in the third phrase the result is that he will send Jesus!

6. This is my translation. The Greek uses eis plus an infinitive, which expresses a purpose clause—a purpose clause indicates that the proposed act (in this case, the act

your "sins" wiped away would not have been understood by Peter's audience in the overly simplistic sense of assuring them of their individual future lives in heaven. For, in the Jewish world of the time, the notion of sins being forgiven was intimately bound up with the restoration of the nation from exile.[7] Since, as Deuteronomy and the latter prophets affirm, Israel was sent into exile for their sins,[8] it necessarily follows that the restoration of the nation would come only after the nation repents. Hence, the Gospels begin with John the Baptist announcing the return from exile: "Behold, I send My messenger before Your face, who will prepare Your way; The voice of one crying in the wilderness, 'Make ready the way of the Lord, make His paths straight'" (Mark 1:2–3; Matt 3:3; Luke 3:4–6; citing Isa 40:3).[9] Yet, in Mark's account the restoration of Israel demands repentance. Thus, he immediately notes that, "John the Baptist appeared in the wilderness preaching a baptism of repentance for the forgiveness of sins" (1:4).

Therefore, when Peter notes that by repenting your sins will be wiped away, he is affirming that the Isaianic promise of the restoration of God's people is at hand. To participate in this restoration, which the NT equates with the kingdom of God, one must simply repent. It is through repentance, then, that God would wipe away their sins, and in doing so they would become members of the kingdom of God!

The second purpose for the repentance of the people is "in order that times of refreshing may come from the presence of the Lord."[10] The "times

---

of repenting) is intended to bring about the following. Though the NAS translates the phrase as "so that" (note that many of the translations use "so that," though the ESV and NKJ employ a simple "that"), a slightly more emphatic translation that brings out the nature of this clause is "in order that." This first phrase then stresses that they should repent "in order that your sins may be wiped away."

7. The exile refers to the conquering of the northern tribe of Israel in the eighth century BC and the subsequent deportation of many of the leading families to remote parts of the Assyrian Empire, as well as the conquering of the southern tribe of Judah in the seventh to sixth century BC and the subsequent deportation of many of the leading families to remote parts of the Babylonian Empire.

8. Cf. Deut 28:15–68; esp. 15, 36–37, 49, 64–65; Jer 3:11–25; 29:10–14; Dan 9:3–19; Hos 5:15—6:2; 14:1–7.

9. Isa 40–66 places great stress on the fact that though the people of Israel have been sent into exile because of their sins, God will indeed bring them back (cf. Isa 40:1–3)!

10. The Greek in this clause employs *hopos*, meaning "in order that," which also indicates a purpose clause. The major English translations vary between the simple "that" (ESV, NIV), "so that" (NET, NKJ), or "in order that" (NAS). The relationship with the previous clause and its context suggests that a purpose clause is intended and

of refreshing" are themselves characteristic of the New Age.[11] Thus, again Peter is not merely offering them the opportunity to experience a personal salvation.[12] Instead, he is exhorting them to experience the restoration that characterizes the end of the ages!

Thirdly, Peter explicitly adds to his exhortation that they should repent "in order that" "he may send Jesus."[13] That is, Peter emphatically declares that the return of Christ is dependent upon the repentance of the people! That is, the reason or purpose for your repenting, says Peter, is *so that* "he may send Jesus."

Consequently, we see that one of the reasons for the delay in the return of Christ is that he is awaiting the repentance of the nations![14] When will Jesus return then? Jesus will return when the kingdom of God has encompassed the nations.

The Completion of the Suffering of God's People

A second reason found in the NT for the delay in the return of Christ is that God is awaiting the fullness of the suffering of the people of God. This may sound strange to many. Neither is this encouraging news! Nonetheless, the notion of the messianic woes and completion of the suffering of

---

thus hopos is best rendered "in order that."

11. Bruce, Book of Acts, 84.

12. This is not to deny that they indeed received a personal salvation. Of course, those who repented surely did.

13. This clause is connected with the hopos of the previous clause by the use of *kai* ("and"). Consequently, the NKJ, which translated the previous clause with "so that," translates this clause with "and that." Note that the NET Bible repeats "so that."

14. This delay in the return of Christ for the sake of the conversion of the nations is one for which I am eternally grateful. For, if God would have deemed it time in 1813, then neither myself nor any of you could have even had the opportunity to enjoy eternity in his presence. Now, of course, one could simply extend this reasoning ad infinitum and conclude that God in his mercy will never return. True indeed. But God in his wisdom has set forth an end. The Scriptures are clear: the end will come. Nonetheless, I and many of you are to rejoice that God has indeed delayed the time of his return.

As for those who ridicule this reasoning, God remains merciful in granting them time to repent. Just as they mocked Jesus on the cross, so too they mock the notion of Jesus' return. Yet, in both cases, what God has done for us he has done for them too. If Jesus would have come down from the cross as they suggested (Mark 15:30–32; Matt 27:40–42), it would only have meant their condemnation. His suffering meant that they too had the opportunity for repentance. So too, those who scoff today are granted one more day to repent as long as Christ tarries.

the righteous was present in the Jewish world of the first century, and it appears in the NT. The NT, in fact, affirms that once the suffering of God's people has reached its climax Christ will return.

We see this first in Revelation 6, where the souls of those who have been martyred for the kingdom are crying out to God, "How long, O Lord, holy and true, wilt Thou refrain from judging and avenging our blood on those who dwell on the earth?" (6:10). As we read Revelation, we realize that the avenging of the blood of the people of God occurs at the return of Christ. So, in effect, the question could be understood as, "When are you going to return and end all this?" The answer is somewhat shocking to the readers of Revelation. "And there was given to each of them a white robe; and they were told that they should rest for a little while longer, until *the number of their fellow servants and their brethren who were to be killed even as they had been, should be completed also*" (6:11). That is, Jesus will not return until all those who are to be killed for the gospel have been killed.

Secondly, as was noted in chapter 8, the NT strongly associates the suffering of the people of God with the coming of the kingdom of God. Paul, in fact, seems to be convinced that the people of God must in some sense fulfill the suffering of Christ. Thus, he notes, "Now I rejoice in my sufferings for your sake, and in my flesh I do my share on behalf of His body (which is the church) in filling up that which is lacking in Christ's afflictions" (Col 1:24). What does he mean by "filling up that which is lacking in Christ's afflictions"? Paul seems to be indicating that the messianic woes are to be endured by the people of God until they have accomplished the full measure of that suffering.[15] The implication is that when the suffering of God's people has been completed the kingdom is consummated. The notion of the messianic woes suggests that whenever God acts in association with the covenant, the people of God suffer the "birth pangs" of the coming age. This may be the allusion behind the account of Matthew 24, where the presence of birth pangs is immediately followed by the statement that "all these things are *merely* the beginning of birth pangs. Then they will deliver you to tribulation, and will kill you, and you will be hated by all nations on account of My name" (Matt 24:8–9). Thus the link between the messianic woes and the suffering of God's people.

In fact, throughout the Jewish literature of the Second Temple Era, there appears a common theme that the presence of "birth pangs"—i.e., the suffering of the people of God—will characterize the final period

---

15. For a detailed look at the notion of messianic woes and 1 Peter, see Dubis, *Messianic Woes in First Peter*.

of distress leading up to the end of the age. That the "birth pangs" of Matthew 24:8 are best associated with the inauguration of the kingdom will be defended in chapter 10 as we look at the Olivet Discourse more deeply. At this point it is worth reiterating that the NT consistently associates the suffering of the people of God with the consummation of the kingdom of God. Here we see that once the full measure of suffering has been accomplished Christ will return.

The Holiness of God's People

Finally, the return of Christ is awaiting the holiness of God's people. The people of God are explicitly told that as they achieve a level of holiness Christ will return. Peter notes:

> the day of the Lord will come like a thief, in which the heavens will pass away with a roar and the elements will be destroyed with intense heat, and the earth and its works will be burned up. Since all these things are to be destroyed in this way, what sort of people ought you to be in holy conduct and godliness, looking for and hastening the coming of the day of God, on account of which the heavens will be destroyed by burning, and the elements will melt with intense heat! (2 Pet 3:10–12).

This is of great importance. For, instead of focusing on the newspapers and the signs of times, the NT exhorts us to live godly lives! In fact, Peter asserts that the return of Christ is not only awaiting the holiness of his people, but that such holiness among the people of God may even "hasten" the day!

This creates havoc, however, for those who wish to predict the time of Christ's return. For, we cannot even attempt to measure the holiness of God's people; nor do we know how much holiness is required for Christ to return. In all honesty, Peter is somewhat vague on this point.[16] The point is that Peter exhorts the people of God to live godly lives, saying that the result will be the hastening of the coming of Christ.

Now, if the readiness of the people of God is understood as their doing the work of the kingdom of God, then it should not be surprising that the NT asserts that the return of Christ is awaiting the holiness of

---

16. This may be an example in which the writers of Scripture (Peter in this instance) were writing to a people who perhaps knew what they were referring. Thus, Peter may well have been referring to something with which his readers were already familiar.

the people of God, the conversion of the nations, and the full number of martyrs. That these three elements go hand in hand with the return of Christ is clear from the NT. Namely, that the holiness of the people of God, which cannot be divorced from the faithful proclamation of the kingdom of God, will result in the conversion of the nations. However, the faithful proclamation of the kingdom of God will also result in the full number of martyrs! Once all this has been completed, Christ will return!

Conclusion

The return of Jesus is an act of God's mercy. The focus on the NT teaching of Jesus' return is on the readiness of the people of God. But readiness in the NT is tied with doing the work of the kingdom and not merely knowing the alleged signs of the times. Thus, instead of reading the newspapers to determine if the signs of the times point to the imminent return of Christ, the NT focuses on whether or not we are indeed busy doing God's work in the world: bringing about justice, faithfully proclaiming the gospel, and caring for God's creation. That is, the NT affirms that once God has finished building his kingdom through the faithfulness of his people, Jesus will return. At that time, we will know that the people of God have achieved the holiness that will usher in the kingdom. This holiness, it must be noted, is instrumental in the conversion of the nations. But, such will not only result in the conversion of the nations; it will also lead to the suffering of God's people. From all of this we may derive several significant implications.

First, the return of Jesus will not happen while we the people of God sit idly by reading our newspapers to see if he is coming today. It will not happen as we callously watch wars and rumors of war destroy nations. It will not occur as we secretly rejoice in the alleged increase of famines and earthquakes. Instead, the return of Christ will occur once God's people have faithfully lived out, proclaimed, and suffered for the kingdom. This means that we must show Jesus to those who are ravaged by floods, pestilence, and war. We must seek justice, and help for the helpless. We must "walk in the same manner as He walked" (1 John 2:6).

Secondly, the when of Christ's return must be unknown. For, who can know when the complete number of martyrs has been reached? How might we know when the repentance of the nations has been fulfilled? Without such knowledge, one cannot know even the approximate time of Christ's return. Nor should we be concerned with the time of Christ's return. The NT is far more concerned with the readiness of the people of God at the time of Christ's return than with the time of Christ's return. Thus, we must ask not "When will Christ return?" but "Are we ready?"

So, if we want to speed Jesus' coming, we should be engage in discipleship and evangelism: we should be living holy lives, and we should be prepared to be martyred.

Excursus: Will Not Christians Know the Time?

Introduction

Though I will look more carefully at Jesus' words in Mark 13 in the next chapter, it seems pertinent here to address some common questions that may still be lingering in the back of many minds. For, we have been told by many a popular end-times teachers that the Bible provides us with definite signs that will indicate the time of Jesus' return. From this understanding, it is also concluded that, since we will be able to observe these signs, we Christians, though not knowing the precise time of Jesus' return, will not be surprised by the return of Christ.

Can We Know the Time of Jesus' Return?

Can we know the time of Jesus' return? In short, no. The message of the NT is emphatic: the time of Christ's return is unknown. No one will be able to discern the time—however loosely one wants to define "time"—of Jesus' return. How can we be certain of this? Easy: even Jesus did not know the time of his return. Jesus, in fact, said, "No one knows, not even the angels in heaven, nor the Son, but the Father *alone*" (Mark 13:32).

Nonetheless, many popular writers and teachers want us to believe that Jesus' sermon in Mark 13 and Matthew 24 provides a detailed list of events that will occur immediately prior to his return.[17] Without even looking at the details of this sermon I am already confident that Jesus could not have been giving his disciples specifics as to the events that would immediately precede his return, for he did not know when he would return![18]

---

17. See, for example, Walvoord, *Prophecy Knowledge Handbook*, 380–401.

18. I will address the Olivet Discourse in detail in ch.10. For those who are aware of such things, I am not advocating preterism or any such school of thought. For now, I will note that the details of events that Jesus was referring to in Mark 13 referred to the events related to the destruction of Jerusalem (which occurred in AD 70). That

Understanding the Second Coming of Christ

At this point some will suggest that we need to study the details that Jesus allegedly provides in order that we might discern the times. But, I might ask, for what purpose? Well, one might respond, in order that we might be prepared. But this is part of the problem. We are commanded to live every day prepared for Christ's return. Knowing or not knowing the time of Christ's return should not affect my Christian life. After all, the message of Jesus in the Gospels is: "when the Son of Man comes, will He find faith on the earth?" (Luke 18:8). We as Christians should not be living any differently today. We should be living everyday day as though it were our last. For it might well be! We are commanded to live each day faithfully proclaiming the kingdom of God, which will result in the salvation of the nations, and the suffering and martyrdom of the church. To propose that we might increase our faithfulness if we knew that Jesus were coming tomorrow suggests that we are not doing enough today.

We must also note that Jesus warned his disciples that false prophets will arise saying that Christ has come:

> "Then if anyone says to you, 'Behold, here is the Christ,' or 'There He is,' do not believe him. For false Christs and false prophets will arise and will show great signs and wonders, so as to mislead, if possible, even the elect. Behold, I have told you in advance. So if they say to you, 'Behold, He is in the wilderness,' do not go out, or, 'Behold, He is in the inner rooms,' do not believe them." (Matt 24:23–26)

Thus, there is an inherent danger in seeking to know the time. Namely, that we will be led astray. The history of the church is littered with many such false prophets and false Christs. The very thing we must do is to avoid such speculations.

The notion that knowing the time of Christ's return will enable us to be more prepared is foreign to the NT. In fact, from the perspective of the prophets, who were ultimately concerned with the behavior of the people, it would not be wise for the Scriptures to give any details as to the time of Jesus' return. Ironically, the NT exhorts the people of God to righteousness in light of the return of Jesus, not by giving signs that indicate when he will return, but by noting that his return is unknown! Hence, Jesus says, "For this reason you be ready too; for the Son of Man is coming at an hour

---

is, Jesus was telling them what would happen before Jerusalem was about to be destroyed—which is the very question they had asked (Mark 13:1–4; Matt 24:1–4; Luke 21:5–7). As for the events that are to precede his return, which I do believe he finally addresses, even Jesus did not know when that would be.

when you do not think *He will*" (Matt 24:44). This exhortation is very emphatic: be ready, because you do not know the time!

Some suggest that though we cannot know the day or hour, we are able to know the week, month, or year, etc.[19] A careful look, however, into Matthew 24:42–44 demonstrates that this conclusion finds no justification. For, Jesus used the terms "day," "hour," and "time" interchangeably. In 24:42 Jesus says, "Therefore be on the alert, for you do not know which *day* your Lord is coming." Then in the next verse he adds, "But be sure of this, that if the head of the house had known at what *time* of the night the thief was coming, he would have been on the alert and would not have allowed his house to be broken into." Then he adds, "For this reason you also must be ready; for the Son of Man is coming at an *hour* when you do not think *He will*" (Matt 24:43). The alteration of the terms "day," "hour," and "time" confirm that these terms are used interchangeably. Therefore, Jesus was not merely suggesting that the "day" and "hour" were not known, but that the "time" of his return was not known.

Furthermore, the immediate context in Matthew's account confirms that Jesus was declaring that the time of his return was unknown. Though I will look at this more deeply in chapter 10, it is worth noting at this juncture that Jesus was contrasting the time of the destruction of Jerusalem, which as we will see, was to happen in the disciples' lifetime,[20] with the time of his return, which even he did not know when it would occur.

Thirdly, Matthew records that Jesus also compared the time prior to his return with the time prior to the flood.[21] In doing so, Jesus affirmed that in the days prior to his return, which even he did not know when it was, life will continue on as usual for the world just as it was in "the days of Noah" (Matt 24:37). Jesus notes that they will continue "eating and drinking, marrying and giving in marriage" (24:38). This comparison with the days of Noah affirms that the time of his return is not marked by eschatological signs. For the point of comparison is that his return will come as a surprise, just as Noah's flood did.

Someone may well suggest that the reference to Noah applies only to unbelievers. That is, unbelievers will continue on with life as normal. But that Jesus is reiterating a general point that life will indeed proceed as normal until his return—a point that applies to the people of God as

---

19. For example, Franklin Minor states, "Jesus stated that we will not know the 'day or hour' of his coming; so, can the Holy Spirit reveal to us the year and the month of [sic] rapture? The answer is yes!" (*After Armageddon*, 73).

20. The destruction of Jerusalem occurred in AD 70.

21. Cf. Matt 24:37–41.

well—is indicated in that the next verse states, "Therefore be on the alert, for you do not know which day your Lord is coming" (24:42). As noted previously, Jesus continues in 24:44 with: "For this reason you be ready too; for the Son of Man is coming at an hour when you do not think *He will*." This exhortation is very emphatic. The people of God must also be ready, because even they do not know the time! Therefore, to say that we can know the week or the month, but not the day, is to completely miss the point.

Though many propose that the Olivet Discourse contains details as to the events that will precede the return of Christ, even specifying that his return will occur within a particular generation, I believe that a deeper look into these texts will reveal that Jesus is not giving any indication as to the time of his return. That is, Jesus is not concerned with whether or not his disciples, or us, know when he will return. Instead, he is concerned with what we are doing until he returns.

I Thought Christians Will Not Be Surprised at the Return of Jesus?

Many have concluded that the people of God will not be surprised at the return of Christ. This is indeed true. The question is: are we not surprised because we have carefully discerned the signs of the times and will have a good awareness as to the approximate time of the return of Christ, or will we not be surprised because we are ready? That is, we must ask: what does it mean to say "surprised"?

One could be surprised at the arrival of another from the fact that one did not know that this person was even coming. In such an instance, the person may be surprised in two senses. First, they are surprised to see the person in the general sense of not even knowing that the person was coming, let alone when. But they could also be surprised in the sense that they were unprepared for this person's arrival. Perhaps, the person is coming as a guest and expecting a room to stay in and a meal prepared. For the unbeliever the return of Christ will indeed be a surprise in both of these senses.

For the believer, however, who knows that Christ is coming—though not when—and is living expectantly for his coming, the return of Christ will not be a surprise in either sense. We may be surprised in the sense that we didn't know that he was coming today—the when—but since we know that he is coming and that he asked us to be prepared, we will indeed have a room and a meal prepared.[22]

This understanding of "surprised" is confirmed by a careful reading of the NT. For, both Jesus and Paul note that Jesus' return will be like a "thief in the night" (Matt 24:43–44; 1 Thess 5:2–6). But in each case the context is clear: the people of God are not to be surprised by the thief. Now, they will not know when he is coming, but they will also not be surprised. Jesus notes,

> But be sure of this, that if the head of the house had known at what time of the night the thief was coming, he would have been on the alert and would not have allowed his house to be broken into. For this reason you be ready too; for the Son of Man is coming at an hour when you do not think He will. (Matt 24:43–44)

We see here that "being alert" means that since we do not know when Christ is coming, we must be ready at all times—have a room and a meal prepared![23]

Paul affirms that the people of God must be ready at all times and, hence, not surprised in the latter sense.

> For you yourselves know full well that the day of the Lord will come just like a thief in the night. While they are saying, 'Peace and safety!' then destruction will come upon them suddenly like birth pangs upon a woman with child; and they shall not escape. But you, brethren, are not in darkness, that the day should overtake you like a thief; for you are all sons of light and sons of day. We are not of night nor of darkness; so then let us not sleep as others do, but let us be alert and sober. (1 Thess 5:2–6)[24]

---

22. Another analogy that fits appropriately pertains to children who are told to behave in a specified manner while mom and dad are away. When those children are behaving poorly and mom and dad finally arrive home, the children are indeed surprised by mom and dad's presence. But, if the children are doing precisely as instructed, they are not surprised by mom and dad's presence even though they were not sure when they were coming home. Fittingly, in this analogy, the ones who are behaving poorly are most concerned with the time of mom and dad's arrival. Those who are obeying are not in the least concerned with when mom and dad are due to arrive!

23. Hoekema confirms: "When Paul adds that his readers are not in darkness and that therefore the day of the Lord ought not to surprise them like a thief, he implies that if one is always spiritually ready for Christ's return, he will not be upset by that return even though it comes at an unexpected time" (Bible and the Future, 1979).

24. Note the ESV, NIV, and NLT use "surprise" instead of "overtake" in 5:4.

Understanding the Second Coming of Christ

The NT, then, is concerned with whether we are ready for the return of Christ and not with whether we are aware as to when it will take place. The use of the thief imagery confirms this. The point is that since one does not know when the thief is coming, the wise person will stay awake. Furthermore, thieves come at night, and since Paul says we are the children of the day, this should not be an issue for us! Now it is also worth observing one further dimension of the thief imagery. Namely, a thief comes to make one poorer. But, if one has been storing up treasures in heaven, then the return of Christ does not make one poorer but richer. For, only those who store up treasures in the kingdom of this world are robbed at the return of Christ.[25]

This does not mean that the people of God will know which night Jesus is coming back—or even the season of his return. The point is that the unbelievers will be getting drunk and acting immorally. And, by contrast, the people of God are to be sober and alert, so that when he comes, even though we do not know exactly when that will be, we will be ready!

Practical Reasons Why We Should Not Attempt to Determine the Time of Jesus' Return

Beyond the fact that the NT does not provide us any details as to the time of Jesus' return, the church would do well to forsake such predictions. For, nearly every generation since the time of Christ has witnessed some group attempting to predict the time of the second coming. And, to this day, they have all been wrong! Despite this lesson from history, the church has been riddled with attempts to predict the time of Christ's return.[26] The twentieth century, and now the twenty-first century, has been no different.

What is it that causes many to continue to make such predictions in the face of not only the history of such failures, but also in light of Jesus' seemingly clear declaration that "no one knows" (Mark 13:32; Matt 24:36)? For some, the predictions of the timing of Christ's return begins with a faulty hermeneutic. That is, many begin with the assumption that our generation is the last generation. That is, it is often assumed that everything that the prophets have written has as the primary meaning a focus on our generation.

---

25. Cf. Luke 12:16–21.

26. Ironically and tragically, I am writing the first draft of this chapter on May 23, 2011—just two days after a popular prediction for the end of the world.

I have already noted that this is not the proper way to read the Scriptures. The prophets were speaking first to the people of their day. They were not concerned with forecasting the future. When they did, we have seen that the prophecies point primarily to Christ.

The dangers of those who predict the date for Jesus' return only to see such not happen are abundant. For one, many make a mockery of the church. These wild speculations about the time of the Lord's return draw negative attention to the church. The media is quick to point out the falsity of the latest prophetic pundit who has allegedly deciphered the time of Christ's return. And with every false prediction in the name of Christianity, we have explaining to do. When a recent preacher forecasted May 2011, his organization spent millions on advertising. Such advertisements were especially abundant in the San Francisco Bay Area. Throughout the Bay Area billboards counted down the days till the final judgment. Many of the signs had an accompanying note: "The Bible guarantees it."

But we must realize that people are led away from the gospel when Christians falsely predict the return of Christ only to see nothing happen. I was in an interview about two weeks before the predicted judgment day, when I was asked what I thought May 21, 2011, would be like. I responded that it wasn't a matter of what we would do on May 21, but what we would do on May 22 when we had to begin cleaning up the mess. When it is suggested that "the Bible guarantees it," the result is that many conclude this is what most Christians must believe.[27]

My own journey as a young Christian in the 1970s and the early 1980s was one of eventual disillusionment. I had read anxiously during those years wanting to know the signs of the times. Jesus was coming back and we were all excited. We were the generation to which all these prophecies pointed. I searched the Scriptures so that I could discern how all that was happening in the world was fulfilling endless prophecies. I wrote letters to loved ones who did not know Christ telling them how everything would transpire in case I was raptured. Then the 1970s and early 1980s gave way to the mid and late 1980s. Things were not only not happening as all those whom I read and listened to had said they would, but they seemed farther from happening. The Russians were not about to invade Israel. They were now having trouble feeding their own people. When the Berlin wall fell, so also did my trust in these prophesy experts who predicted the end of

---

27. At the same time, I do acknowledge that the Lord works in the midst of such events. I know of instances where coworkers asked those whom they respected as Christians what they thought about the May 2011 date. This allowed them an opportunity to share the gospel with their coworkers!

the world. As I look back on this time, I thank God that he was merciful to me. For, instead of this wrecking my faith in Christ, it was only my faith in such teachings that was wrecked. But, for many their faith is wrecked.

Another problem that arises with the sensationalism often associated with end-times paranoia is that it has caused us to focus on the newspapers and not the Word and our readiness. Discipleship and fulfilling the mission of God should be our focus, not endless speculations regarding the future.

Such false predictions then are dangerous. They give unbelievers reasons for rejecting the church. And, they can cause serious harm to believers.

Conclusion

The second coming of Christ is indeed the "blessed hope" (Titus 2:13) of the New Testament. As Christians we should live in anticipation of Christ's return. We long for the time when all tribulation will cease, when death is done away with, and when our tears will be wiped away. We call out, "Amen. Come, Lord Jesus" (Rev 22:20), and we cry *maranatha* ('Come O' Lord"; 1 Cor 16:22).

Christ will return once the people of God have fulfilled the mission of God, are characterized by holiness and the bringing forth of the kingdom of God to the nations, for which they will suffer greatly. When these have been fulfilled, the kingdom of God will come and God will "send Jesus" (Acts 3:20).

It is not wrong for us to anticipate the return of Jesus. In fact, we are called to do so! For Paul, living with the hope of the second coming is a hallmark of the Christian life. "For the grace of God has appeared, bringing salvation to all men, instructing us to deny ungodliness and worldly desires and to live sensibly, righteously and godly in the present age, looking for the blessed hope and the appearing of the glory of our great God and Savior, Christ Jesus" (Titus 2:11–13). The question, however, is: are we busy living out the kingdom in anticipation of the return of Christ (which in itself will actually hasten his return), or are we simply sitting idly by and "watching the signs of the times" (which in itself will actually delay his return)?

10

Understanding the "Signs of the Times"[1]

The admonition "to watch" indicates that the purpose of the eschatological discourse in Mark 13 is not primarily to provide a timetable or blueprint for the future so much as to exhort readers to remain faithful in the present.[2]

Mark cautions his readers that the community is to find its authentic eschatological dimension not in apocalyptic fervor but in obedience to Jesus' call to cross-bearing and evangelism in the confidence that this is the will of God which must be fulfilled before the parousia.... Vigilance rather than calculation is required of the disciples.[3]

Introduction

IN THIS CHAPTER, WE will venture into an examination of the Olivet Discourse. The Olivet Discourse is Jesus' speech presented in Mark 13, Matthew 24–25, and Luke 17, 21. It is sometimes suggested in popular Christian thought that this speech presents Jesus' words detailing the events that will precede his return. As we will see, Jesus does not give any indication as to when he would return or what signs might indicate that his return is near. After all, he affirms that "of that day or hour no one

---

1. This chapter is an excursus of sorts. I have included it because I realize that many readers have a number of lingering questions. In particular, I have suggested that the NT does not give any detailed "signs," at least in the popular sense, that will precede Jesus' return. Many will immediately object and cite the Olivet Discourse as evidence that Jesus gave us at least some basic signs that will provide us with some indication as to when he might return. Thus, it is important to include in our study of the second coming a look at Mark 13.

2. Edwards, *Gospel According to Mark*, 384.

3. Lane, *Gospel of Mark*, 447–48.

Understanding the "Signs of the Times"

knows, not even the angels in heaven, nor the Son, but the Father *alone*" (Mark 13:32).

Throughout this sermon, then, Jesus was primarily informing his disciples of the events that would lead to the destruction of the temple—an event that took place in AD 70—and how difficult life would be for them in the interim. As for his return, Jesus explains that he does not even know when it will occur, only that when it does it will be unmistakable. As was set forth in the previous chapter, the message of Jesus to the people of God today is that since we do not know when he will return, we must "be ready" (Matt 24:44)!

Herein lies the significance of the Olivet Discourse for the people of God today: we too must "be ready." For, the Olivet Discourse, instead of providing us with details as to what will transpire in the "last days" leading up to the return of Christ, it informs us that since we do not know the time of Christ's return, we must "Therefore, be on the alert—for you do not know when the master of the house is coming, whether in the evening, at midnight, at cockcrowing, or in the morning—lest he come suddenly and find you asleep. And what I say to you I say to all, 'Be on the alert!'" (Mark 13:35–37).

Understanding the Olivet Discourse

As we look into the Olivet Discourse, I will primarily examine the account in Mark 13—with references to Matthew 24 and Luke 21 as appropriate. I will not endeavor, however, to provide a thorough analysis of these chapters. Instead, the goal is to ascertain three factors: First, what was Jesus trying to convey his disciples? Second, did Jesus intend to provide his disciples with any indications as to when he will return? Finally, how does all of this translate to us today?

In looking at the Olivet Discourse in Mark 13, as with any biblical text, our first concern must be to discern what the biblical writers were trying to convey to their readers. That is, what did the text mean both to Mark and to his original audience?[4] This understanding must precede any attempt to bring the text into the contemporary world. In the case of the Olivet Discourse, however, we have an added component. Namely, we

---

4. Though postmodernism challenges the ideas that the main point is to discern what the author meant, it will take us too far afield to attempt to address the nature of biblical interpretation in the twenty-first century. For a discussion of postmodern hermeneutics, see McCartney and Clayton, *Let the Reader Understand*; Vanhoozer, *Is There Meaning in This Text?*; and Kaiser and Silva, *Introduction to Biblical Hermeneutics*.

have both the meaning of the Gospel writers and their audiences, and we have the words of Jesus to his disciples. That is, we must examine both: what was the message of Christ to his disciples in AD 30,[5] and what were the Gospel writers trying to communicate to their readers in AD 65–85?[6]

Context for Olivet Discourse in Mark 13: Judgment on the Temple for the Lack of Fruit

The narrative of Mark 13 opens with Jesus declaring that the temple in Jerusalem will be destroyed.[7] Mark states, "And as He was going out of the temple, one of His disciples said to Him, 'Teacher, behold what wonderful stones and what wonderful buildings!' And Jesus said to him, 'Do you see these great buildings? Not one stone shall be left upon another which will not be torn down'" (Mark 13:1-2). This pronouncement surely puzzled the disciples, who then inquired, "Tell us, when will these things be, and what *will be* the sign when all these things are going to be fulfilled?" (Mark 13:4).[8] Jesus' speech that follows is in response to these questions.[9] That is, the disciples wanted to know both when this might happen and what the signs might be that it was about to happen.

---

5. We, of course, are not certain as to when Jesus preached this message to his disciples. Since AD 30 or 33 are the likely dates for the death and resurrection of Jesus, we know that this message was not spoken later than that. It is my conviction that AD 30 is the latest date for Jesus' sermon, but it is well beyond the scope of this writing to contend for one date over the other.

6. The dates for the writing of the Gospels of Mark, Matthew, and Luke are also quite secondary to the present book. Suffice it to say that most scholars place the writing of the Synoptic Gospels (Matthew, Mark, and Luke) between AD 65–85.

7. It is essential for Christians to understand that the destruction of the temple and Jerusalem was a judgment of God upon the people of that day for their rejection of the covenant. Such an act of God in no way provides a basis for any of the acts of anti-Semitism that have too often characterized church history. The Jews as a race were not morally responsible for the crucifixion of Jesus. Jesus' death was the result of all of our sins. It was only the covenantal relationship between God and the house of Israel, and the fulfillment of the covenant in Jesus, that led God to declare that the temple was incurring judgment and that those who adhered to it instead of Jesus would be expelled. This, however, provides no justification for any continued condemnation for the Jewish people any more than anyone of Roman descent remains guilty for the injustices of Pilate and the Romans.

8. Cf. Matt 24:3; Luke 21:7.

9. Though it appears that the disciples' are asking two separate questions, in one sense the questions themselves both relate to the one event—the destruction of the temple. See below.

It is important to note that the disciples' questions could not have been asking for an indication as to when Jesus might return. After all, they had no conception of a dying Messiah.[10] Since they could not fathom the idea that Christ was going anywhere, they could not have been inquiring as to when he was to return.[11] And since neither Jesus' statement nor his reply offers any details pertaining to his leaving, it does not appear that he was concerned with answering the question of when he was going to return. This leaves us, then, with the understanding that both the disciples' question and Jesus' reply were concentrated on Jesus' declaration that the temple was going to be destroyed.[12]

That the focus of the Olivet Discourse in Mark pertains to the destruction of the temple is also clear from the larger context of Mark 11–13. The speech of Jesus in 13:5–37 closes a larger section, which began in 11:11, and centers on the temple. This is supported by several factors. First, 11:11 notes that Jesus "entered Jerusalem and came into the temple; and after looking around, He departed." This somewhat strange editorial note leaves the reader with more questions than answers. Why did he enter only to leave? What did he see when he looked around? And why does Mark even bother to mention this? After all, nothing seems to have happened!

10. This is especially clear in Mark's Gospel. For, when Jesus announces his impending death and resurrection (9:9), Mark notes: "And they seized upon that statement, discussing with one another what rising from the dead might mean" (9:10). Then in 9:31-32 Mark states, "For He was teaching His disciples and telling them, 'The Son of Man is to be delivered into the hands of men, and they will kill Him; and when He has been killed, He will rise three days later.' But they did not understand *this* statement, and they were afraid to ask Him." The continuous failure to grasp the impending death and resurrection of Jesus is a theme in the Gospel of Mark. At Jesus' first announcement of his death in Mark's Gospel, it states, "And He began to teach them that the Son of Man must suffer many things and be rejected by the elders and the chief priests and the scribes, and be killed, and after three days rise again. And He was stating the matter plainly. And Peter took Him aside and began to rebuke Him. But turning around and seeing His disciples, He rebuked Peter, and said, 'Get behind Me, Satan; for you are not setting your mind on God's interests, but man's'" (8:31-33).

11. Now it is true that Jesus might well have responded by explaining to them that he was indeed going to die and leave and that such and such would be the signs of his return—all the while knowing that they would not have understood them until after the resurrection. The point here, however, is that the question, as posed by the disciples, could not have been asking for Jesus to give them a description of the events that would lead up to his return, since they had no concept of his leaving, let alone his returning.

12. It is true that the disciples likely did not understand fully that Jesus was predicting the destruction of the temple. Nonetheless, they did perceive that this is what Jesus was declaring, as they inquired both as to when this might be and what are the signs that it is imminent.

Upon closer examination, however, we find that Mark's reference to Jesus entering the temple and looking around in 11:11 serves to set the stage for the larger narrative that continues through Mark 13. The speech in Mark 13, which closes this larger section, begins with reference to Jesus' "going out of the temple" (13:1). Therefore, the seemingly obscure reference that Jesus "came into the temple; and after looking around, He departed" (11:11) serves alongside the statement of Jesus' "going out of the temple" (13:1) to bracket the entire unit of Mark 11–13 within the context of the temple.

That Mark 11–13 is a larger narrative section concentrated on the temple and the temple establishment is also evident from Mark's account of Jesus cursing the fig tree and "cleansing" the temple.[13] Mark, in his typical style, narrates Jesus' cursing of the fig tree for its failure to bear fruit in two segments (11:12–14; 11:20–21). In between these two segments Mark interjects (or sandwiches) the episode of the cleansing of the temple (11:15–19). Mark's use of this sandwiching, in which he narrates a separate event in the middle of another event, is well known by commentators.[14] Mark employs this technique in order to allow the readers to see these two episodes in light of one another. In this instance, Mark wants the reader to understand that the failure of the fig tree to bear fruit corresponds to the failure of the temple establishment to produce fruit. Jesus' "looking around" then signifies his effort to find fruit. The cursing of the fig tree, then, serves to highlight Jesus' activities in the temple.[15]

The connection between the speech of Jesus in Mark 13 and the events in the temple in Mark 11 is further supported by reference to Peter's exclamation to "behold" the fig tree (11:21), which is paralleled by the exhortation of an unnamed disciple who encourages Jesus to "behold" the beautiful temple (13:1). Other details that confirm that Mark 11–13 provides an extended look at the temple and the lack of fruit include the reference to the fig tree in the close of Jesus' speech in the Olivet Discourse (13:28). This too is a common literary technique whereby an account is

---

13. I use "cleansing" to refer to Jesus' activity in the temple simply because that has been the common designation for this event. The act itself, however, was that of a prophetic sign-act—which refers to the actions of a prophet performed in order to symbolize what will transpire. Thus, Jesus' overturning the tables and causing mild havoc in the temple signifies the time when Rome would come and do the same, on a much larger scale, to the temple. This "cleansing" of the temple, then, is best viewed as a pronouncement of judgment on the temple.

14. Edwards, *Mark*, 11–12.

15. The sandwiching of the cursing of the fig tree around the account of the "cleansing" of the temple, then, suggests that Jesus was pronouncing judgment/cursing on the temple just as he cursed the fig tree.

Understanding the "Signs of the Times"

framed by reiterating an earlier term or phrase. For Mark, it serves to link the speech of Mark 13 to the larger unit—corresponding in particular to the cursing of the fig tree in Mark 11.

Furthermore, that the main focus of the narratives of Mark 11–13 centers around the temple is evident from the fact that the temple is the theme, explicitly or implicitly, throughout these narratives. For instance, in 11:15 Jesus "entered the temple." In 11:23, Jesus' allusion to "this mountain" likely refers to the temple. In 11:27, Jesus was "walking in the temple." The parable of the vineyard in 12:1–12 has many temple allusions and must be understood against the backdrop of Jesus' condemnation of the temple for its failure to produce fruit.[16] The reference to the "stone" (Mark 12:10; citing Ps 118:22) corresponds to the stone of Daniel 2 and is filled with allusions to the temple.[17] Also, in Mark 12:35 we see that Jesus was teaching in the temple. Then, in 12:41 Jesus sits opposite the treasury, which was in the temple. Finally, we see that the entire speech of Mark 13 begins with explicit references to the temple in each of the opening three verses.[18]

The only possible exception to the consistent theme of the temple in these chapters relates to the accounts of the Pharisees, Sadducees, and scribes questioning Jesus (12:13–34). But these accounts, themselves presented in the midst of the consistent references to the temple and Jesus' acts therein, likely serve to provide evidence that the religious establishment has failed in their mission of making the temple "a house of prayer for all the nations" (11:17).

Thus, Mark 11–13 is a larger narrative unit focused on Jesus' condemnation of the temple for its failure to produce fruit. Jesus' speech in Mark 13 provides a fitting conclusion to this larger section. For, Jesus has entered the temple and found no fruit. Thus, he pronounces judgment upon the temple. The disciples then inquire, "when will these things be, and what *will be* the sign when all these things are going to be fulfilled?" (13:4).

---

16. Note that this parable comes in the midst of the accounts of Jesus in the temple and the cursing of the fig tree in Mark 11. Jesus' prophetic pronouncement of the impending destruction of Jerusalem in Mark 13 also confirms that this parable should be read in light of the theme of the temple.

17. For the connection between the "stone" of Dan 2 and the temple see the discussion in ch. 6.

18. Mark 13:1 opens with "And as He was going out of the temple"; 13:2 notes, "Do you see these great buildings"; and 13:3 says, "And as He was sitting on the Mount of Olives opposite the temple."

Understanding the New Testament and the End Times

Discerning Both Jesus and the Gospel Writers' Intent Regarding His Coming

One of the difficulties in understanding the Olivet Discourse and its interpretation for the contemporary reader is the fact that we must discern both what it was that Jesus was exhorting his disciples when he spoke this message, and what the later Gospel writers wanted their readers to understand from this message. This is significant because a careful reading confirms that they are not identical. Jesus' response, in fact, is subject to great misunderstanding among contemporary interpreters when this contextual background is overlooked.

As we read the Olivet Discourse we discern that Jesus' message to his disciples was pertinent to their immediate concerns. Jesus' message stressed the fact that Jerusalem and the temple were about to be destroyed.[19] His intent includes a warning to them of the magnitude of the coming events and the distress it will bring upon them, their need to flee Jerusalem once these events reached a certain severity, and their need to be discerning so that they are not deceived.

Jesus does, however, address the time of his "coming."[20] His words, contrary to many of the popular writers, were not intended to instruct his disciples, or any future readers, as to the time of his return. Instead, his primary intent was to disassociate the time of his "coming" with the destruction of the temple. Thus, Jesus informs them that the events surrounding the destruction of the temple do not mark the time of his "coming." He notes, in fact, "And then if anyone says to you, 'Behold, here is the Christ'; or, 'Behold, *He is* there'; do not believe *him*" (Mark 13:21). Matthew's account adds the caveat, "For just as the lightning comes from the east, and flashes even to the west, so shall the coming of the Son of Man be" (Matt 24:24). That is, Jesus explains that the destruction of the temple will not mark the time of his "coming"; instead, his "coming," when it does occur, will be unmistakable. Consequently, the disciples and the readers of the Gospels are not to be deceived by anyone who claims that the Christ has come.

Why was it important for Jesus to clarify that the destruction of the temple was not an indication as to the time of Christ's "coming"? Most likely the answer is to be found in the fact that the temple was considered

---

19. Mark 13:2.

20. The use of quotes for "coming" here is important because, as noted above, the disciples would not have understood Jesus initially in terms of a future "coming" because they did not understand that he was going anywhere.

Understanding the "Signs of the Times"

to be inviolable/indestructible. Thus, the exhortation to flee Jerusalem was likely very important for the disciples. For without the instruction from Jesus to flee Jerusalem—because these events were not a sign that he was about to "come"—they may well have attempted to stay and defend the city. That is, if Jesus had not instructed them that the fall of the temple was a result of his judgment on the city for its failure to bear fruit, they may well have stayed.

This is the thrust of Jesus' words to his disciples. Jesus informs his disciples that the judgment of the temple was the result of the lack of fruit among the leaders of Israel—in particular, their failure to make the temple a house of prayer for the nations.[21] The disciples, once they see these things being fulfilled, must flee! Now, again it is essential to understand that the disciples would have perceived any references to Jesus' "coming" not in terms of a return, but in relation to the time of Jesus' enthronement as king. They were most certainly convinced that Jesus was heading to Jerusalem to become king.[22] They, of course, did not understand that this meant that he had to die. When Jesus explained that the temple must be destroyed, the disciples would likely have considered this as a sign that Jesus was about to become king. Instead, Jesus explained, these events are not an indication that he is "coming," but that they are to take flight.

The Gospel writers, then, writing years later, and perceiving the distinction made by Jesus pertaining to the destruction of Jerusalem and the time of his "coming," drew out the significance of these events for their readers.[23] The readers must first understand the implications of Jesus as the temple of God and the consequences of this for the physical temple and those who have failed to produce fruit. But, the Gospel writers affirm, they must also understand that Jesus warned that the destruction of the temple would also be a grave ordeal both for the disciples and, by extension, the Christian community.[24] Later readers of the Gospels have the benefit of

---

21. Mark 11:17.

22. This is evident in the brothers James and John's request to sit on his right and on his left when they arrived in Jerusalem (Mark 10:37).

23. The Gospels writers have two advantages that enabled them to discern the distinction between the destruction of the temple and the "coming" of Christ. First, they have the benefit of history. Jesus has been crucified and risen. Something that was unfathomable to the disciples before the cross has happened. Secondly, since Pentecost (Acts 2), they have the indwelling of the Spirit, whom Jesus promised "will teach you all things, and bring to your remembrance all that I said to you" (John 14:26).

24. It is not essential that we determine the time of the writing of the Gospels. If the Gospels were written before or after AD 70, then their message relayed that Jesus warned them of the severity that the people of God would encounter or did encounter.

hindsight in order to understand that the cross was necessary—which the disciples at the time of Jesus' speech did not understand—and that any reference to the "coming" of Christ was to his return.

Now in looking at the words of Christ more carefully, we first observe that the disciples' questions were about when "these things" will happen and what will be the sign when "these things" are to be fulfilled (Mark 13:4).[25] The "these things" in the disciples' question refers back to Jesus' affirmation that "these great buildings" (13:2) will be destroyed.[26] Thus, in Mark, the disciples' question is simply to be understood as asking when the temple will be destroyed and what will be the signs of its impending destruction.[27] It is important to note that in Mark's account there is nothing in the disciples' question regarding the "coming" of Jesus.

Now Matthew's Gospel, which most scholars have concluded was written after Mark, includes an additional question. In Matthew's account the disciples ask, "Tell us, when will these things be, and what *will be* the sign of Your coming, and of the end of the age?" (24:3).[28] As we can see, the disciples' questions here include a reference to the sign of Jesus' "coming."

Now, what is essential to reiterate at this point is that at this time the understanding of the disciples was such that the destruction of the temple and the "coming" of Christ were likely the same. The disciples, at the time of their questioning, had no concept of Jesus' leaving—let alone of him returning, i.e., a second coming. They, in fact, were still expecting that Jesus was going to be some sort of a political-messianic ruler. Though they likely did not fully comprehend Jesus' reference to the destruction of the temple either, their questions serve to associate the destruction of the temple with the time of Jesus' "coming." Thus, the "coming" of the disciples' question

---

25. The demonstrative pronoun *tauta* (these things; Mark 13:4, 8, 29; Matt 24:3) or *tauta panta* (all these things; Mark 13:4, 29, 30; Matt 24:2, 8, 33, 34) is vital to understanding this discourse.

26. In each of the Synoptic accounts, Jesus utters the demonstrative pronoun *tautas* ("these"; cf. Mark 13:2; Matt 24:2; Luke 21:6). The reference to "buildings" likely includes both the temple building itself and the other structures of the temple mount, including the royal stoa.

27. The question as posed by Luke is virtually identical to Mark's.

28. Though the English translation appears to have three questions (when will these things be?; what is the sign of your coming?; and [what is the sign] of the end of the age?), the Greek suggests that the last "and" is separating the second question into two parts. Thus, the disciples were asking, when will these things be, and what is the sign of your coming/end of the age (which suggests that the coming of Jesus *is* the end of the age)?

must have at the time referred to Jesus' inheriting the throne of David. That is, what they appear to have understood regarding Jesus' pronouncement of the impending destruction of the temple was that it was directly linked with the time of his rise to the throne. So, they were in effect asking, "When will this happen?" (the destruction of Jerusalem and the coming of Christ; i.e., inheriting the throne of David), which they likely expected to be soon, and "What will be the signs?"

The readers of the Gospels are aware that Jesus' answer to the question pertaining to his "coming" refers to his return. But, they have the advantage of history and an awareness that Christ indeed died and will come again, and, consequently, they have come to understand that Jesus was going to return in the future. That is, the disciples at the time in which they asked the question would have conceived of the time of Jesus' "coming" as the time of his enthronement. The readers of the Gospels, however, which were written years later, could understand that Jesus' answer regarding the time of his "coming" refers to the time of his return. Hence, Matthew makes this explicit for the sake of his readers.

Overview of the Olivet Discourse in Mark 13

Mark's version of the Olivet Discourse, then, contains two distinct emphases. First, there is the exhortation of Jesus to his disciples about the events leading up to and beyond the destruction of the temple. This is the thrust of 13:5–23, which addresses the events that will transpire during the lifetime of the disciples and climax with the destruction of the temple.[29] Secondly, there are Jesus' words about his "coming." This is the thrust of 13:24–27, which specifies that the "coming" of Jesus will occur in the days "after that tribulation" (13:24). As we will see, these two events are distinct. Throughout 13:5–24, however, Jesus does not answer the second question of *when*. The reference to the when, of both the time of the destruction of the temple and the time of his "coming," occurs in 13:28–32. The sermon then closes in 13:33–37 with a final exhortation.

Mark 13:5–23: Jesus' Words to His Disciples

In examining Jesus' message in the Olivet Discourse, one is first struck by the repeated concern of Jesus for the well-being of his disciples. His

---

29. The temple was destroyed by the Romans in AD 70.

concern for them was because he foresaw a time of great distress that was about to come upon them.³⁰ That Jesus was addressing the plight that would confront the disciples themselves is evident from the numerous commands throughout this speech. The disciples are told: "be on their guard" (13:5, 9, 23),³¹ "do not be frightened" (13:7), "do not be anxious beforehand" (13:11), "pray" (13:18), and "do not believe" (13:21).³²

In regard to the significance of these commands, we must first note that the imperative to "watch out" (13:5, 23) brackets this section. Mark begins and ends this section with the same command. This repetition serves to accent and stress this particular command. Thus, Jesus was quite concerned that his disciples were to be on their guard.

Throughout this speech the use of second-person commands also affirms that it is the disciples themselves who are going to face difficult times during which they must "watch out." It is they who, in the face of these trials and difficulties, must stand firm. Hence, Jesus exhorts them, "do not be anxious beforehand" (13:11), but instead "pray" (13:18). As Lane observes, Jesus is preparing "his disciples for a period which entails both persecution and mission."³³

The main thrust of 13:5–23 relates to the events surrounding the destruction of Jerusalem. That these events relate to the lifetime of the disciples and the destruction of the temple (which occurred in AD 70), and not a future "coming" of Jesus, is further justified in light of several additional factors.

First, in Mark's Gospel the disciples question Jesus only about the temple and its destruction. Jesus' response serves to prepare them for what they were to do and how they were to conduct themselves until this event transpired. This event would not happen immediately, hence the need for Jesus to prepare them for what they were to do in the interim (of course, Jesus knows that he will not remain present with them for much longer, hence the need for him to prepare them now).

Secondly, that 13:5–23 relates to the disciples themselves is clear from the use of language and historical references that find their primary relevance within a first-century context. For example, they are told, "let

---

30. Cf. Mark 13:13; Matt 24:9; Luke 21:16–18;

31. Though translated differently in the NAS, all three of these verses use the same Greek word *blepete*.

32. These commands take the form of the imperative in Greek—in particular they are second-person plural imperatives. A second-person plural imperative is one in which more than one person is directly commanded regarding something.

33. Lane, Mark, 447.

those in Judea flee" (13:14), "do not let the one who is on the housetop go down" (13:15), and "do not let the one who is in the field turn back to get his cloak" (13:16). All of these commands relate to the geographical, historical, and cultural context of first-century Palestine. Thus, Jesus was warning his disciples of things that would take place among them during their lifetime.

Furthermore, there is nothing in 13:5–23 that relates to the second coming of Christ. For, the events that are depicted are those that directly impacted the disciples. They were exhorted to "watch out," to "not be alarmed," and to "pray." The message of Jesus to his disciples in 13:5–23 first informs them that the destruction of the temple was not going to happen immediately.[34] Jesus further explains that until the destruction of the temple there would be many false speculations concerning the end. The disciples were not to be misled.[35] Instead, they were to be on their guard.[36] Furthermore, Jesus informs them that this period was going to be a time of great difficulty for them. You will be delivered "to *the* courts, and you will be flogged in *the* synagogues. . . . And you will be hated by all on account of My name" (13:9, 13).

Jesus Indicates That Jerusalem Will Not Be Destroyed Immediately

That the destruction of Jerusalem was not going to occur in the immediate future is evident from Jesus' declaration,

> And when you hear of wars and rumors of wars, do not be frightened; *those things* must take place; but *that is* not yet the end. For nation will arise against nation, and kingdom against kingdom; there will be earthquakes in various places; there will *also* be famines. These things are *merely* the beginning of birth pangs. (Mark 13:7–8)[37]

---

34. This was important for them because they had likely come to conclude that Jesus' arrival in Jerusalem was an indication that the establishing of his kingdom was imminent—even if they did not understand the nature of his kingdom. This is evident in the request of the brothers James and John to sit on his left and on his right (Mark 10:35–40). They must have thought that Jesus was approaching Jerusalem and preparing to be crowned king—which, of course, he was. But in a manner that they were not expecting!
35. Mark 13:6.
36. Mark 13:9.
37. Cf. Matt 24:6–8; Luke 21:9–11.

Understanding the New Testament and the End Times

These words, instead of providing an explicit indication as to when the temple would be destroyed, serve to indicate that in some regards life would continue on as normal. The presence of wars, earthquakes, and famines, then, were not signs of the end. They were merely the "beginning of birth pangs" (Mark 13:8; Matt 24:8). In fact, "the end does not follow immediately" (Luke 21:9). Furthermore, Jesus notes that as time proceeds false speculations about the end would arise. During this time, many would claim to be the Christ and attempt to deceive many.[38] The disciples were not to believe them.

Mark 13:24–27: Jesus' Message Concerning His Coming

It is widely acknowledged that Jesus' words in 13:24–27 relate to the time of his coming.[39] As was noted, the disciples would not have understood this in the sense of the Jesus' return, though we, along with the early readers of the Gospels, having the advantage of hindsight, may certainly do so. The key, for our interests, is that Jesus does not give any indication as to when he will return. All he states is, "But in those days, after that tribulation, . . . they will see the Son of Man coming in clouds with great power and glory" (13:24–26). The only detail Jesus provides is that his coming will be "after that tribulation." The problem here, of course, is that "after that tribulation" provides no indication as to when. The time of Jesus's coming here is totally undefined.

Mark 13:28–31: When Will the Temple Be Destroyed?

Jesus' answer to the disciples' question as to *when* these events will occur is then given in 13:28–32. That is, 13:28–32 provides the answer to the question of when both the temple will be destroyed and when he will come back. First, in 13:28–31, Jesus provides insights into the *when* related to the time of the destruction of the temple. Then, in 13:32, he addresses the *when* in regard to the time of his "coming."

That 13:28–31 transitions back to the temple in order to inform the disciples as to when its destruction will occur is evident in light of several features. First, Jesus explains that the disciples must "learn" (13:28). This

---

38. Cf. Mark 13:5–6, 21–22; Matt 24:4–5, 23–24; Luke 21:8.

39. N. T. Wright dissents and argues that this section refers to Jesus ascension to heaven and not his return from heaven. He suggests that the coming on the clouds is a coming to heaven. See Wright, *Jesus and the Victory of God*, 361.

Understanding the "Signs of the Times"

command again reflects something that Jesus wanted his disciples to know or do. If the passage related to the events that would transpire two thousand years or more in the future, why would he bother telling them to learn?

This is also indicated by the similar statement, "when you see" (13:29). Again, the "you" must indicate the disciples whom Jesus was addressing and something that they will themselves "see." This concern for the disciples strongly suggests that Jesus has transitioned back to the issue of the destruction of the temple. This is something that pertains to them.

Furthermore, that Jesus has transitioned back to the issue of the temple in order to provide them the when of its destruction is confirmed by the reference to the fig tree. Jesus exhorts them, "Now learn the parable from the fig tree: when its branch has already become tender, and puts forth its leaves, you know that summer is near" (13:28). I have already noted that the fig tree in Mark 11 represents the temple.[40] The reference to the fig tree, then, confirms that Mark has transitioned back to the topic of the destruction of the temple.

Furthermore, Jesus' statements that "even so, you too, when you see these things happening" (13:29), and "this generation will not pass away until all these things take place" (13:30) affirm that Jesus has transitioned back to the issue of the destruction of the temple. Furthermore, the term "these things"[41] serves as a catchword that draws the reader's attention back to the use of "these things" in 13:4. There, the disciples asked, "when will these things be?"—clearly referencing Jesus' pronouncement that "these" buildings will all be torn down (13:2). The reference to "these things" in 13:29, then, directly connects Jesus' words to the disciples' question and confirms that Jesus is again referring to the destruction of the temple.

When would the temple be destroyed? First, it must be noted that it is the destruction of the temple that was indeed to occur with definitive signs.[42] As a result, the disciples will, in fact, be capable of discerning the signs of the imminence of the destruction of the temple. As already noted, this event was not to happen immediately. However, as time progressed, it would become more apparent that the destruction of the temple was near.

---

40. That the cleansing of the temple is sandwiched by the account of the cursing of the fig tree suggests that the lack of fruit on the fig tree corresponds to the lack of fruit in the temple. Thus, just as the fig tree was cursed and withered, so the temple was to be destroyed.

41. Remember that this is one word in Greek (*tauta*).

42. Cf. Mark 13:14, 28–31.

Understanding the New Testament and the End Times

The disciples are then warned that when the imminent destruction of the temple becomes apparent, they must "flee to the mountains" (13:14).

Furthermore, that the destruction of the temple would occur with definitive signs derives from the fact that Jesus was describing an event that was part of a military campaign by the Romans. As with any impending military conquest, one should, in fact, expect that there would be particular signs that will alert the inhabitants that an enemy is approaching. Mark's account observes that the signs would include: "when you see the abomination of desolation standing where it should not be" (13:14). Now, it is beyond our scope to delineate precisely what the "abomination of desolation" might have referenced. Suffice it to say, however, that the abomination of desolation must have referred to a definitive event that the disciples would have been able to discern. They were, in fact, warned that when they see it they must "flee to the mountains." Luke's account is much less ambiguous. There Jesus simply notes, when "you see Jerusalem surrounded by armies, then recognize that her desolation is near" (Luke 21:20).

What then did Jesus mean when he told them to "learn"? And what might he have meant when he said, when they "see these things happening"? In context, then, it appears that the signs themselves point to the fact that when they see the things indicated by Jesus, they should know that the destruction of Jerusalem is near. These signs related to the military conquest of Jerusalem. Therefore, what the disciples were to look for and to see would actually be fairly apparent. In the interim, they were not to be misled by the threat of "wars and rumors of wars" (Mark 13:7).

Mark's transition, then, in 13:28–31 back to the issue of the temple occurs in order to answer the question as to when this will take place. With regard to the destruction of the temple Jesus explains that just as one is able to observe the season by examining the blossoming of the fig, so they too should discern that once they "see these things happening" (13:29), that the destruction of the temple is near.

This statement in Mark, however, has unfortunately been muddled both in the translations and in much of the interpretation. For, Jesus continues, "when you see these things happening, recognize that He [it?] is near, *right* at the door" (13:29). The problem here is related to the translation of he/it. The question is whether or not the Greek verb *estin* should be translated "he is" or "it is."[43] That is, whether or not Jesus is referring to the nearness of his own return ("he is"), or the destruction of Jerusalem ("it

---

43. Both are correct in general. The context must be the final determiner.

is"). The Greek is unclear and can be translated either way. The ambiguity in the Greek is demonstrated by the variations in English translations: "he is near" (ESV, NAS, NET) and "it is near" (NIV, NKJ).

Several arguments may be raised to affirm that indeed Jesus was most likely referring to the nearness of the destruction of the temple ("it is") and not the nearness of his return ("he is"). That Jesus is indicating the nearness of the destruction of the temple and the coming of the kingdom of God is supported by the fact that Luke's Gospel, in a parallel citation, explicitly states, "Even so you, too, when you see these things happening, recognize that the *kingdom of God* is near" (Luke 21:31).[44] Luke, then, makes explicit what Mark has implicit. Thus, though Mark's account is unclear even in the Greek, it is apparent that Luke, who likely wrote after Mark, clarified for his readers that Jesus was indicating the nearness of the kingdom of God, which includes the destruction of the temple, and not the nearness of Jesus' return. N. T. Wright affirms, "'It' is near: is both natural and obvious."[45]

That Jesus signals that the destruction of the temple is near once "you"—which must refer to the disciples—"see these things happening" (Mark 13:29) is further evident from the fact that this event transpired within the lifetime of most of the disciples. That the fulfillment of "these things" does not indicate the imminence of his return is further suggested by the fact that the disciples did not witness the "coming" of Christ in their lifetimes. Hence, for any of them to "learn" and "see" in order to discern the imminence of the coming of Christ would have been superfluous at best and erroneous at worst.

What, then, did Jesus mean when he referred to the fact that "this generation will not pass away until all these things take place" (Mark 13:30)? First, I have already noted that the term "these things" references Jesus' prediction of the temple's destruction. Furthermore, it is apparent that 13:28–31 transitions back to the issue of the destruction of the temple and the accompanying signs that will serve to affirm its imminence. Therefore, since "these things" refers to the destruction of the temple, Jesus' words that

44. That the "it" refers to the kingdom of God is clear from Luke. What I have argued throughout this chapter is that in Mark 13 Jesus is referring to either the destruction of the temple or to his return. That Luke understands this as referring to the kingdom of God seems to present another option. However, it stands to reason that the presence of the kingdom of God itself necessitates that the temple must be destroyed likely provides the basis for Luke's interpretation. That is, Luke is concerned not with just the destruction of the temple, but with the more global reality that the destruction of the temple affirms that the kingdom of God has come.

45. Wright, *Victory of God*, 364.

"this generation will not pass away" (13:30) must refer to the generation alive at the time Jesus spoke, many of whom were still alive later to witness the destruction of the temple. That the temple was destroyed in AD 70, exactly forty years after the death of Jesus, provides further attestation.[46]

Mark 13:32: When Will Jesus Return?

Now, I have argued throughout the last two chapters that neither Jesus nor the NT provides any indication as to the *when* of his return.[47] That the Olivet Discourse does not provide any details as to when Jesus will return is equally evident. Mark 13:32, in fact, closes the main section of the speech of Jesus by turning to address the time of his "coming."[48]

As to the time of his "coming," we first observe that Jesus disassociates his coming from the destruction of the temple. Jesus' transition to address the when of his "coming" must be understood in light of the contrast between the destruction of the temple and the "coming" of Jesus. The distinction between these events is that the destruction of the temple will be accompanied by the invasion of the Roman army and will be apparent, while the time of his "coming" is unknown. Jesus affirms, "But of that day or hour no one knows, not even the angels in heaven, nor the Son, but the Father *alone*" (13:32). There is, then, a clear contrast between all "these things" that must happen within a generation and the "that day," which no one knows when it will occur!

The only indication that Jesus gives for the time of his coming is that it will be "after that tribulation" (13:24).[49] But, as for how long "after that tribulation" the return of Jesus will occur, no one knows. The relationship, then, between the destruction of the temple and the "coming" of Jesus is such that the advent of the first does not indicate the time of the second.

This point was significant for the disciples. For, the disciples certainly would not have understood that the two events were separated in any manner. As noted previously, the disciples were likely under the conviction that Jesus' rise to power was imminent. Suddenly, Jesus was indicating that

---

46. As mentioned previously, the date of the crucifixion of Jesus was either AD 30 or 33. A biblical generation is forty years as established in the Exodus wanderings. Thus, the destruction of the temple in AD 70, whether we affirm AD 30 or 33 as the date of the crucifixion, affirms the accuracy of Jesus' prediction.

47. That is, beyond the three factors mentioned in ch. 9.

48. The change in topic is mildly suggested by the use of the conjunction *de* (but).

49. Cf. Matt 24:29.

Understanding the "Signs of the Times"

the temple would be destroyed. Thus, they likely considered that these two events went hand in hand. Jesus informed them, however, that they were not the same. The temple would be destroyed in their lifetime, though not as soon as they might have expected. Therefore, one of the key points that Jesus was iterating in this speech is that the destruction of the temple would not mark the time of his coming. The time of his coming would be merely "after that tribulation" (13:24). As for the time of his coming, "no one knows" (13:32).

Mark 13:33–37: Conclusion to the Olivet Discourse

This speech of Jesus, then, closes with the reiteration of the command to "watch out" (13:33). Jesus adds to this that they are to "stay on the alert" (13:33, 34).

The speech then concludes with the admonition:

> Therefore, *be on the alert*—for you do not know when the master of the house is coming, whether in the evening, at midnight, at cockcrowing, or in the morning—lest he come suddenly and find you asleep. And what I say to you I say to all, *Be on the alert!* (Mark 13:35–37).

The framing of these three verses with the command to "be on the alert" serves to highlight this as the key command. The disciples should take what they have heard and "be on the alert"!

Jesus' intent, then, in the Olivet Discourse was to prepare and exhort his disciples for the trials that they were to encounter in the years leading up to the destruction of the temple. They must "watch out" (13:5, 9, 23, 33), "not be alarmed" (13:7), and "pray" (13:18). For, false teachers would come (13:22) attempting to mislead them (13:5). There is nothing in this speech instructing and preparing the disciples for the return of Jesus.

Conclusion: What Does All This Mean for Us?

The importance of this speech of Jesus for us is multifaceted. First, the speech serves to demonstrate Jesus' concern for his disciples—and, by extension, for us as well. We too must "be ready." What does it mean to "be ready"? Being ready certainly entails maintaining a diligence in our focus on the mission of God. As Edwards affirms, "The admonition 'to watch' indicates that the purpose of the eschatological discourse in Mark

Understanding the New Testament and the End Times

13 is not primarily to provide a timetable or blueprint for the future so much as to exhort readers to remain faithful in the present."[50] It does not mean, however, that we are enlightened as to the events that will precede the return of Jesus so that we will know the approximate time of his return and, thus, not be surprised at his coming.

---

50. Edwards, *Mark*, 384.

11

The War of Armageddon

So the dragon was enraged with the woman, and went off to make war with the rest of her children, who keep the commandments of God and hold to the testimony of Jesus. (Rev 12:17)

The final battle is preeminently spiritual in character. Attempts to correlate it with the maneuvers of particular national armies misses the point. The battle is between the servants of God and the enemies of God, not between two nations of the world.[1]

Introduction

THE TOPIC OF ARMAGEDDON has aroused much speculation. Armageddon is commonly believed to be the final, cataclysmic battle, which climaxes with the visible return of Christ. The war/battle[2] of Armageddon is described in Revelation 16:14, 16: ". . . which go out to the kings of the whole world, to gather them together for the war of the great day of God, the Almighty. . . . And they gathered them together to the place which in Hebrew is called Har-Magedon."

The first problem in determining what this war refers to arises with the translation of the term "Armageddon" itself.[3] The literal rendering of "Har Magedon," meaning "mount of Megiddo," is somewhat problematic,

---

1. Poythress, *Returning King*, 157.

2. The NAS reads "war," while most other English translations read "battle." The Greek term is *polemos*, which may be translated as "war" or "battle."

3. The NAS and NRS both render the word "Har Magedon," which is certainly the proper translation.

for there is no "Mount of Megiddo."[4] This may explain why most English translations employ "Armageddon," meaning "battle of Megiddo."[5] In addition to the problem of determining what Armageddon refers to is the fact that Revelation 16:16 is the only occurrence of "Armageddon" in the Scriptures. This means that any attempt to determine the biblical teaching of Armageddon should be met with great caution.

It is at this point that many Christians suggest doing a word study on "Armageddon." Though word studies have a place in the study of Scripture, they are also subject to great abuse. The result of such inquiries is, on occasion, a reading into the passage some subtle nuance of the meaning of a word or its form—which often transcends the contextual meaning.[6] Oftentimes, a much more profitable exercise for determining the meaning of a word or phrase is to compare the use of that word or phrase elsewhere within the particular book one is studying, and from there to compare its use throughout Scripture.[7] That is, instead of attempting to determine the lexical, or dictionary, meaning of a word and reading that meaning into the text, it is more profitable to determine how the author uses that word elsewhere. From there, one can then compare the use of that word or phrase throughout Scripture.

When it comes to Armageddon, of course, this cannot be done because the word occurs only once. But we can survey the meaning of other

---

4. See Beale, *Revelation*, 839; Fee, *Revelation*, 224–25; Mounce, *Revelation*, 301; Smalley, *Revelation*, 412; among many others. Note: not only is there no "mount Megiddo," but there is also no reference to such in the entire OT or any ancient Jewish literature. The apocalyptic indications of a final battle are in Zech 12:11 (the only apocalyptic reference to "Megiddo"—though there it is the *plain* of Megiddo) and Ezek 38–39 (where the final battle in history takes place on the "mountains of Israel"). See Beale and Carson, *NT Use of the OT*, 1136.

5. For the sake of simplicity I will adopt the more common designation "Armageddon," with the full knowledge that "Har Magedon" is the preferred reading of the Greek. The choice of Megiddo may result from the fact that it was the place where the righteous Israelites repeatedly fought off attacks by wicked nations (cf. 2 Kgs 23:29). See my entry for "Armageddon" in the *Baker Illustrated Bible Dictionary*.

6. What must be understood is that words have meaning only when they are used in a sentence. The context determines the meaning of a word and the nuance of the aspect (tense). Those who attempt word studies too often determine the meaning of a word and then read that meaning into the context. See Carson, *Exegetical Fallacies*, ch. 1. Moises Silva, discussing the nature of verbs and the subtleties of Greek aspect (or tense), notes that "No reasonable Greek author, when wishing to make a substantive point, is likely to have depended on his reader's ability to interpret subtle syntactical distinctions" (*Philippians*, 11).

7. Even here one must proceed with caution. For, an author may use a word or phrase with two different senses.

significant terms in 16:14, 16, most notably, the use of "war." After all, "Armageddon" is the name for the "war of the great day of God the Almighty" (16:14).

The War of Armageddon

A closer examination of the account of the war (Armageddon) in 16:14, 16 indicates that whatever "war" is being referred to, it is one that is known to John's readers/hearers.[8] This is indicated by the presence of the article ("the" war).[9] Thus, 16:14 refers to "the war," which is tantamount to John saying, "you know the one that I am talking about." The use of the article in 16:14; 19:19; and 20:8 further suggests that the war in each of these verses refers to the same war. This is helpful in that we can now begin to compare these verses with one another in order to gain a more complete understanding.

In the effort to determine what the war of Armageddon in 16:14, 16 might refer to, it is important to note that the identical phrase, "to gather them together for the war" (16:14), is repeated in 20:8.[10] Furthermore, a similar, though not identical, phrase occurs in 19:19: "And I saw the beast and the kings of the earth and their armies assembled *to make war* against Him who sat on the horse and against His army." Thus, a comparison of 19:19 and 20:8 with 16:14, 16 may shed some light on the war of Armageddon. A look at these parallel accounts (19:19; 20:8) suggests that John is describing the final climactic battle at the end of history.[11] This war has two key features: it is waged by the kings of the earth, and it is waged against Christ and his people.

That the war in Revelation is waged against Christ and his people by the kings of the earth is clear in the account of 19:19. For one, it is explicitly

---

8. The book of Revelation, as with most ancient literature, was meant to be read aloud. Thus, most people would be hearing the book (see 1:3).

9. The nature of Greek is such that use of the article ("the") is not always needed or employed. The use of the article here is known as an anaphoric article, or an article of previous reference. This means that the author is referring to "the war"; which would indicate one that is known to the readers/hearers. This would be similar to someone asking you to bring "the book" as opposed to "a book." "The book" references a particular, or known, book.

10. In both passages the Greek reads, *sunagagein autous eis ton polemon*.

11. That John is describing the final battle in history is also supported by a comparison with the OT prophecies of the final battle. See the chart in Schnabel, *40 Questions*, 234–35.

stated that the war is against Christ ("him who sat upon the horse"; 19:19) and his followers ("and against His army"; 19:19). Furthermore, those waging the war against Christ and his army are "the beast and the kings of the earth and their armies" (19:19).

That this war is waged against Christ and his people is evident from the account in 20:8. Because 16:14 and 20:8 both employ the identical phrase "to gather them together for the war" a comparison of these two accounts is justified.[12] Here again it appears that the war is waged against Christ and his people. For 20:9 notes, "And they came up on the broad plain of the earth and surrounded the camp of the saints." That this war is also waged by the kings of the earth is likely connoted by the reference to "Gog and Magog" (20:8).[13] That the two parallel accounts of 16:14, 16 and 19:19 both depict the kings of the earth (the "kings of the whole world"; 16:16) gathered for battle suggests that Gog and Magog may also refer to the kings of the earth. This is also justified, as Smalley notes, by the fact that Gog and Magog represent in Jewish tradition the "hostile nations from across the world."[14]

The most significant insight gained from comparing 16:14, 16; 19:19; and 20:8 is that the war is explicitly stated as waged by the kings of the world against Christ and his army. That this represents the final battle of history based on these passages is certainly warranted. For, the war is described as "the war of the great day of God" (16:14). This is also confirmed by the parallel uses of the final battle as "the great day of God" in the OT.[15] Since the war of Revelation 19 appears to occur at the visible return

---

12. It is well beyond our purpose to determine if these two wars are indeed identical. The fact that the same phrase occurs in both places suggests that the basic features of the wars are worthy of comparison. Whether or not they both depict the same actual war is beyond our interests.

The major debate is whether or not 20:8 takes place at the end of a thousand-year physical millenial reign of Christ on the earth. Those who affirm this position place the battle of Armageddon as taking place one thousand years before the battle of 20:8. Those who identify the two battles as the same would then suggest that the millenial reign of Christ refers to his present spiritual reign from heaven by means of his people. As noted earlier, it is well beyond the scope of this book to wade in the waters of this debate. Among the many books on this topic one may consult are Bock, *Three Views on the Millennium*; and Clouse, *Meaning of the Millennium*.

13. For a discussion of Gog and Magog, see Schnabel, *40 Questions About the End Times*, ch. 27, "Who Are Gog and Magog in Revelation?"; also Beale, *Revelation*, 1024–26; Mounce, *Revelation*, 372; Smalley, *Revelation*, 512.

14. Smalley, *Revelation*, 512.

15. Cf. "The day of the LORD is indeed great" (Joel 2:11), "the great and awesome day of the LORD" (Joel 2:31), and "the great day of the LORD" (Zeph 1:14).

of Christ, we may reasonably conclude that the war of Armageddon in Revelation 16 likewise entails the final battle in history. Thus, the war of Armageddon in 16:14, 16 references a final climactic battle waged by the nations against Christ and his people immediately prior to Christ's return.

However, a look at the use of "war" in the rest of the book of Revelation expands our conception of war beyond that of merely the final battle.

The Use of "War" Throughout Revelation

The noun *polemos* (war/battle) is used nine times in Revelation.[16] The uses in 9:7, 9 and 12:7, however, do not contribute anything essential to our conversation. Thus, having already looked at the three instances above (16:14; 19:19; and 20:8), we will turn our attention to the other three uses in 11:7; 12:7; and 12:17. In doing so, we again find that the war of the book of Revelation is directed at the people of God. In fact, we could go so far as to conclude that Satan's waging war with the people of God serves as one of the primary themes in the book of Revelation.

That is, though we have seen that the kings of the earth wage war against Christ and his people, we now find out that it is actually the work of the devil. For, it is he who empowers the kings of the earth. We, also, see that the focus of this war is actually the people of God. Finally, these verses inform us that the war of Revelation against Christ and his people is not solely relegated to the end of time. Instead, the war is that which Satan has always waged, and still does, against the people of God. Thus, though it is true that the war in Revelation climaxes with the final battle of Armageddon, it is also true that this war is presently being fought by the devil against the people of God.

The War in Revelation 13

That the war of Revelation is that which Satan presently wages against the people of God is also affirmed in 13:6–7. Here the beast, who is empowered by the devil,[17] is said to have "opened his mouth in blasphemies against God, to blaspheme His name and His tabernacle, *that is*, those who dwell in heaven. It was also given to him to make war with the saints and to

---

16. See Rev 9:7, 9; 11:7; 12:7, 17; 13:7; 16:14; 19:19; 20:8. This does not include the verbal cognate used in Rev 2:16; 12:7 (2x); 13:4; 17:14; 19:11. We are only interested in determining the meaning of Armageddon and, thus, the use of "war" as a noun.

17. Rev 13:2.

overcome them, and authority over every tribe and people and tongue and nation was given to him." Note, the NAS (along with the ESV, NET, NLT, and NRS) includes the phrase "that is" in 13:6.[18] The inclusion of "that is" is explanatory, i.e., it is an effort to clarify that the following phrase ("those who dwell in heaven") serves to make clear whom the beast is actually blaspheming. Thus, the beast, when he blasphemes God's "name and His tabernacle" (13:6), is actually blaspheming "those who dwell in heaven" (13:6). That "those who dwell in heaven" refer to the people of God, whom the beast blasphemes, is made explicit in the following verse where the beast is said to make "war with the saints" (13:7). Thus, Satan, in his effort to blaspheme God, attacks God's people. This accords with what we have seen in 16:14, 16; 19:19; and 20:8. Namely, that the war in Revelation is Satan's attack on God's people.

That 13:6–7 also affirms the war is fought by the nations against the people of God is evident from a comparison of the narrative in 13:1–7 with the clear parallel account of Daniel 7. In Daniel 7 there are four beasts that wage war against the people of God.[19] These four beasts are explicitly described as "These great beasts, which are four *in number*, are four kings *who* will arise from the earth" (Dan 7:17). That the beast of Revelation 13 is a composite of all four beasts of Daniel 7 is virtually undisputed.[20] Thus, if the beasts of Daniel 7 represent nations, then one may reasonably infer that the beast of Revelation 13 does so as well. Therefore, the account of 13:6–7 affirms that the war of Revelation is that which the kings of the earth wage against Christ and his people. Now, however, it is more emphatic that this war is directed at the people of God as the means by which Satan attacks Christ.

---

18. The Greek has the conjunction *kai*; which is commonly translated as "and." However, the conjunction may also be explanatory; that is, it may serve to introduce a clause that itself is explaining something in the previous clause (note: my use of "that is" in this sentence would have been rendered as *kai* in Greek). Hence, the translation "that is." Most English translations, correctly in my opinion, render it "that is"; cf. ESV, NET, NLT, and NRS. The NIV and the NJK both translate it as "and." The translation of "and" here suggests that the beast blasphemes three things: God's name, his tabernacle, and those who dwell in heaven. The translation "that is" suggests that "those who dwell in heaven" constitute God's tabernacle.

19. Dan 7:21.

20. One must simply compare the description of Daniel's four beasts in 7:3–8 with John's lone beast in Rev 13:1–2.

The War in Revelation 12

That the war against Christ in Revelation is directed specifically at the people of God is also confirmed by the reference to "war" in 12:17. In 12:17, it explicitly states that the dragon "went off to make war with the rest of her offspring, who keep the commandments of God and hold to the testimony of Jesus." This clearly depicts that the war of the devil is against the people of God—for only the people of God may be properly designated as those "who keep the commandments of God and hold to the testimony of Jesus" (12:17).

The War in Revelation 11

Finally, that the war in Revelation is directed at the people of God is also evident from the reference to the war against the two witnesses in 11:7. Though this passage is somewhat difficult, it is apparent that the two witnesses are best understood, not as two individuals, but as representing the entirety of the people of God.[21]

For one, the two witnesses are described as "the two lampstands" (11:4). This description is made easy in light of the fact that in Revelation 1–2 the seven lampstands were explicitly identified with churches.[22] Thus, the description of them in language used to describe entire churches suggests that the two witnesses also are not individuals but a group. But, why are they only two lampstands and not all seven? The most probable suggestion is that they are two here because two is the number of a credible witness in Scripture.[23] That is, they represent all of the people of God. They are depicted as "two" to connote that the testimony they proclaim is true.

Also, the war of 11:7 against the two witnesses can hardly be against two people. For how does one wage a war against only two people? This, also, corresponds to the fact that every occurrence of the war against Christ and his people in Revelation is always against the entirety of the people of God. Thus, it stands to reason that this war is also against the entirety of the people of God.

---

21. I have argued extensively that the two witnesses represent all of the people of God in history. See my *Revelation and the Two Witnesses*, 34–40.
22. See Rev 1:20.
23. Deut 17:6; 19:15.

Finally, that the war in 11:7 against the two witnesses describes the war against the entirety of the people of God is evident from the continuity of the account in 11:7 and 13:5–7. First, both the war against the two witnesses in 11:1–14 and the beast's war against the people of God in 13:1–7 relate to the same time period of "forty-two months" (11:2; 13:5). Also, both accounts reference a "beast" (11:7; 13:7) who wages war against the people of God. Furthermore, in both accounts the beast not only wages war with the people of God, but he is said to "overcome" (11:7; 13:7) them. Therefore, if the war in Revelation 13 is waged against the entirety of the people of God, then the war against the two witnesses in Revelation 11 is also against the entirety of the people of God.

The result is that there are ample reasons to conclude that the war of 13:7 is the same war as that of 11:7. If so, then, the fact that the war in 13:7 is against the entirety of the people of God strongly suggests that the war against the two witnesses also describes a war against the entirety of the people of God.

Finally, beyond the scope of whether or not the two witnesses or those who dwell in heaven constitute the entirety of the people of God is the fact the war in Revelation is not simply some future battle to be waged in the fields of Israel. In fact, the entirety of the message of Revelation is The that the dragon is currently waging war against the people of God.

The War in Revelation Is That Which Satan Wages Against the People of God Throughout History

The narrative of 12:1–17 is best understood in part as an expansion on the war of the beast against the two witnesses in 11:7.[24] The reference to the war against the two witnesses in Revelation 11 somewhat surprisingly intrudes itself into the narrative. Consequently, one of the major functions of Revelation 12 is to provide the background for this war. In short, Revelation 12 informs the readers that the war against the two witnesses is none other than the war that the dragon has waged against the people of God throughout history.

Revelation 12 begins by explaining that the dragon (Satan) stands before a woman.[25] Thus, we see that the dragon opposed the people of God, for the woman represents the people of God before Christ, in history

---

24. See my *Revelation and the Two Witnesses*, 80–82.
25. Rev 12:3–4.

The War of Armageddon

prior.[26] Next, the dragon attempts to devour the Christ child.[27] When this is unsuccessful,[28] the dragon then pursues the woman who gave birth to the child.[29] The dragon pursues not just the woman, but "went off to make war with the rest of her offspring, who keep the commandments of God and hold to the testimony of Jesus" (12:17). That this depicts the historical, current, and future plight of the people of God derives from the most natural reading of the Revelation in general and the account of Revelation 12 in particular.

This is further affirmed by what was argued in our chapter on prophecy.[30] There we saw that the nature of prophecy is such that it was relevant to the original readers. Though prophecy may also predict events that will find a fulfillment in the future, its primary function is to speak to the people of that day. This is equally true for the book of Revelation.

For one, the book of Revelation is called a prophecy. John, in fact, begins his book with the exhortation, "Blessed is he who reads and those who hear the words of the prophecy, and heed the things which are written in it" (1:3). John is clearly encouraging his original readers to listen and do what is commanded in this book. If Revelation merely depicted events that would transpire some two thousand or more years later, it is very difficult to see how John's exhortation would have had any force.

Furthermore, the book of Revelation ends with the repeated exhortation, "Blessed is he who heeds the words of the prophecy of this book" (22:7).[31] Thus, Revelation opens and closes with the reminder that it is a prophecy that needs to be heeded. That this exhortation applied to John's readers is further justified in light of the fact that Revelation 2–3 contains seven letters to seven churches of John's day. This further substantiates the fact that Revelation was written to the churches of the first century just as much as it was to the present. Thus, the war in Revelation most likely had some present application to John's readers.

---

26. This accords with Jesus' warning to the disciples that "they persecuted the prophets who were before you" (Matt 5:12; Luke 6:23). See also Heb 11:36–38.
27. Rev 12:4.
28. See Rev 12:5.
29. Rev 12:13.
30. See ch. 5.
31. See also Rev 22:10, 18, 19.

Winning the War

One final thought: according to Revelation the people of God are caught in the midst of a war with the devil. The question must be asked, "How are we to win this war?" The answer in Revelation is simple: through death. The people of God "overcame him because of the blood of the Lamb and because of the word of their testimony, and they did not love their life even when faced with death" (12:11). The means of winning in Revelation is not by some show of force according to the standards of this world. It is by being lambs!

Conclusion

We have seen that the "war" in Revelation is against the people of God. This is evident in 11:7; 12:17; and 13:7. Thus, though the description of Armageddon in Revelation 16 is in accord with the final battle waged by the kings of the earth against Christ and his people, the use of war in Revelation has a broader scope. That is, war in Revelation is what the dragon is currently waging against the people of God! It is not some futuristic battle to be fought with swords on some battlefield in Israel. It is the constant, daily, battle of Satan against the people of God!

This is of the utmost significance. Namely, that war in the book of Revelation is the battle of the kings of the earth—"nations" might be a better designation in the twenty-first century—against God's people! That is, though Satan gathers his minions to wage war against Christ, the means by which he wages this war against Christ is not by attacking Christ himself—as though that would do any good—but by attacking God's people!

We must be cautious then to overly literalize Revelation and conclude that it only refers to some future battle fought in the land of Israel. To do so may well mean that we neglect the present war of the devil against the people of God.

Excursus: Is Armageddon a Literal Battle?

Most scholars indeed affirm that "Armageddon" does not refer to a literal physical battle fought in the plains of Megiddo. This is evident from a number of factors. First, the literal rendering "mount of Megiddo" is problematic since there is no such mountain in the OT or Jewish literature.[32]

---

32. This oddity may account for some of the differences in the manuscripts.

Secondly, the OT consistently portrays the final battle as taking place, "without exception, in the immediate vicinity of the city of Jerusalem and mount Zion or its surrounding location."³³ This corresponds with Rev 14:20 and 20:8-9, which depict the final battle as taking place in the vicinity of Jerusalem.³⁴ Why, then, does Revelation place this battle in Megiddo? The primary reason why it appears that John is depicting this final battle as taking place in Megiddo is because it is in the valley of Megiddo that the righteous Israelites fought the wicked nations.³⁵ Thus, to symbolically depict the final battle of Satan against Christ, or the nations against God's people, John describes a war taking place where the people of God have always done battle against the nations. Thus, Armageddon in Revelation refers to a symbolic battle, which is waged constantly by the devil against the people of God, and climaxes in the defeat of Satan at the return of Christ.

There are a number of different spellings of the word in the Greek manuscripts, which may suggest that the copyists, knowing that there was no such mountain, made slight emendations to the text in order to "correct" it. See Beale, *Revelation*, 839–41.

33. Beale and Carson, *NT Use of the OT*, 1136.

34. Rev 14:20; 20:8, 9—where the city is most likely Jerusalem.

35. This is most prominent in Judg 5:19. Beale and Carson affirm, "The Judges 5 passage provides the most probable OT typological pattern for Rev 16:16, since there God defeats an overwhelmingly powerful foe who had formerly oppressed defenseless Israel" (*NT Use of the OT*, 1136). The importance of Ezekiel cannot be overlooked either. See the reference to a climactic battle on the "mountain of Israel" (Ezek 38:8; see also Ezek 38:30, 21; 39:2, 4, 17).

12

Understanding The New Testament and the End Times: Why It Matters!

The expectation of deteriorating conditions prior to the soon-approaching rapture is morally corrosive, encouraging pessimism, fatalism, and the forsaking of political responsibility. Disengagement from the problems of the world is ethically indefensible.[1]

God gave to Jesus' people the assignment he had given to Adam and Eve. They were Eikons like Adam and Eve but with a major difference: they had the Holy Spirit. This Holy Spirit could transform them into the visible likeness of Jesus himself.[2]

But if Christians are the actual beginning of the end-time new creation, they must act the way new creatures act.[3]

Introduction

THE OBJECTIVE OF THIS book has been to contend that understanding the end times matters. I have intended to provide what I believe is a proper foundation for interpreting Scripture in general and understanding the end times specifically. That foundation is Christ. I have also argued that the NT is wholly eschatological. Thus, understanding the end times is essential because it is the fabric upon which the NT is penned. As such,

---

1. Craig Hill, *In God's Time*; cited in Witherington, *Revelation and the End Times*, 1.
2. Scot McKnight, *The King Jesus Gospel*, 152.
3. Beale, *New Testament Biblical Theology*, 303.

an end times, or eschatological, perspective is foundational to a proper interpretation of the Scriptures.

In our study of the temple we saw that at the climax of God's kingdom God will dwell both among all his people and throughout the entirety of creation. Hence, the centrality of the temple in Scripture. Furthermore, in our study of tribulation we saw that this kingdom, contrary to the manner in which the kingdoms of this world are established, triumphs both through the suffering and death of Jesus Christ and through the suffering of the people of God. Hence, the significance of tribulation as part and parcel of the present experience of the people of God. In our study of the second coming of Christ we saw that the return of Christ in glory awaits the fullness of the kingdom of God. Hence, the necessity for the people of God to be steadfastly devoted to lives of love and humility, which are to characterize the people of God! Finally, in our study of Armageddon we saw that the war in Revelation is not some wholly future war to be fought out by the nations, but that it is directed at the people of God in the present. The result of all this is that the people of God are called to live lives of holiness in the midst of a hostile world, working towards the kingdom of God, and all the while awaiting the return of Christ and the climax of his kingdom, while the world wages war against us.

A proper understanding, then, of the end times, the nature of the temple, the tribulation, the second coming of Christ, and Armageddon is central to the nature of the kingdom of God, to our mission as followers of Christ, and for our spiritual and ethical lives. Eschatology, therefore, matters!

In this chapter I will summarize the arguments of this book and further contend that understanding the end times matters because the mission of God's people is to carry out the end times mission of Christ in the present. That is, the end times are not something future to the life of the believer, but they are inherently present. To live in the kingdom of God is to live in the eschatological end. Therefore, in closing I intend to review each of the core chapters and to explore why it is so important that we have a proper end times framework for understanding the temple, the tribulation, the second coming of Christ, and Armageddon.[4]

---

4. Without this chapter, this book may well provide a proper framework for understanding Jesus and the Scriptures. In doing so, I may have even persuaded some to accept my theological perspective on such matters. But, if that is all we accomplish, then I am not sure that we have accomplished much. We have enough theological bantering going on in the church. For, if our theology fails to truly translate into Christian living, then it is nothing more than a "noisy gong or a clanging symbol" (1 Cor 13:1).

Understanding the New Testament and the End Times

Understanding the Temple: Why It Matters

Jesus is the temple. And, by means of his giving us the Spirit, we too are temples. Why does this matter? Understanding this should greatly affect the life of the church today. Not only does this have implications for how we read our Bibles and what we are, or are not, expecting to happen in the future, but it has great relevance for how we live today. After all, the very nature of a temple is such that it demands holiness. Holiness, in fact, is to be the defining feature of God's people. Peter exhorts his readers, "but like the Holy One who called you, be holy yourselves also in all *your* behavior; because it is written, 'You shall be holy, for I am holy'" (1 Pet 1:15–16). Therefore, since God dwells within us and God is holy, we too must be holy.

This is, also, the conclusion of the Apostle Paul. In 2 Corinthians, when Paul makes his appeal to the fact that we are the temple of God by citing Leviticus 26:11–12 and Ezekiel 37:24–28, he then cites Isaiah 52:11: "'Therefore, come out from their midst and be separate,' says the Lord. 'And do not touch what is unclean; And I will welcome you. And I will be a father to you, And you shall be sons and daughters to Me,' Says the Lord Almighty" (2 Cor 6:17). Just as importantly, after citing these verses to make his point that we are the temple of God, Paul adds, "Therefore, having these promises, beloved, let us cleanse ourselves from all defilement of flesh and spirit, perfecting holiness in the fear of God" (2 Cor 7:1).

We are the temple of God. We already experience through the Spirit God's presence among us. We must carry forth this commission to the nations that they too may enjoy the restoration of God's presence among them. To do so, we must live in holiness. After all, this is what it means to be a temple! And, this is the essence of what it means to be the people of God.

Understanding the Tribulation: Why It Matters

The fact that the kingdom of God has come means that we already enjoy life as members of God's kingdom. However, the fact that the kingdom of the world remains means that these two kingdoms live in tension with one another. Most notably, the kingdom of this world stands opposed to the kingdom of God. The result is the suffering and persecution of the people of God.

In the chapter on tribulation I noted that the NT clearly stresses that tribulation and suffering are the lot of the Christian life. We also observed that in the NT the suffering of Christ is the example that the suffering church is to follow. We are to "follow the Lamb wherever He goes" (Rev 14:4). This includes the fact that each one of us must "take up his cross" (Mark 8:34).

We also saw that the suffering of the people of God for the gospel is the means by which God builds his kingdom! The kingdom of God does not spread in the same manner as the kingdoms of this world. "You know that the rulers of the Gentiles lord it over them, and *their* great men exercise authority over them. It is not so among you, but whoever wishes to become great among you shall be your servant, and whoever wishes to be first among you shall be your slave; just as the Son of Man did not come to be served, but to serve, and to give His life a ransom for many" (Matt 20:25–28).

Therefore, a proper understanding of the role of tribulation in the life of the people of God is vital both to grasping the nature of the NT teaching regarding the end times and for understanding the nature of discipleship in Scripture. Very simply put: the nature of life in the kingdom of God is one of tribulation![5]

Understanding this is essential for a variety of factors. For one, from a pastoral perspective it is important for the people of God to come to terms with suffering. The potential for many to become disillusioned when their Christian life fails to result in the blessedness and happiness that many propose can be catastrophic. Jesus, of course, was manifestly clear that the one who is blessed is the one who is persecuted.[6]

---

5. In light of this it is somewhat perplexing to see Christians debating whether or not we will face the tribulation or be raptured. The notion of a rapture and its tendency towards an escapist theology did not arise in the history of the church until the nineteenth century, primarily because it could not have arisen. The church has virtually always suffered. To establish a theology in which the church is somehow exempt from suffering is beyond imagination both for the historic church and for much of the non-Western church today! Paul, in fact, says, "Indeed, all who desire to live godly in Christ Jesus will be persecuted" (2 Tim 3:12). For some, then, to propose that Christians are dismissed from the earth before the "Great Tribulation" fails to properly understand the nature of the kingdom of God. To be a member of Jesus' kingdom, one must suffer. Such sufferings are in accord with the sufferings of Christ. Jesus informed his disciples on numerous occasions that "the Son of Man *must* suffering things" (Mark 8:31; cf. Matt 16:21; Luke 9:22; also Luke 17:25). In fact, Peter's failure to properly understand the role of suffering led him to "rebuke" Jesus (Mark 8:32; Matt 16:22), to which Jesus replies, "Get behind me, Satan" (Mark 8:33; Matt 16:23).

6. Matt 5:10–12. Note that Jesus relates the persecution of the NT people of God

Understanding the New Testament and the End Times

Secondly, it seems as though many, especially among us in the West, are content living a life of relative comfort. Yet, a life that is committed to living out the kingdom as Christ has called us to will often result in persecution and suffering. Such a life, in fact, constitutes the forsaking of the things in this world that bring us comfort.[7] Jesus stated:

> Blessed *are* you *who are* poor, for yours is the kingdom of God. Blessed *are* you who hunger now, for you shall be satisfied. Blessed *are* you who weep now, for you shall laugh. Blessed are you when men hate you, and ostracize you, and cast insults at you, and spurn your name as evil, for the sake of the Son of Man. Be glad in that day, and leap *for joy*, for behold, your reward is great in heaven; for in the same way their fathers used to treat the prophets." (Luke 6:20–23)

This is not to say that the suffering of the people of God is good or even to be sought out. In fact, the church is called to care for our brothers and sisters in Christ who are suffering. We are to visit them while in prison, feed them when they are hungry, clothe them when they are naked, etc.[8] The point is that we are to expect suffering and certainly not to be surprised when it comes.[9]

Overcome

This brings us to a point of great significance in understanding the nature of the kingdom of God. Namely, that the people of God are constantly exhorted to "overcome."[10] That is, we must be prepared to endure the great tribulation. This is one reason why we must be so passionate about a proper understanding of the kingdom of God and the end times. Those who view the tribulation as something purely future often fail to exhort the people of God with one of the most fundamental charges in the NT: namely, to overcome. The exhortation to overcome is one of the more seminal commands in the book of Revelation. In fact, each of the seven letters in Revelation 2–3 contain the exhortation to "overcome."[11] It is only when we grasp the

---

with the persecution of the OT people of God.

7. Cf. Matt 16:24–26; Mark 8:34–38; Luke 9:23–26.

8. Cf. Matt 25:31–46.

9. Beale notes, "tribulation always comes because of the believers' faithful witness to Jesus" (Beale, *Revelation*, 434).

10. The Greek *nikao* means to "overcome" or to "conquer."

11. Cf. Rev 2:7, 11, 17, 26; 3:5, 12, 21.

reality that the kingdom of God is one of "tribulation, and kingdom, and perseverance" (1:9) that we gain an insight into the need to overcome. To suggest that this is something future and not pertinent to the life of the believer today is to look past one of the most fundamental exhortations for the people of God in the NT.

Prepared for Tribulation

An important derivative of understanding the nature of tribulation as part of the consequence of being members of the kingdom of God is that we are prepared for it so that we will not fall away when tribulation arises. According to the Parable of the Sower (Mark 4:1–20), enduring the tribulation means that we have our seed planted in the good soil of Jesus Christ.

> And in a similar way these are the ones on whom seed was sown on the rocky *places*, who, when they hear the word, immediately receive it with joy; and they have no *firm* root in themselves, but are *only* temporary; then, when affliction [*thlipsis*, "tribulation"] or persecution arises because of the word, immediately they fall away.... And those are the ones on whom seed was sown on the good soil; and they hear the word and accept it, and bear fruit, thirty, sixty, and a hundredfold. (Mark 4:16–17, 20)[12]

The NT, then, exhorts the people of God to be prepared in the present for the tribulations that are inherent to the Christian life.

But What About the Fact That I Am Not Suffering?

Many Christians in the West enjoy the unique situation of relative ease in their Christian experience. This certainly has increased the notion that Jesus promised us peace and prosperity.[13] So why is it that many in the West experience little to no suffering?

---

12. The seed on the rocky soil sprang up and bore a plant but faded away without producing fruit because of tribulation (*thlipsis*). The message of the Parable of the Sower is that only those who are willing to endure tribulation for the kingdom of God will bear fruit.

13. Certainly a digression into the unbelievable teachings of the prosperity gospel is well beyond the confines of this work. It stands as very apparent from what I have noted here that such teachings fly in the face of the NT emphasis on blessings for the poor and suffering (cf. Luke 6:20–23, referenced above).

Understanding the New Testament and the End Times

Is it because we live in a Christian family and have a strong supportive Christian environment—or at least one that is tolerant of our faith? Or, perhaps we have been transformed by the gospel to the point in which everyone respects and appreciates us. Or, is it because we are not really living out the gospel in our own life? We must look inwardly and ask ourselves if we are truly living out the gospel faithfully. Perhaps we have so compromised the gospel in our daily lives that the world sees no reason to persecute us. A group persecutes others and not themselves. If we are so much like the world, then the world has no reason to persecute us. For, we are just like them. We certainly do not represent a threat to their way of life.[14]

Or, perhaps God has placed us in a position of relative peace, so that we can aid our brothers and sisters in Christ who are suffering—that is, after all, what the body does. For, if one member suffers, we all suffer, and we must all come to the aid of those in need. I would suggest that we might consider that perhaps God has blessed us so that we might be in a position to bless others in the body of Christ who are not as fortunate.

Any one or more of these factors may account for the relative peace experienced by Christians in much of the western world.

How Does This Affect My Walk Today?

In regards to tribulation and our walk, we should note several things. First, we should anticipate suffering on account of the gospel and not be surprised when it comes. Secondly, as we have already noted, tribulation is a means of growing in Christ. Therefore, we should embrace it. This does not mean that we seek it out, but that we should rejoice when it comes. Finally, we must recognize that Jesus taught us that the way to the throne is through the cross. The Lion is the Lamb!

Therefore, an understanding of the nature of the kingdom of God is essential for proper discipleship and growth in Christ. When the NT speaks of the "deeds of the flesh" and the "fruits of the Spirit" (Gal 5:16–26), these should be understood in terms of the contrasting kingdoms.

Also, understanding the tribulation as a present reality for the people of God means that we must constantly remember our brothers and sisters in Christ around the world who are suffering greatly from *thlipsis/*

---

14. This point is difficult to articulate. For it is also possible that we are so lovingly living out the gospel that we do not pose a threat to our neighbors either. I do not suppose that many would want to persecute Mother Teresa if she were still alive.

affliction/persecution. The fact is that suffering is the lot of the people of God, and this has not only been historically true, but that it remains true throughout much of the world today. For, indeed, "if one member suffers, all the members suffer with it; if *one* member is honored, all the members rejoice with it. Now you are Christ's body, and individually members of it" (1 Cor 12:26–27).

Therefore, if our brothers and sisters in Christ are imprisoned or suffering on account of the gospel, we must come to their aid. In fact, I would strongly contend that this is one of the primary distinctions of the judgment. This is the essence of the Parable of the Sheep and the Goats in Matthew 25:31–46. Jesus informs us that God rewards or punishes men for how they have treated "the least of these brothers of mine" (25:40, 45).[15] This theme runs through the book of Revelation, where the judgment of the world is because of how they have treated God's people.[16] Therefore, we must think and live eschatologically, with a full awareness that the suffering of God's people is something we must attend to.

> Then the King will say to those on His right, "Come, you who are blessed of My Father, inherit the kingdom prepared for you from the foundation of the world. For I was hungry, and you gave Me *something* to eat; I was thirsty, and you gave Me drink; I was a stranger, and you invited Me in; naked, and you clothed Me; I was sick, and you visited Me; I was in prison, and you came to Me." Then the righteous will answer Him, saying, "Lord, when did we see You hungry, and feed You, or thirsty, and give You drink? And when did we see You a stranger, and invite You in, or naked, and clothe You? And when did we see You sick, or in prison, and come to You?" And the King will answer and say to them, "Truly I say to you, to the extent that you did it to one of these brothers of Mine, *even* the least *of them*, you did it to Me." (Matt 25:34–40)

---

15. The phrase "least of these" without exception in Matthew refers to followers of Jesus (cf. Matt 10:42; 18:6, 10, 14; 5:19; 11:11). Likewise the phrase "brothers of mine" also indicates followers of Christ (cf. Matt 5:22–24, 47; 7:3–5; 12:48–50; 18:15, 21, 35; 23:8; 28:10).

16. E.g., Rev 6:10; 16:5–6; 17:6–18:24. Note: the people of God in Revelation are defined as those who "hold to the testimony of Jesus" (Rev 12:17).

Understanding the New Testament and the End Times

Understanding the Second Coming: Why It Matters

The key with regards to the biblical teaching on the second coming is that we are not to sit idly by awaiting the return of Jesus, but we are to be diligently engaged in the process of transformation now. The problem here is that for many Christians transformation is conceived of as something that takes place at the return of Christ. This line of thinking, however, can be quite dangerous. After all, it promotes, whether by intention or not, apathy. Many become content knowing that someday they will go to heaven where everything will be all better. In the interim, it is often suggested that we should try to do good.

I suggest that in the New Covenant Christ is not concerned with what we do, but with who we are! It is in the New Covenant, which Christ has already established,[17] that Christ writes his law upon our hearts: "But this is the covenant which I will make with the house of Israel after those days," declares the LORD, "I will put My law within them, and on their heart I will write it; and I will be their God, and they shall be My people" (Jer 31:31). Ezekiel adds,

> Moreover, I will give you a new heart and put a new spirit within you; and I will remove the heart of stone from your flesh and give you a heart of flesh. And I will put My Spirit within you and cause you to walk in My statutes, and you will be careful to observe My ordinances. (Ezek 36:26–27)

Another way of looking at this is to contend that if the end times/eschaton have already begun, then whatever is true of the end times/eschaton have already begun. Thus, it matters greatly what kind of persons we are. For we are not merely awaiting that day when Christ returns and restores all things. The process of restoration has already begun. We must then strive for such a transformation of heart in the present.[18]

Furthermore, as we have seen, in the New Covenant we are the agents of that restoration! But, we can only do so when we ourselves have undergone that transformation and are in the process of implementing it among ourselves! Therefore, if in the end times/eschaton there will be peace, then we must begin in the present to be peacemakers. And, if the

---

17. Luke 22:20; 1 Cor 11:25.

18. Interestingly, there is a renewed emphasis on the role of spiritual formation in the evangelical world. The thesis of this book actually provides a theological, or eschatological, grounding for such. Namely, that the kingdom of God has arrived and God has given us of his Spirit, so that our hearts are circumcised and through the Spirit we can faithfully live out the kingdom's ethics.

end times/eschaton have already begun, then we must diligently strive to be "a chosen race, a royal priesthood, a holy nation, a people for *God's* own possession, that you may proclaim the excellencies of Him who has called you out of darkness into His marvelous light" (1 Pet 2:9). And, if the end times/eschaton have already begun, then we must begin to be the community who loves and cares for one another so that "there should be no poor person among" us (Deut 15:4).[19] Such living should characterize the people of God today.

Understanding Armageddon: Why It Matters

Understanding Armageddon and the biblical teaching of "war" is fundamental to the NT and the life of the people of God. The war of Revelation is waged against the people of God. It is not some physical battle waged on the plain of Megiddo,[20] among the nations. Instead, it is waged by the devil against Christ and his people.[21] Therefore, an understanding of Armageddon matters. After all, the people of God must be prepared for this war! That many of us are unaware that we are at war can only mean that the devil is winning.

What is interesting is that many discussions of Armageddon gloss right over Revelation 16:15. This verse, which is clearly parenthetical, states, "'Behold, I am coming like a thief. Blessed is the one who stays awake and keeps his clothes, so that he will not walk about naked and men will not see his shame.'" Thus, in the midst of describing the war against God's people, which is then named "Armageddon", John quotes Jesus, who exhorts the people of God to be ready! But, being ready assumes that it pertains to us!

This creates a stark contrast with many of the popular conceptions of Armageddon, which suggest that it refers to a literal battle. But, those who suggest that Armageddon refers to a physical war among the nations cannot really make sense of the exhortation to be ready in Revelation 16:15. It is only by understanding Armageddon as a war of the devil against the

---

19. Cf. Acts 4:34, which appears to be citing Deut 15:4. The church in Acts was already in the process of living out what God had called his people to be!

20. Recall that the Greek of Rev 16:16 says "mount of Megiddo," which is problematic since there is no such mountain. See ch. 11.

21. The nature of this battle is unfortunately well beyond the scope of this book. Suffice it to say that the devil is not using the sophisticated weapons of nuclear arsenals, but is engaged in far more insidious measures to bring the people of God to destruction. Suffice it to say that he will wage war in any manner that he can.

people of God that we can really affirm that we too must be ready. We must be ready not simply because Christ is coming back. We must be ready because we have an enemy who is already at war with us!

The popular conception of Armageddon is, perhaps, the one area of eschatology that is most alarming among many evangelicals today. The implications of a faulty perspective of Armageddon are worthy of an entire book. Certainly, the political ramifications, for example, are indeed grand. For, too many Christians are not actively seeking peace in the world because they are convinced that war and the signs of war are themselves an indication that Jesus' return is imminent. But being peacemakers is one of the hallmarks of being a follower of Christ![22] Nonetheless, this excitement over war is consistently promoted by such teachers as Hal Lindsey.[23] Lindsey himself stated, "The dispute to trigger the war of Armageddon will arise between the Arabs and Israelis over the Temple Mount and Old Jerusalem (Zechariah 12:2–3), the most contested and strategic piece of real estate in the world. Even now we are witnessing the escalation of that conflict."[24]

The effect of this thinking is overwhelming. The Middle East is a region in great turmoil. What is of great concern is that our brothers and sisters in Christ are caught in the midst of all this. They are suffering greatly from this conflict. Yet, many Christians in the West are excited about this because of the prospects of an approaching Armageddon![25]

22. Matt 5:9.

23. Now, I realize that Hal Lindsey does not in any way reflect the teachings of the scholarly community. The reason for citing him here is that his teachings have had a dramatic effect upon the popular Christian world in the West. What I have attempted to do in this book is to provide a positive framework for interpreting Scripture that will equip the pastors and leaders to address such aberrant teaching.

24. Lindsey, *Israel and the Last Days*, 19. Someone may attempt to cite Matt 10:34 at this point: "Do not think that I came to bring peace on the earth; I did not come to bring peace, but a sword." But to take this verse as though Jesus were advocating war is preposterous. First off, Jesus is not addressing civil governments and their wars with one another. He is suggesting that the gospel that he brings will create strife in the world. But that strife is directed at Jesus and his followers. This follows from the fact that the context of Matt 10:24–42 is about discipleship. Jesus goes on to say that "he who receives you receives Me, and he who receives Me receives Him who sent Me" (Matt 10:40). See Morris, *Matthew*, 264–65. Thus, this passage affirms what was argued in our discussion on Armageddon. Namely, that the focus of the hostility is directed at Christ and his followers. Thus, this passage has nothing to do with wars among the nations.

25. John Walvoord stated in his book *Armageddon, Oil and the Middle East Crisis*, under the heading "Armageddon Countdown," that "First, the Middle East must become the number one crisis in the world" (27). He then went on to list other factors

Efforts to bring peace to the region, which would benefit not only our brothers and sisters in Christ, but also the people of Israel and Palestine, and even the greater Middle East, as well as the US, are looked down upon because they compromise what is a false reading of Scripture. I am not sure I can say this strongly enough. But, such thinking is quite dangerous. The Scriptures teach that the "war" in Revelation is waged against God's people by the devil, who uses the nations of the world to do his bidding. Here we see God's people suffering at the hands of the nations and, yet, many Christians are excited about this!

We must be reminded that our victory in this war against the devil is through death and resurrection. We are victorious lions, as Jesus is, only when we become slain lambs.

Conclusion

There is a revival of sorts among the evangelical community. That revival is of the emergence and growth of the role of spiritual formation and discipleship. Essentially, many of its proponents are claiming that the people of God must be about making disciples and not merely making converts. I applaud this move. This book, surprisingly, is joining that conversation. How might a book on the end times participate in, or even contribute to, the questions of spiritual formation? I am glad you asked! Quite easily. The message of the NT, as I have seen it, is that the end times kingdom of God has come in Christ and that we, the people of God, are called to carry it forth to the ends of the earth. The bringing of the kingdom of God to the earth is eschatological! Thus, I hope that I have provided an eschatological and hermeneutical framework that the leaders in spiritual formation may use to further the dialogue.

This closing chapter has admittedly only begun a conversation that is worthy of a book, or many books, in itself. I hope that I have begun to tease out some of the implications that derive from an eschatological understanding of Scripture. I have not intended so much to provide answers as much as I have attempted to provide a framework for the conversations. These are conversations that the people of God must get on board with soon or else the church will be relegated to irrelevance—as I fear it already has in some places. We have lost our voice in many arenas today. This is, in part, because we have lost sight of our mission as the end times people of God.

---

that would follow, eventually leading to the rise of the Antichrist.

Many others have faithfully searched more deeply into some of the missional, ethical, social, and political implications of the kingdom of God. I have only attempted to provide an eschatological foundation for their work. Suffice it to say for now that when we, the church, are not advocating for justice in our families, in our communities, and in our world, we are not engaged in the restoration of God's kingdom for which he has called us. When we are not advocates of peace, we are not acting as members of Christ's kingdom who are called to be the peacemakers. When we do not care for the poor, the widows, the orphans, those in distress, the sick, and all humankind, we are not effectively building the kingdom of God. And when we are not advocating for the proper care of God's creation, we are failing to live as those made in God's image and entrusted with the task of caring for his creation.

If our eschatology promotes war, or in the least advocates that war is so inevitable that we have no need to actively pursue peace, then our eschatology is not in accord with Scripture. If our eschatology leaves us contentedly ignorant of the injustices of sex trafficking and human slavery, then our eschatology is not in accord with Scripture. If our eschatology tells us that the earth will be burned up and that God really only cares about humankind and, thus, we can use and abuse the earth and its resources, then our eschatology is not in accord with Scripture.

This book has had one primary concern: to present a biblical view of the end times and to highlight the implications of such for the church. This view, as I have set forth, has radical implications for the people of God. God has begun his kingdom in Christ and he has called us to be the means by which he builds his kingdom. What we have hopefully learned is that a proper eschatological framework constitutes a call to action for the church. For, if Jesus is the fulfillment of the temple, and through the Spirit we are too, then we should be busy living lives characterized by holiness! For, temples demand holiness. If the kingdom of God was established through the cross, then we too should be bearing our crosses and, in doing so, building God's kingdom. For the kingdom comes through suffering. If the return of Christ is awaiting the suffering of his people, the conversion of the nations, and the holiness of the church, then we should be striving to live lives of holiness in order to be God's witnesses to the world—knowing full well that we will suffer for it. For, Jesus will return when he finds faith on the earth. If the war of Revelation is currently fought against the people of God, then we must be prepared and "stay awake."

Indeed, the eschaton has arrived. God is already in the process of bringing his kingdom to the earth! Lord Jesus, have mercy on your church! Lord Jesus, continue your work of building your kingdom through us. Help us to overcome just as you overcame!

"These are the ones who follow the Lamb wherever He goes!" (Rev 14:4).

BIBLIOGRAPHY

Select Resources for Further Study

Allison, Dale C., *The End of the Ages Has Come: An Early Interpretation of the Passion and Resurrection of Jesus*. Philadelphia: Fortress, 1985.

Baker, David W., ed. *Looking Into the Future: Evangelical Studies in Eschatology*. ETS Studied. Grand Rapids: Zondervan, 2001.

Beale, G. K. *A New Testament Biblical Theology: The Unfolding of the Old Testament in the New*. Grand Rapids: Baker Academic, 2011.

Beale, G. K. *The Temple and the Church's Mission: A Biblical Theology of the Dwelling Place of God*. New Studies in Biblical Theology 17. Downers Grove, IL: InterVarsity, 2004.

Beale, G. K., and D. A. Carson, editors. *Commentary on the New Testament Use of the Old Testament*. Grand Rapids: Baker, 2007.

Boyd, Gregory A., and Paul R. Eddy. *Across the Spectrum: Understanding Issues in Evangelical Theology*. Grand Rapids: Baker, 2002.

Brower, Kent E. "Eschatology." In *New Dictionary of Biblical Theology*, edited by T. Desmond Alexander and Brian S. Rosner, 459–64. Downers Grove, IL: InterVarsity, 2000.

Brower, Kent E., and Mark W. Elliot. *Eschatology in Bible and Theology*. Downers Grove, IL: InterVarsity, 1997.

Caird, G. B. *The Language and Imagery of the Bible*. Philadelphia: Westminster, 1980.

Clowney, Edmund P. "The Final Temple." *Westminster Theological Journal* 35 (1973) 156–89.

Dumbrell, William J. *The End of the Beginning: Revelation 21–22 and the Old Testament*. Homebush West, NSW: Lancer, 1985.

Dumbrell. William J., *The Search for Order: Biblical Eschatology in Focus*. Grand Rapids: Baker, 1994.

Erickson, Millard J. *A Basic Guide to Eschatology: Making Sense of the Millennium*. Rev. ed. Grand Rapids: Baker, 1998.

Guthrie, Donald. *New Testament Theology*. Downers Grove, IL: InterVarsity, 1981.

Hays, J. Daniel, and Tremper Longman. *Message of the Prophets: A Survey of the Prophetic and Apocalyptic Books of the Old Testament*. Grand Rapids: Zondervan, 2010.

Hays, J. Daniel, J. Scott Duvall, and C. Marvin Pate. *Dictionary of Biblical Prophecy and End Times*. Grand Rapids: Zondervan, 2007.

Kyle, Richard. *The Last Days Are Here Again: A History of the End Times*. Grand Rapids: Baker, 1998.

Bibliography

Ladd, George Eldon. *The Presence of the Future: The Eschatology of Biblical Realism.* Grand Rapids: Eerdmans, 1974.
Ladd, George Eldon. *A Theology of the New Testament* Grand Rapids: Eerdmans, 1974.
McKnight, Scot. *The King Jesus Gospel: The Original Good News Revisited.* Grand Rapids: Zondervan, 2011.
Pate, C. Marvin. *The End of the Age Has Come: The Theology of Paul.* Grand Rapids: Zondervan, 1995.
Pitre, Brant James. *Jesus, the Tribulation, and the End of Exile: Restoration Eschatology and the Origin of the Atonement.* WUNT, ser. 2, 204. Grand Rapids: Baker Academic, 2005.
Ridderbos, Herman N. *The Coming of the Kingdom.* Translated by H. de Jongste, edited by Raymond O. Zorn. Philadelphia: P&R, 1962.
Schnabel, Eckhard J. *40 Questions about the End Times.* Grand Rapids: Kregel, 2011.
Schreiner, Thomas R. *New Testament Theology: Magnifying God in Christ.* Grand Rapids: Baker, 2008.
Waldron, Samuel E. *The End Times Made Simple: How Could Everyone Be so Wrong about Biblical Prophecy?.* Amityville, NY: Calvary, 2003.

Works Cited

Aune, David. "The Apocalypse of John and the Problem of Genre." *Semeia* 36 (1986) 65–96.
Barnett, Paul. *The Second Epistle to the Corinthians.* NICNT. Grand Rapids: Eerdmans, 1997.
Bauckham, Richard. *The Climax of Prophecy: Studies on the Book of Revelation.* Edinburgh: T. & T. Clark, 1993.
Block, D. I. "My Servant David: Ancient Israel's Vision of the Messiah." In *Israel's Messiah in the Bible and the Dead Sea Scrolls*, edited by Richard S. Hess and M. Daniel Carroll R., 17–56. Grand Rapids: Baker, 2003.
Bock, Darrell L. editor. *Three Views on the Millennium and Beyond.* Grand Rapids: Zondervan, 1999.
Boersma, T. *Is the Bible a Jigsaw Puzzle: An Evaluation of Hal Lindsey's Writings.* St. Catharines, Ontario: Paideia, 1978.
Bruce, F. F. *The Book of Acts.* NICNT. Rev. ed. Grand Rapids: Eerdmans, 1988.
Burge, Gary M. *John.* NIV Application Commentary Series. Grand Rapids: Zondervan, 2000.
Carson, D. A. *Exegetical Fallacies.* 2nd ed. Grand Rapids: Baker, 2002.
Clouse, Robert G., editor. *The Meaning of the Millennium: Four Views.* Downers Grove, IL: InterVarsity, 1977.
Collins, C. John. *Genesis 1–4: A Linguistic, Literary, and Theological Commentary.* Phillipsburg, NJ: P&R, 2006.
Collins, J. J. "Towards the Morphology of a Genre: Introduction." *Semeia* 14 (1979) 1–20.
Cullman, Oscar. *Christ and Time: The Primitive Christian Concept of Time and History.* Philadelphia: Westminster, 1950.
Dalrymple, Rob. "John." In *The Baker Illustrated Bible Dictionary*, edited by Tremper Longman. Grand Rapids: Baker, 2012.

Bibliography

Dalrymple, Rob. *Revelation and the Two Witnesses: The Implications for Understanding John's Depiction of the People of God and His Hortatory Intent.* Eugene, OR: Wipf and Stock, 2010.

Davies, W. D. *The Gospel and the Land: Early Christianity and Jewish Territorial Doctrine.* Berkeley: University of California Press, 1974.

Dubis, Mark. *Messianic Woes in First Peter: Suffering and Eschatology in 1 Peter 4:12–19.* SBL 33. New York: P. Lang, 2002.

Edwards, James R. *The Gospel According to Mark.* Pillar New Testament Commentary. Grand Rapids: Eerdmans, 2002.

Evans, Craig A. *Mark 8:27—16:20.* WBC 34B. Nashville: T. Nelson, 2001.

Fee, Gordon. *Revelation.* New Covenant Commentary Series 18. Eugene, OR: Cascade, 2011.

Goldingay, John E. *Daniel.* WBC 30. Nashville: T. Nelson, 1989.

Gorman, Michael. *Reading Revelation Responsibly: Uncivil Worship and Witness: Following the Lamb into the New Creation.* Eugene, OR: Cascade, 2011.

Green, Gene L. *The Letters to the Thessalonians.* Pillar New Testament Commentary. Grand Rapids: Eerdmans, 2002.

Green, Joel B. *The Gospel of Luke.* NICNT. Grand Rapids: Eerdmans, 1997.

Hays, Richard B. *The Conversion of the Imagination Paul as Interpreter of Israel's Scripture.* Grand Rapids: Eerdmans, 200.

Hoekema, Anthony A. *The Bible and the Future.* Grand Rapids: Eerdmans, 1979.

Jamieson, Robert, A. R. Fausset, and David Brown. *A Commentary, Critical and Explanatory, on the Old and New Testaments.* Oak Harbor, WA: Logos, 1997.

Jeffrey, Grant R. *The New Temple and the Second Coming.* Colorado Springs, CO: WaterBrook, 2007.

Kaiser, Walter C., and Moises Silva. *An Introduction to Biblical Hermeneutics: The Search for Meaning.* Rev. ed. Grand Rapids: Zondervan, 2007.

Keener, Craig S. *Revelation.* NIV Application Commentary. Grand Rapids: Zondervan, 2000.

Kline, Meredith. *Glory in Our Midst: A Biblical-Theological Reading of Zechariah's Night Visions.* Eugene, OR: Wipf and Stock; Overland Park, KS: Two Age, 2001.

Lacocque, André. *The Book of Daniel.* Translated by David Pellauer. Rev. ed. Atlanta: John Knox, 1979.

Lane, William L. *The Gospel of Mark.* NICNT. Grand Rapids: Eerdmans, 1974.

Lindsey, Hal. *Israel and the Last Days.* Eugene, OR: Harvest House, 1983.

Lindsey, Hal. *The 1980's: Countdown to Armageddon.* Toronto: Bantam, 1982.

Lindsey, Hal. *There's a New World Coming.* Eugene, OR: Harvest House, 1984.

Longman, Tremper, editor. *The Baker Illustrated Bible Dictionary.* Grand Rapids: Baker, 2012.

Lucas, Ernest C. *Daniel.* Apollos Old Testament Commentary. Downers Grove, IL: InterVarsity, 200.

Marshall, I. Howard, A. R. Millard, J. I. Packer, and D. J. Wiseman, editors. *New Bible Dictionary.* 3rd ed. Downers Grove, IL: InterVarsity, 1996.

McCartney, Dan, and Charles Clayton. *Let the Reader Understand: A Guide to Interpreting and Applying the Bible.* 2nd ed. Phillipsburg, NJ: P&R, 2002.

Minor, Franklin. *After Armageddon.* Self-published with Xlibiris, 2010.

Moltmann, Jürgen. *Theology of Hope: On the Ground and the Implications of a Christian Eschatology.* Translated by James Leitch. New York: Harper & Row, 1967.

Bibliography

Morris, Leon. *The Gospel According to Matthew*. Pillar New Testament Commentary. Grand Rapids: Eerdmans, 1992.

Pearcey, Nancy. *Total Truth : Liberating Christianity from Its Cultural Captivity*. Wheaton, IL: Crossway, 2005.

Poythress, Vern S. *The Returning King: A Guide to the Book of Revelation*. Phillipsburg, NJ: P&R, 2000.

Poythress, Vern S. *Understanding Dispensationalists*. 2nd ed. Phillipsburg, NJ: P&R, 1993.

Roberts, Vaughan. *God's Big Picture: Tracing the Storyline of the Bible*. Downers Grove, IL: InterVarsity, 2002.

Ryken, Leland, James C. Wilhoit, and Tremper Longman, editors. *Dictionary of Biblical Imagery*. Downers Grove, IL: InterVarsity, 1998.

Schmitt, John W., and J. Carl Laney. *Messiah's Coming Temple: Ezekiel's Prophetic Vision of the Future Temple*. Grand Rapids: Kregel, 1997.

Silva, Moises. *Philippians*. Baker Exegetical Commentary on the New Testament. Grand Rapids: Baker Academic, 2005.

Smalley, Stephen S. *The Revelation to John: A Commentary on the Greek Text of the Apocalypse*. Downers Grove, IL: InterVarsity, 2005.

Smith, Ralph L. *Micah–Malachi*. WBC 32. Nashville: T. Nelson, 1984.

Stordalen, T. *Echoes of Eden: Genesis 2-3 and Symbolism of the Eden Garden in Biblical Hebrew Literature*. Leuven: Peeters, 2000.

Swihart, Stephen D. *Armageddon 198?*. Plainfield, NJ: Haven, 1980.

Taylor, Richard A., and Ray E. Clendenen. *Haggai, Malachi*. New American Commentary 21A. Nashville: Broadman & Holman, 2004.

Vanhoozer, Kevin J. *Is There a Meaning in This Text?: The Bible, the Reader, and the Morality of Literary Knowledge* Grand Rapids: Zondervan, 1998.

Walker, Peter W. L. *Jesus and the Holy City: New Testament Perspectives on Jerusalem*. Grand Rapids: Eerdmans, 1996.

Walvoord, John F. *Armageddon, Oil and the Middle East Crisis*. Grand Rapids: Zondervan, 1990.

Walvoord, John F. *The Prophecy Knowledge Handbook*. Wheaton, IL: Victor, 1990.

Wenham, Gordon J. *Genesis 1–15*. WBC 1. Nashville: T. Nelson, 1987.

Wenham, Gordon J. *The Book of Leviticus*. NICOT. Grand Rapids: Eerdmans, 1979.

Witherington, Ben. *Revelation and the End Times: Unraveling God's Message of Hope*. Nashville: Abingdon, 2010.

Wright, Christopher J. H. "A Christian Approach to Old Testament Prophecy Concerning Israel." In *Jerusalem Past and Present in the Purposes of God*, edited by Peter W. L. Walker, 1–19. 2nd ed. Grand Rapids: Baker, 1994.

Wright, Christopher J. H. *The Mission of God: Unlocking the Bible's Grand Narrative*. Downers Grove, IL: InterVarsity, 2006.

Wright, N. T. *How God Became King: The Forgotten Story of the Gospels*. New York: HarperOne, 2011.

Wright, N. T. *Jesus and the Victory of God*. Vol. 2 of *Christian Origins and the Question of God*. Minneapolis: Fortress, 1996.

Wright, N. T. *The New Testament and the People of God*. Vol. 1 of *Christian Origins and the Question of God*. Minneapolis: Fortress, 1992.

www.ingramcontent.com/pod-product-compliance
Lightning Source LLC
Chambersburg PA
CBHW062042220426
43662CB00010B/1620